THE
10 - DAY HOTEL
MANAGEMENT

NEERAJ CHANDHOK

INDIA • SINGAPORE • MALAYSIA

Notion Press

No.8, 3rd Cross Street,
CIT Colony, Mylapore,
Chennai, Tamil Nadu - 600004

First Published by Notion Press 2021
Copyright © Neeraj Chandhok 2021
All Rights Reserved.

ISBN 978-1-64892-997-7

WHAT YOU WILL LEARN IN THIS BOOK:

- Fundamentals of Hotel Management
- Professional Hotel Terminology
- Management Concepts

THIS BOOK SERVES:

- Those doing INTERVIEW PREPARATION
- Those who want to revise HOTEL BASICS
- Beginners who are about to join HOTEL JOB
- To learn KEY MANAGEMENT CONCEPTS
- To brush up knowledge FOR EXAM PREPARATIONS

Contents

Acknowledgement

The objective of this book is to provide essential fundamentals of hotel management in one concise book. As a student, as a teacher and as a hospitality professional I always felt, that there was a need for a book that provides a brief, handy information about the basics & fundamentals of hotel management. That is how the concept of **"The 10 Day Hotel Management"** was born. The book contains selective relevant information across different functions of a hotel providing an overall understanding of basics of hotel management. It gives an overview of all aspects and departments, key terms & working of all departments.

A big "Thank You" to the following people to have assisted me in the execution of the book, without them this book would not have been possible.

Our Team at Building Block Customer Services LLP.

Book Edited by Ms Priyanka Vishnoi

MBA in Culinary @ Indian Culinary Institute (2019-2021).

Ms Akshita Tiwari- PhD Research Scholar (Hospitality)

Sagar Sachdeva -MBA in Culinary @ Indian Culinary Institute (2019-2021)

Himanshu Kaushal & Yugal Kishore-MBA in Culinary @ Indian Culinary Institute (2019-2021)

Arjun Lalhall- M.sc. Hospitality Administration@ IHM Pusa (2020-2022)

Ms Chandrokala Biswas Assistant lecturer @IHM Mumbai for your assistance & support

Thanks to Ocean Glass Public Co Ltd, Thailand for providing pictures of the glassware

Thank You Mr Satish Arora -Director K.I.Glassware India Pvt. Ltd.

A big thank you to Jason, the publishing guide from Notion Press for his valuable assistance.

Please access more information and Quiz Bank at

www.the10dayhm.com (T&C Apply)

Testimonials

Mr, Neeraj Chandhok, Sir: He is my mentor and professor for more than 17 years. His positive attitude and amiable personality always create a superior learning environment and lasting impression with everyone.

A very well-structured and organized textbook with an innovative approach to Hotels that examines the fundamentals of all the operational departments in a commendable way. It will quickly become a must-read for all students and academicians associated within Hospitality space

– Dr Anjana Singh-Head of School Hospitality-Vedatya

"I had the privilege of working with Mr. Neeraj Chandhok during my days at Inter-Continental, he always exhibited loads of enthusiasm, positivity, focus and passion towards his work and colleagues. He was always exceptional with his understanding of guests and sensitivity towards their expectations. He is multi-talented as he understands the needs and expectations of almost all stakeholders of hospitality from guests, employees, owners to educational institutes. As a trainer he brings loads of refreshing & energetic change as he speaks with so much enthusiasm & passion & out of his experience in the most simple but extraordinary ways challenging the thinking capacity of each person he trains.

His books also display the condensed wisdom which comes from his experience of more than 25 years in the industry covering hotels, corporates and educational institutions. With his eye for detail there is no way he misses to encourage and motivate each person he meets. With his presence in industry and academics not just across the country but even internationally, he perfectly bridges the gap between industry and academics and the ever-changing trends of hospitality."

– **Ritika Singh-Director-Faculty of Hotel Management**
Manav Rachna International Institute of Research and Studies

When I look down the line, I only see one person telling us; you guys need a paradigm shift.

The person with no orthodox textbook teaching technique, he educated us with his contemporary style of facilitating whether it was sharing every real life situation examples he had in his vast career or having discussion over coffee out of monotonous classroom sessions. The teacher who taught me how to teach or I would rather say a facilitator who facilitated us to be a facilitator. Yes that's what farsightedness meant when he told us about the bird's eye view approach. He played an important role in turning our learning style from pedagogy to andragogy.

Some educators just teach you, some just inspire you but very few analyze your potential/ acumen & lead you towards a suitable career path. They play the role of a continuous guiding torch whenever you are lost.

Furthermore, very rarely you get associated with people who invest themselves in your career building, treat you as their own asset & see your success as their own success. That's a true facilitator, a guide, a mentor; that's Mr. Neeraj Chandhok Sir for me.

– **Amarjeet Kundu-Faculty Institute of Hotel Management,**
Catering Technology & Applied Nutrition, Lucknow UP
(Under Ministry of Tourism, Government of India)

A few words can-not describe my association with Neeraj Chandhok sir as a mentor, guide and motivator towards not only in career but also in life. I was lucky enough to be his student during my masters in IHM Pusa. His energetic classes and futuristic views change any of his session into a life lesson. A multi-talented personality having a bouquet of skills in customer service, quality assurance, leadership, consultancies and decades of experience in hospitality sector makes him a perfect guide to write this book. This book will give a strong foundation for all the core departments of hotel management, giving a conceptual clarity and holistic view of each area with a strong base. A must-read book for all the aspirants of the industry for their better growth and excelling in it. It's my honour and privilege to write about it and be associated with it.

– Shreya Prasad-Assistant Lecturer-IHM Bhubaneswar

I've attained so much knowledge and information while helping you out for this book. Thank you doesn't adequately express my gratitude for the experience that I've had. It has made me confident and a better person. Your inspirational tone makes everyone charged up and ready to learn. You have challenged me to shock up the world and make my life matter in my own way.

– Priyanka Vishnoi-MBA,
Culinary Arts from Indian Culinary Institute, Noida

This book covers all the essential elements of the hospitality industry. Each and every page is packed with useful information which would prove to be highly useful for an individual's professional life! Wish this book was there when I was pursuing my Hospitality education! Kudos to Mr. Neeraj Chandhok Sir for creating this masterpiece!

– Akshita Tiwari, PhD Research Scholar (Hospitality)
M.sc. (H.A) IHM PUSA 2017-19 Batch

Neeraj Chandhok Sir has been my inspiration. He has been a guiding force for all the budding professionals like me. Sir you have shaped our character, calibre and confidence with your massive knowledge and experience that you have shared with us. We all have been fascinated with your different style of inculcating knowledge into your students. Thank you for shaping us into the professionals we are today. In this book Chandhok sir has touched all the basics of all the departments which are very important for every student to understand before he/she enters the industry. The book in itself is unique in its presentation. With its simple effective presentation, it can be understood by all.

– Deeksha Khatri PhD, Research Paper
Maharishi Dayanand University

I have known Neeraj sir since 2011 when I started my M.sc in Hospitality Administration from IHM Pusa. He was the General Manager at the Lutyens, New Delhi. He is an excellent educator, motivator & trainer and has expertise in several domains like customer service, leadership, food and beverage management etc. Neeraj sir has all the qualities which we seek in our teachers & leaders in today's time. Not many teachers are able to stimulate the students to the extent which Neeraj sir does, so he provides a great environment to learn. He has great communication skills and explanations are very helpful. Thank you sir, for always being there for us and being so helpful, kind and a great motivator all the time.

This text book aims to cover all the basic aspects and essentials of various departments of the fast-growing hotels and provides Fundamentals of Hotel Management in one Book. It will help readers to develop the skills they need in the dynamic industry. It is an ideal and highly recommended book for the hospitality students and as well as professionals in the industry.

– Dr. Nidhi Nayna-Assistant Professor,
Le Cordon Bleu School of Hospitality,
G D Goenka University, Gurugram.

Mr. Chandhok sir always play a role of my mentor in my life, Chandhok sir, he is an inspiration, an idol, a true mentor, guide and what not .....He is available to help all his students and in my case he played a different role for me. He believes in me and made me what i am today. His teaching pattern is almost new to me and make me more confident in term of knowledge. His last publication helped me a lot to know what i really want to be.(Leadership Plus) That book was a game changer for me and boosted me with positive confidence. The book gave me ability to think over my career goal and make them more clearer than. Now I am clear about my career goals and started working as HR Executive in Flipkart that is my first step towards my real goal.

– Sumit Rohilla (Masters of Science in Hotel Administration)
M.sc. (H.A) 2017-19 (IHM Pusa)

It is really like an opportunity for me to share something about this wonderful person, I met Mr. Chandhok in my MSc. days at IHM PUSA. As said, "First Impression is the Last Impression" he has created that impression on very first day and it still continues. The way he used to teach us was very different from others, and he used to get mingle with each and every student present there. I really liked the way he shares the live and practical examples with us, as well as those comparative studies.

If you are willing to opt your career in Hotel Management and want first hand advice from experienced professional, then this book is perfect for aspirants like you.

In this piece of art, you will learn about the fundamentals of hotel management

Mr. Chandhok's earlier books "Customer Plus" & "Leadership Plus" totally focuses on Customer Satisfaction & Leadership, which was very handy and helpful for me to set my goals as well as it also helped me to clear my vision to prosper in my career.

– **Ms Jyotishikha Singh-Assistant Professor,**
Amity School of Hospitality, Lucknow

"questions are more important than answers "This is A point that impacted me. Your teachings made me look at management and businesses in a completely different perspective. Even though it was so obvious that the dots were always there you just made me realise how to connect them. Interactions with you were very insightful and quite a quest into my own thinking and you continue to provide great value to me as your student

– **Ms Vaishnavi C. U- MBA in Culinary,**
Indian Culinary Institute Tirupati

Mr. Chandhok has been an inspiration & mentor for young minds and always encourages them to think outside the box and look out for the prospects & lessons that exist outside the syllabus as well. As his books are an extension of his conscience, they too fulfill the same purpose. This book reflects the mind & soul of this wise author, who always encourages self-learning & inspires to excel and challenge the status-quo. This book comprises of fundamentals of hotel management which students & professionals of hospitality would find, of immense value.

– Ms Chandrokala Biswas-Assistant lecturer-IHM Mumbai

At Times words cannot articulate our enormous gratitude towards a person.
"Mr. Neeraj Chandhok... A Man with Ocean of Knowledge".
Sir, For Me you first became a Teacher during my M.Sc. days at IHM Pusa, after that you have always turn out to be an Inspiration... a motivation... a friend... a well-wisher...
You had that spirit that brings the best out of students. You gave me the requisite motivation and learnings to move ahead in life. Your classes were always informative and unique with real examples of the industry. *Mr. Chandhok is Indeed, A Passionate Trainer, An Entrepreneur, A Leader, A Musician and A Creative Author...* who has already authored various articles and two well-known and must-read books entitled Customer Plus & Leadership Plus, which gives an actual extract of Customer Satisfaction and Leadership Styles required for today's competitive corporate world. In the streamline, This Book on Fundamentals of Hotel Management will enlighten the true world of

Hospitality along with the New Normal in every department of the Hotel.

**– Dr. Ashutosh Sharma (Ph.D., M.Sc. in Hospitality Administration
from IHM Pusa)
Programme Leader, HOD (Front Office) & Assistant Professor,
Amity School of Hospitality,
Amity University Lucknow, Uttar Pradesh.**

To Hospitality Professor
Mr. Neeraj Chandhok,

I consider myself a fortunate enough that I got the chance to learn from an author which I never experienced before and your true experience you shared with me in class during your lectures. On academic point of view, it was very effective but what I really admire is, a positive change you brought into my attitude.

I promise you I will remember all your lessons throughout my life and especially that sportsman spirit. All I can say on precise note that your lessons on both customer and leadership approach is key to successful business in this competitive professional world.

– Pranjul Gaur, Msc previous, IHM PUSA.

About

www.the10dayhm.com

A Quiz Based Online Learning Centre for Hotel Management Fundamentals

- An ONLINE HOTEL MANAGEMENT QUIZ PLATFORM
- To test your knowledge OF HOTEL MANAGEMENT FUNDAMENTALS
- To earn online E-CERTIFICATION FOR EACH QUIZ COMPLETED
- To earn E-BADGE

Login/Register @ www.the10dayhm.com (T&C Apply)

Online Quiz Learning Centre for Hospitality Fundamentals & Management is a separate feature and is to be accessed subject to the Terms & Conditions Applicable at the Time of Registration at the website. For Eligibility of membership / fee structure / quiz access please access the website

ACCESS ONLINE QUIZZES
HOTEL MANAGEMENT FUNDAMENTALS

www.the10dayhm.com

SAMPLE CERTIFICATE

INDIVIDUAL QUIZ

www.the10dayhm.com

Individual Quiz Certificate is a certificate that is achieved on successful completion of an Individual Quiz

One can Download & Print the Certificates with Name

You can print the E-Certificate sitting at your home any number of times

One can Take repeated Quiz to improve score

Terms & Conditions Apply

www.the10dayhm.com

SAMPLE CERTIFICATE

MASTER CERTIFICATE

www.the10dayhm.com

Master Certificate is a certificate that keeps updating all the Quiz successfully completed.

One can Download & Print the Certificates with Name

As you successfully complete more quizzes , those topics get updated into your certificate. You can print the E-Certificate sitting at your home any number of times

One can Take repeated Quiz to improve score

Terms & Conditions Apply

www.the10dayhm.com

Essentials Terms in Hotel Management

AI (All inclusive): All inclusive, term in hospitality means a kind of package that includes more than solely the price of a room into the price per night, but also three meals per day (Breakfast, Lunch and Dinner), services and activities. (Depending on the specified inclusions/customised all-inclusive package)

AMENITIES: Commonly used to describe hotel facilities. The correct use of this term is for personal toiletry items such as shampoo, toothpaste, mouthwash, shoe shine kit, sewing kit, and shower cap, with no additional cost to the guests.

ATRIUM: An interior design in which there are public areas, that overlooks the lobby from anywhere above.

B&B: A bed and breakfast is a small lodging establishment that offers accommodation and breakfast.

BANQUET: Banquet means, meal hosted in recognition of a special occasion. Banquet is an area in hotels which is meant for hosting & serving large formal and informal meals for events.

BARISTA: A coffee specialist and knows about coffee blends/varieties. He is an expert in coffee beverages and has good knowledge obout types of coffee and coffee making process

BEO (Banquet Event Order): A Banquet Event Order, is a document that outlines the details of your event. It serves as a guideline for the hotel to execute and communicate details of a particular event to all necessary hotel departments.

BLACK OUT DATES: Dates where special rates or promotional offers do not apply, existing around holidays, peak seasons, or special events.

Many loyalty programs have blackout dates when rewards may not be redeemed. These dates are typically heavy demand dates for example holiday season dates/special occasion dates.

BOH (Back of the house): A term used to describe the functional areas of the hotel, which are in the back area of the hotel and the employees have limited or no guest contact. These include areas such as kitchen, engineering and accounts etc.

BOT (Bar order ticket): This ticket provides information of the beverage order, name of the drink ordered and number of each drink ordered along with any special instructions if any.

BOUTIQUE HOTEL: A type of hotel, usually smaller yet sophisticated with a stylish décor and aiming to provide personalized service to its guests

BUFFET: A buffet is a system of serving meals in which food is placed in a public area where the diners serve themselves or service may be aided by the service staff

BUTCHERY: A department of kitchen area which processes meat, fish, poultry etc. and are also cut, cleaned, prepared as per the demands and requirements of different restaurants.

BUTLER SERVICE: Is a dedicated service which assists guests with varied guest requests like a personal assistant. Their position involves everything from light housekeeping, unpacking guest cases, preparation of light meals, and usually available 24hrs a day. This is a service often found in the highest standard hotels.

CDP: A Chef de partie, also known as a "station chef". He is in-charge of a particular area of production. In large kitchens, chef de partie might have several cooks and/or assistants under him

COFFEE SHOP: Often Coffee shop is the main dining place in a Hotel, often open 24 hours and serving multi-cuisine menu including global dishes to make it attractive to all guests. It provides a-la-carte and an elaborate buffet option for breakfast, lunch & dinner.

COMMIS: A junior chef in larger kitchens. May have just completed training or part of a training process

CONCIERGE: Dedicated staff members who can assist guests with dinner reservations, show tickets, and booking tours and transfers. He is stationed at front office and manages special guest request and is a go getter and extremely resourceful member of the front office.

CORKAGE: Corkage is the fee that restaurants charge customers who bring their own wine/alcohol to a restaurant.

COVER: Cover is the place where complete set of cutlery, crockery & glassware is placed and the space that a customer requires to have his meal. It also refers to the table cover size that is 24-30 inches wide.

DAY GUEST: Guests that arrive and depart the same day without spending the night at the hotel.

DIGESTIVE: A drink taken after meal.

DISCOTHEQUE: A party place where people dance at recorded music.

DOILY: - A mat lace paper, round shaped with pattern of tiny holes placed under the cakes or bowls

DOSM: Director of Sales and Marketing.

DUTY MANAGER: Duty Manager is the one who has to ensure that the hotel runs smoothly in the absence of the General Manager of the hotel.

EXPRESS CHECK-OUT: This means that at the time of leaving the hotel the process is quicker than it is during a normal check out. The guest under express check out will not have to wait at the front office.

F&B OUTLET: This term is used in Food and beverage for areas where food and beverages are served and sold to in-house as well as walk in guests. For example -coffee shop, tea lounge, bar all of these are F&B outlets

FF&E: Furniture, Fixtures and Equipment.

FINGER BOWL: A small bowl filled with warm water with a slice of lemon. It is served with a cloth napkin when food is eaten with fingers for the purpose of cleaning the fingers after a meal

FLOOR PANTRY: A service room provided on each floor for housekeepers and service staff, to store cleaning agents, equipment, guest supplies, guest room linen and housekeeping trolleys.

FOH (Front of the house): A term used to describe any functional and visible areas of the hotel, in which employees have extensive guest contact. These include but not limited to Front Desk/Reception, Restaurant, Bars, Lobby, and any accessible areas to the public.

FP (Function Prospectus/function sheet): It provides details of a function in detail to all relevant departments of the hotel. It is sent to the Chef, Concierge, Food controller, Accountant, Housekeeping, Engineering, and any other relevant department.

FREE CANCELLATION: Is a booking condition, which permits cancellation without penalty or charges, provided the reservation is cancelled before a specified date/time

FSSAI: Food Safety Standards Authority of India.

FULL BOARD: This stay plan rate includes bed, breakfast, lunch and dinner, (drinks or minibar) may or may not be included unless specified in the stay plan or accompanied with special instructions.

GARDE MANGER: Is an area of kitchen which takes care of cold food production like cold meat cuts, salads, cheese, cold soups, dressings etc.

GM: General Manager.

GOURMET: Producing or serving food that is of very high quality.

GRE: Guest Relation Executive job is to welcome guests as they arrive, co-ordinate check in and check outs and inform guests about various facilities of the hotel and helps them have a comfortable stay.

GREEN HOTEL: Generally, refers to hotels making an active effort to operate sustainably and reduce their environmental impact.

GUEST EXPANDABLES: These are supplies such as bathroom toiletries, tea and coffee sachets, stationery, magazines, slippers, laundry bags, that are expected to be used up or taken away by guest while leaving the property.

HACCP: Hazard Analysis Critical Control Point.

HALF BOARD: This stay plan rate includes bed, breakfast and either lunch or dinner.

HAPPY HOURS: This is a marketing/promotional term which refers to special offers on alcoholic beverages during a particular day or time or even restricted only on certain items in a restaurant, bar etc.

HOD: Head of Department

HUMIDOR: A cigar humidity control cabinet/a cigar case in which the cigars are kept in prime smoking condition.

HWC (Handle with care): This is a practice to flag or highlight guests who may have had previous negative experience or has some specific requirements to be provided for or simply extremely important for the hotel. This designation is given to the guest in the hotels computer system, for reminder of their stay, and remains in the 'Comments/Notes' field for future stays.

INDEPENDENT HOTEL PROPERTY: An individual hotel that is not a part of a chain/group of hotel.

INVENTORY: Inventory represents one of the most important assets of a business because the turnover of inventory represents one of the primary sources of revenue generation and subsequent earnings for the company's shareholders.

KITCHENETTE: It is a term used to describe a small kitchen facility in an apartment styled room. A kitchenette may not be in a separate area to the living area.

KOT (Kitchen Order Ticket): This ticket provides information with regard to the guest food order, name of dishes, quantity/portions ordered along with special instructions if any.

LIMITED SERVICE HOTEL: A hotel that may not offer the full range of services typically expected of a hotel. e.g. restricted room service, no health club or a pool or just one multi cuisine coffee shop.

MARINATE: To change the taste of salads, vegetables or meat and fish by way of putting them in flavour or sauce for a period of time to add flavour or to make them tender i.e to soak in a marinade

MICE (Meetings Incentives Conferences & Events): MICE represent a sector of tourism which includes business events and activities. Meeting planners and hotels often refer this term to denote an event, meeting or a conference. This is a special niche segment of business for hotels.

MINI-BAR: Is an in-room fixture, i.e a mini fridge refrigerator, stocked with juices, liquor, and snack for the convenience of guests. The contents of the bar could be miniature bottles of whisky, gin, vodka, rum and soft beverages. The mini bar may also be stocked with some packaged snack options like almonds, cashews & chocolates, waffers etc. & are individually priced

MOD (Manager on Duty): The Manager on Duty or the Night Manager is responsible for the overall operations of the hotel and its guests during the night time. Also ensures the smooth and efficient operation of the hotel during the night shift.

MOMENT OF TRUTH: Moment of truth, is the moment when a customer/user interacts with a brand, product or service & forms or change an impression about that particular brand, product or service.

MYSTERY GUEST: A quality control measure whereby an undercover Guest (usually of an external organisation representative that has expertise in service standards audit) poses as a guest to evaluate the performance of a hotel.

NIGHT CLUB: A night club in a hotel is primarily an entertainment venue serving beverages and food that usually operates late night. It may have live music, a dance floor and even a DJ.

NO SHOW: A guest who doesn't show up, despite having a confirmed reservation.

ON THE HOUSE: When guest is given something in a restaurant or bar on the house, they do not have to pay for it. (either services/food/beverage/amenities/mini bar etc.).

ON THE ROCKS: "On the rocks" refers to liquor poured over ice cubes, is a drink served on the rocks. Often a drink which is undiluted and served only with ice cubes.

OOO (OUT OF ORDER): Out of Order means that the room is not for sale because is under repair and maintenance.

OOS (OUT OF SERVICE): The Out-Of-Service status is used if you want to block a floor or wing in the hotel due to low season, cleaning, etc.

The out-of- service room is a room which is under short term maintenance but the room stays in the availability, of course, because an Out of Service room can be sold if the need arises.

OTA (Online Travel Agents): A 3rd party who often sells a hotels room inventory on their behalf (and is paid a commission for any bookings referred) Examples of some of the main OTA's include Expedia, Booking.com, Hotels.com etc.

OVER BOOKING: Overbooking is when the number of rooms booked exceeds the number of room available for sale for a particular period. Overbooking is sale of a good or service in excess of actual supply. Overselling is a common practice in the travel and hospitality sectors, in which it is expected that some people will cancel their bookings.

PAID OUT: A charge processed to a guest account, whereby external services are paid for, by the hotel on the guest behalf, and then charged to the guest account. This accounting process is also used to refund, cash balances left on a guest account at time of checkout

PATISSERIE: A place where cakes & pastries are sold.

PATISSIER: This word means Pastry Chef- one who is skilled in the art of making pastries, breads, desserts, tarts and other baked goods.

PAX: Number of people/passengers. e.g. 6 pax would be 6 people/passengers or guests

PMS: Property Management System.

POS (POINT OF SALE): Point of sales is the place where the transaction, of goods or services is executed. It's the point at which the customer pays for the services and products purchased and taxes are applied on the purchase. At this point the seller calculates the amount to be charged and generates invoice.

RACK RATE: Also known as the standard or default rate, often called as "Published Tariff" for a room, before any discounts (for example, advance purchase discounts) are applied. It is often the maximum price that is chargeable for a room.

RDM: Room Division Manager.

ROOM MOVE: It is the task of having to change the guest room, whether it is requested by the guest or is done by the hotel for some reasons.

SERVICE CHARGE: A service charge is a fee collected by an establishment for services related to the primary product or service being purchased. The charge is added at the time of the transaction. Generally, it is charged between 5% - 10 % bracket and may be optional to pay.

SIGNATURE DISH: Special dish of the restaurant or it is a recipe that identifies an individual chef or his unique way of creating a dish

SIGNATURE DRINK: A special or most appreciated or best-selling drink which contains a branded liquor or a special ingredient which makes it stand out among competition

SNAG LIST: Generally, refers to a list of problems/issues that need to be addressed. For example, a repair & maintenance detailed list of maintenance of rooms, restaurant etc.

SOMMELIER: A wine expert, who is knowledgeable wine professional. He is an expert in pairing wine with food and specializes in all aspects of wines. Generally employed in upscale/fine dining restaurants.

SOUS CHEF: Sous Chef is the second in command in the kitchen after the Executive Chef.

SPECIALITY RESTAURANT: A food outlet in a hotel which specialises in a particular cuisine could be Indian, Chinese, Japanese, Thai etc. Often the menu in such outlets is a la carte. Striving to be one of its kind. They aim to be up-scale & offer more personalized experience in its unique ways.

STUDIO: Is a term used for room types, which have a designated living area and sleeping area, but does not have walls separating them.

SUITE: Technically suite is a hotel room which has more space than a regular room. Ideally a suite should also have sitting room with a sofa but often suites are interpreted differently by different hotels.

SUPPER: A light informal evening meal especially when the dinner is taken mid day

T.I.P.S: To Ensure Prompt Service. This is the extra money/gratuity paid to the service as recognition/reward to good service provided.

TEA LOUNGE: Is a place which serves primarily tea & coffee and some light refreshments and is generally seen in the lobby of the hotel. They have a strong personality of its own to stand out amongst the competition.

TIP: A gratuity given to waiters from their guests for a great service.

TOUCH POINTS: The opportunities a hotel has, to establish a genuine connection and rapport with each guest is called as "guest touchpoints"- the moments in which a guest is in direct contact with hotel staff.

TURN DOWN SERVICE: Is an early evening service, provided by the housekeeping department. The guest room is refreshed, restocked with supplies, and bedcovers are removed for guest sleep. Guests often receive 'gifts' such as goodnight chocolate, mints, as part of the Turn Down service.

UPGRADE: Process by which a guest is offered a better room than what has been booked. Term used for a room reservation, whereby a guest is provided complimentary next category of room type above what was originally booked (at no extra charge)

VALET DRY CLEANING: It is a charged laundering and dry-cleaning service for guest clothing and garments.

VALET PARKING: Is a hotel parking service for all guests, whereby the vehicle is parked on the guest behalf by a designated staff member called valet.

DIFFERENCE BETWEEN SERVICES & PRODUCTS

- A service is produced at the instant of delivery. It can't be created in advance.
- A service cannot be centrally produced, inspected, or stocked in advance. It is usually delivered wherever the customer is.
- Services, cannot be demonstrated, nor can a sample be sent for customer approval in advance.

- The person receiving the service has nothing tangible. The value of the service depends on a customer's personal experience.
- The experience cannot be sold or passed on to a third party.
- If improperly performed, a service cannot be "recalled".
- Delivery of the service usually requires human interaction.
- The receiver's expectations of the service are integral to his or her satisfaction with the outcome.

WHY QUALITY MAINTENANCE IS DIFFICULT IN THE SERVICE INDUSTRY?

- Because service experience is Intangible.
- Because services are produced and consumed at the same time.
- Because services provided are unique as they are delivered by different people at different instances.
- Because it has high customer interaction.
- Because services have Inconsistent definition.
- Because services are affected by the service provider's knowledge.
- Because services are frequently dispersed.
- Because in services reselling is unusual.
- Because services are difficult to automate.

PHRASES TO SERVE GUESTS BETTER

1. It's my pleasure
2. Happy to help
3. Thank you
4. Welcome
5. Is there anything else I can do for you?
6. Thank you for bringing this to our attention
7. We look forward to serve you again Sir/Ma'am!
8. How may I help you today?
9. I'm sorry about that. Let me see how we can fix that right away
10. Thank you and hope to see you again soon.
11. Certainly Sir/Ma'am!

12. Thank you for choosing us, is there anything else I can help you with?
13. I apologize for any inconvenience caused
14. I do not know this, but let me find this out
15. Let me know if you have any other questions
16. Thank you for your appreciation
17. How is your day going?
18. I will keep you updated
19. I will deliver on time
20. We appreciate your business

FRONT OFFICE

FRONT OFFICE: This is the place in lobby where guests arrive in the hotel, and it is at the front desk that they check in. Front office is the face of any hotel and makes the first impression about any hotel. This department directly interacts with the guests at all times. Front desk is also called as the back bone or nerve center of the hotel. Some of the key functions of this department are Reservation, Guest service, Check-in, Check-out, Billing, Foreign exchange, Room assignment, Guest history, & handling miscellaneous guest queries and requests. It also does up-selling and cross-selling of various services and products of the hotel. Front office department is first and last contact point in hotel.

RESERVATION: This department is responsible for reserving a particular category of room for a guest for a given period of time as per the guest booking/confirmation. Reservation handles all accommodation requests and interacts with the customers and stay updated with the room availability/inventory status. Key information required by the reservation for booking a guest room are – guest name & contact number, the expected date of arrival with time & departure dates, the desired room category and the number of rooms required and number of people & booking plan and inclusions. Based on this information the reservation department checks the availability of the rooms and further confirm or decline the booking. The room reservation can be done through various channels like online portals, by calling the hotel directly, through travel agents, through tour operators, through banquets, through hotel sales team, airline crews etc.

RECEPTION: Reception department is responsible for greeting the guest on arrival and informs the guest about the hotel and its facilities and services. Registers guest & allocate room & verifies guest billing details/mode of payment. Manages room booking and process payment of guest accounts. Informs housekeeping timely at the time of guest check out. Issues room keys to guests and directs them or assist them to the room. They listen and attend to various guest requests and requirement on phone and in person. Some of the tasks performed by the reception department are:

- Registers the guest on his arrival.
- Assign rooms to the guest at the time of check-in.
- Issues room keys to the guest.
- Shows check-in, in the booking system.
- Co-ordinate with other departments of a hotel to ensure excellent services as per guest requirements.
- Manage guest complaints.
- Manage guest queries.

BELL DESK: Bell desk/Bell stand/Porter's lodge: Operations at this desk are controlled by Bell captain. In case of large & very large hotels this responsibility is taken care of by the senior bell captain. There are bell boys/porters/page boys working under the bell captain. This small desk is located in the lobby, in front of the front desk, near the entrance & luggage elevator. Bell desk communicates with Doorman, Reception/Information/Cashier & Lobby manager. Responsibilities of the bell desk are following:

1. Assists guest luggage to the front desk
2. Tag guest luggage
3. Transfer of guest luggage to guest room & often escort guest to the room
4. Inform guest of room amenities
5. During Check out- Transfers Guest Luggage to the front desk

KEY TASKS PERFOMED BY FRONT DESK

- Welcomes Guest on arrival to the Hotel.
- Explain to them the services and facilities of the hotel and explain inclusions in their stay rate/plan.
- Perform Check in & Check out of Guests.
- Maintain details of the check out and check in of the guest with billing instructions.
- Allocate guest rooms.
- Upsell Rooms and other facilities to the guests.
- Co-ordinate with different departments like housekeeping for cleaning of rooms and making them ready.
- Extend VIP courtesy and services as required.
- Plan for check in & check out of groups.
- Manage complaints or customer feedbacks with patience and expertise.
- Manage overall guest satisfaction by ensuring a comfortable and safe guest stay.

FRONT OFICE OPERATIONS: 1) Front of the House 2) Back of the House

FRONT HOUSE OPERATIONS: These operations are visible to the guests. The guests can interact and see these operations, hence, the name Front-House operations. Few of these operations include –

- Interacting with the guests to handle request for an accommodation.
- Checking accommodation availability and assigning it to the guest.
- Collecting details of the guests & information while guest registration.
- Creating a guest's account with the accounting system.
- Issuing accommodation keys to the guest.
- Settling guest payment at the time of check-out.

BACK HOUSE OPERATIONS: Front Office staff conducts these operations in which the guest's involvement is not required. These operations involve activities such as –

- Determining the type of guest (fresh/repeat) by checking the database.
- Ensuring preferences of the guest to give a personal touch to the service.
- Maintaining guest's account with the accounting system.
- Preparing the guest's bill.
- Collecting the balance amount of guest bills.
- Generating reports.
- Checking guest credit limit

GUEST CYCLE IN A HOTEL

Generally, a guest's interaction with the hotel is divided into the following sequential phases:

GUEST STAY JOURNEY:

PRE-ARRIVAL & ARRIVAL

DURING STAY

DEPARTURE

PRE-ARRIVAL: It is the stage when the customer is planning to book an accommodation in the hotel. At this stage the guest checks information displayed at hotels website, so it is crucial to have an updated, informative & easy to navigate website. The guest also checks the online reviews of the past guest experiences before making a decision.

The hotel must pay attention to the pre-confirmation communication which is the Booking Confirmation & a welcome e-mail along with all inclusions of facilities & meal plans etc.

At the hotel end, the front office accounting system captures the guest's details & information such as name, age, contact numbers, identification card, Credit Card details etc. and duration of stay for room reservation and so on.

ARRIVAL: The Front Office reception staff receives the guest at the reception and porters bring in the guest luggage. The Front Office registers the guest in the database thereby creating a guest record and a guest account along with it. Front Office hands over keys of the accommodation. After the procedure of registration, the guest begins his room stay.

DURING STAY/OCCUPANCY: During occupancy, accounting system is responsible for tracking guest charges against his/her purchases from the hotel restaurants, room service, bar, etc. On guests' request, the staff also makes arrangement for transportation, babysitting, or local touring while the guest is staying in the hotel. Front office also ensures from time to time that the guests overall stay is comfortable.

DEPARTURE: During guest departure, the front office accounting system ensures payment collection for goods and services provided to the guest. At the time of guest departure, the front office staff thanks the guest for giving an opportunity to serve & helps in smooth checkout and luggage handling. In addition, if the guest requires airport or other drop service, the front office bell desk fulfills it.

FRONT OFFICE HIERARCHY

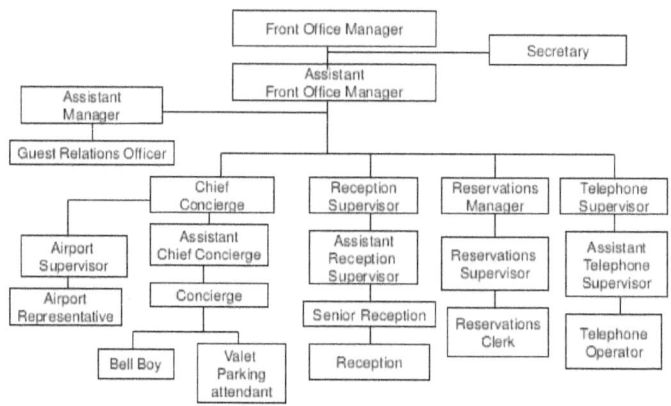

HOTEL

It is a commercial establishment which provides paid lodging to travellers & also provide meals & beverages - in room, in restaurant and also have meeting rooms that are available to the general public and to travellers

TYPES OF HOTELS

AIRPORT HOTELS: These hotels are located near airports and are ideal location for transit guests who wish to stay in a hotel in between their flights or simply ideal for those business travelers who fancy staying near an airport simply to avoid wasting travel time.

BOATELS: A house boat is often termed as a Boatels. A perfect example would be a boat which provide luxurious hotel like accommodation

BOUTIQUE HOTELS: These are distinctly different from the hotels in a way that each room has a distinct personality. These are small but expensive hotels. These hotels offer personal and personalized services by the staff.

CASINO HOTELS: In these hotels, as the name suggests, the focus is on gambling and provision of a casino. These are luxurious class hotels with well- appointed rooms and other top-class service

COMMERCIAL HOTELS: These hotels are located in the heart of the cities and busy commercial areas. The guests coming to stay are mainly commercial and company executives. Duration of stay is short, usually from 2 to 7 days. During weekends the business is slack.

CONVENTION HOTELS: These Hotels have large & extensive banqueting & convention facilities ideal for large conventions, conferences & MICE segment.

ECOTELS: The hotels that are designed and operated with environment friendly practices are called ecotels. For example, they recycle certain items and also request customers to reuse towels to save water.

FLOATELS: This type of hotels are the luxury cruise liners, sailing in seas and rivers. They have luxurious facilities like accommodation, pool, health club, restaurant's, theatre, entertainment, bar & live music etc.

HERITAGE HOTELS: These are hotels running in palaces, forts, haveli's or residences which were built prior to 1950, are called as heritage hotels.

MOTEL: This term is derived from "Motorway Hotels". These are located on the highways and the perimeters of the city. Mostly motorists, road travelers are likely to stay here for a short duration, usually overnight.

RESIDENTIAL HOTELS: These hotels are also located in the heart of the city. The guests are generally long staying guests who have to stay away from their homes for some reason and who make these hotels their homes. Length of stay is very long, 6 months to 1 year or more.

RESORT HOTELS: A destination hotel where people go to relax, rejuvenate or pursue a specific activity to take a break from the hectic city life. The guests generally arrive in these hotels for a long duration of a week to a month or even more.

ROTELS: These are special category of hotels and are also known as Hotels on wheels, for example a luxury train with all hotel facilities like accommodation, dining etc.

SUITE HOTEL: A type of hotel which has only suites, each room often has a sitting area and a compact kitchen well equipped kitchen. Such hotels are used mostly by professionals who often use the suite for their meetings and long stays

TRANSIT HOTELS: These hotels are located near airport or ports of entry in the city. The guests coming to stay are usually transit, layover passengers, airline crew and businessmen who arrive for a short duration of 1 or 2 days or a few hours.

HOTEL TYPES ON THE OWNERSHIP BASIS:

PROPRIETARY OWNERSHIP/INDEPENDENT HOTEL: Proprietary ownership is the direct ownership of one or more properties by a person or company. No affiliations or contract with other property, No tie up with other hotels. Owner has independent control. Profit goes to the owner. Quickly respond to market changes. Centralized control systems are adopted

MANAGEMENT CONTRACTED HOTELS: Management by others. Properties owned by individuals or partners but operated by external professional organization for management fee. Under this association a branded Hotel Chain may associate at management level or at franchise level. In management control they offer their brand name as well as management teams to operate the hotels as per there brands prescribed standards.

Advantages – international recognitions, operating systems, training program, marketing, international expertise, profitable operations, advertisement, reservation system, staff.

CHAIN HOTEL: Group of hotels that are owned or managed by one company is called chain hotel.

Advantages: Large central organization providing central reservation system, management aids, financial strength, expertise, manpower, specialties, promotions

FRANCHISE HOTELS/AFFILIATED: It is the authorization given by a company to another company or individual to sell its unique products and services and use its trademark according to the guidelines given by the former, for a specified time and at a specified place for a certain fee. This association has more flexibility in process & operation as compared to the management association.

Franchise owner (franchisor) grant another hotel (franchise) the right to use its methods & system, technical services, marketing trademark, signs etc. for fees.

Advantages: Opening assistance- architectural, interior designs, Systems and procedure, Staff training, Financial assistance, Advertising and global marketing, Central reservation, Central purchase.

TIME SHARE/VACATION OWNERSHIP/HOLIDAY OWNERSHIP: On payment of a membership fees each member gets to avail holidays (for certain number of their days as per there membership plan) at member properties as per the terms and conditions. Room is owned by several people for different time period. Each owner gets a stay of specific period for a number of years. One-time purchase is made, by paying purchase price & payment of a yearly maintenance fee. Generally located at dream sites like beaches, hill, waterfall etc.

Advantages: Long term accommodation, comfort homes, economical, good location, international exchange possible.

TYPES OF MEAL PLANS

EUROPEAN PLAN (EP): This plan includes room rate only.

EP = Room rate only.

CONTINENTAL PLAN (CP): This plan includes room rate and continental breakfast only. The guest will be charged additional for having lunch and dinner if he has it in the hotel.

CP = Room rate + continental breakfast.

AMERICAN PLAN (AP): In stay plan is about full board stay play as it includes American breakfast, lunch and dinner.

AP = Room rate +American breakfast + lunch + dinner

MODIFIED AMERICAN PLAN (MAP): This stay plan includes Room rate, Breakfast and one meal (either Lunch or Dinner) Guest may have either lunch of dinner that would be inclusive in the stay plan package. If guest consumes both the meals, he will have to pay for either one.

MAP = Room rate + American breakfast + lunch or dinner.

OCCUPANCY TERMS

ROOM STATUS	ABBREVIATION	EXPLANATION
OCCUPIED	O/OCC	Room currently occupied by Guest
STAY OVER		The guest is not expected to check out today and will stay at least one more night.
VACANT & READY		The room has been cleaned, inspected & ready for guest arrival
DO NOT DISTURB	DND	The guest has requested not to be disturbed.
SLEEP-OUT		A guest is registered to the room, but the bed has not been used.
ON-QUEUE		Guest has arrived at the hotel, but the room assigned is not yet ready. In such cases, the room is put on Queue, status in-order for the housekeeping staff to prioritize such rooms first.
SKIPPER		The guest has left the hotel without making arrangements to settle his or her account/bills
VACANT & READY VACANT & CLEANED CHECKED & READY	V/R or V/C or CR	The room has been cleaned and inspected and is ready for an arriving guest.

OUT OF ORDER	OOO	Rooms kept under out of order are not saleable and these rooms are deducted from the hotel's inventory. A room may be out-of-order for a variety of reasons, including the need of maintenance, refurbishing and extensive cleaning etc.
OUT OF SERVICE	OOS	Rooms kept under out of service are not deducted from the hotel inventory. This is a temporary blocking and reasons may be bulb fuse, TV remote not working, Kettle not working etc. These rooms are not assigned to the guest unless these small maintenance issues are fixed.
LOCK OUT		The room has been locked so that the guest cannot re-enter until he or she is cleared by a hotel official.
DID NOT CHECK OUT	DNCO	The guest made arrangements to settle his or her bills (and thus not a skipper), but has left without informing the front desk.
DUE DATE		The room is expected to become vacant after the following guest checks out.
CHECK OUT/ VACATED/ DEPARTED	CO or C/O	The guest has settled his or her account, returned the room keys, and left the hotel.
LATE CHECK OUT		The guest has requested and is being allowed to check out later than the normal/standard departure time of the hotel.

SCANTY BAGGAGE	SB	The guest has very light baggage that could be carried away in his/her hand without indicating an obvious departure, should he/she walk out with it.
SLEEPER/NOT CLEARED	NC	The guest has settled his or her account and left the hotel, but the front office staff has failed to update the room status.
VACANT ROOM	V	A room in which no guest has slept the previous night and which is not yet occupied.
LUGGAGE IN	L	The guest's luggage is in the room but the bed has not been slept in.
UNDER REPAIR	UR	The guest room is not to be assigned to any guest as repair work is being carried out.
NO LUGGAGE/ NO BAGGAGE	NL/NB	The guest is staying in the room but without luggage/baggage.
DOUBLE LOCK	DL	A room which has been double locked. No other key can open this room door except the grandmaster key or the emergency key.
COMPLIMENTARY	Comp.	A guest is occupied but the guest is not being charged for its use.
OVER-STAY		When a guest requested to the management that if possible extend his/her stay over and above his expected departure date

TYPES OF ROOMS

SINGLE ROOM	A room with a standard single bed to accommodate single person.
DOUBLE ROOM	A room which has double bed and provide sleeping comforts for two persons. A double bed is a larger bed.
TWIN ROOM	A room having two single beds separated out by a small bedside table. The room provides sleeping accommodation for two people.
DOUBLE DOUBLE ROOM	A room has two double beds and provides sleeping comfort for 4 people or for the family.
STUDIO ROOM	A room having utility furniture such as sofa-cum-bed. A bed is used as a sofa in the day time and converts into bed at night, meant for business people.
SUITE ROOM	A suite refers to a set of two rooms interconnected to each other out of which one is a bed room and other is a sitting room. Suite is a costly room of the hotel. Size of suite is bigger than the deluxe category but suite may be interpreted differently by different hotels
EFFICIENCY ROOM	A room having a small kitchen facility.
CABANA ROOM	A room situated near the swimming pool of the hotel and normally used by the people who love water games or swimming. These rooms are mainly used for changing.
DUPLEX	Two rooms on two successive floors and is connected to each other with a common staircase. Generally, the sitting room is on the lower floor and the bedroom is on the upper floor.
PENT HOUSE	Room situated on the highest floor of the hotel and often one of the door opening towards the terrace.

LANAI	A room overlooking a landscaped area, a scenic view, a water body or a garden. These rooms are found in resort hotels.
HOLLYWOOD TWIN ROOM	A room with two twin beds but a common headboard meant for two people. If so desired the beds can be joined together to make it appear like a single bed.
ADJACENT ROOM	Rooms close to each other perhaps in the same corridor.
ADJOINING ROOM	Rooms next to each other with an adjoining wall but not having a connecting door
INTER-CONNECTING ROOM	Rooms next to each other with an adjoin wall and an interconnecting door
PRESIDENTIAL SUITE	The best and the most luxurious and accommodation available in the hotel
QUAD	A guest room which is assigned to accommodate 4 guests, and also may have two or more beds

ESSENTIAL TERMS- FRONT OFFICE

AMENITY: Certain items that are placed for the convenience & comfortable stay of the guest at no extra cost are called amenity. For example, shampoo, soap, tooth brush, tooth paste, shaving cream, razor, shower cap, shower gel, conditioner.

AVERAGE ROOM RATE = Total Room revenue/Total Rooms sold

BACK TO BACK: This phrase refers to major guest movement in terms of check in and check outs, for example on a full house day, many guests check in and check out within a short period of time.

BLACK LISTED GUEST: This is the list of unwanted guests. This may comprise of those guests who have a poor guest history of not having paid their bills or may be who are known to damage, misbehave with staff or dispute payments.

CANCELLATION TOUR: The hour after which a property may release for sale all unclaimed non-guaranteed reservations, according to property's policy.

CITY LEDGER ACCOUNT: A collection of accounts receivable of non-registered guest e.g. one who uses the services of the hotel (e.g. Dining Room, Night Club etc.)

COMMISSION: Amount paid to a travel agent as per the agreed terms and conditions for the business of provided to the hotel.

COMPETITION SET: Those hotels who compete for the same category of guest in the market are termed as competition set for a hotel.

CUT-OFF-DATE: Cut off date is that date that which a hotel is legally bind to hold the rooms or venue for a certain booking (may be with and advance payment or may be a mutual understanding between the hotel & the booker) Howevere once the Cut off date passes the hotel has the right to release the room or banquet venue for sale to any other customer.

DOOR KNOB MENU: A kind of room menu designed in a way that it can be hanged at the door knob of the room. For example, a guest can tick requirements in the menu and hang it at the doorknob. The menu will be picked from there by housekeeping and guest order would be placed and served subsequently by food & beverage department

ELECTRONIC KEY CARD: Electronic key card that provides access to the guest room/elevators which has a magnetic strip with its master control desk at front office.

EXPECTED ARRIVAL & EXPECTED DEPARTURE: A daily report that shows the details of the expected arrivals of the guests and the expected departures of the guests

FIT: Free Individual Traveller.

FULL HOUSE: When a hotel is 100% occupied and all its rooms are occupied/sold.

GUEST HISTORY: Recording Information about a guest who has stayed & availed hotel services before also. This helps understand a guest better and to serve him better. This information also includes his room preference & his likes and dislikes.

HOUSE COUNT = Total house count of the previous day + arrivals today-today's departure

HOUSE LIMIT: It is the credit limit of the in-house guest which is established by the hotel management.

MINUS POSITION: When the booking of guests expected to check in, exceed the number of rooms available.

NO SHOW: When a guest does not come appear at the hotel in spite of holding confirmed booking.

OCCUPANY PERCENTAGE = Number of rooms occupied/Total number of rooms available × 100

OVERBOOKING: This is a situation whereby a hotel has booked more number of rooms, than the numbers of rooms available

PLUS-POSITION: When the number of rooms available exceeds the number of guest arrivals.

POSITION: it is the status of the total number of rooms available for selling.

RACK RATE: The printed tariff, or the price at which the hotel rooms are offered without applying any discount.

ROOM BLOCK: A set of rooms that has been blocked especially for a particular group of people that are going to stay with the hotel.

SELF -REGISTRATION: A computerized system that registers a guest & allocates room to the guest and dispenses based on the guest's reservation and credit card information.

SOLD OUT: Means all rooms and sold and there is no inventory of rooms available for selling. Though the amenities would differ from hotel to hotel and depending on its category and level of luxury

UNDERSTAY: A guest who checks out before the stated departure date.

UPSELL: To encourage & convince to customer to buy a higher priced product or service over a product or service which he had earlier anticipated to buy.

UPSELLING: A sales technique where a guest is offered a more expensive room than what was reserved initially and is then persuaded to buy a higher room category based on the benefits & facilties etc in that category.

WALK IN: Refers to a guest who arrives at the reception without any prior room booking.

Housekeeping

HOUSEKEEPING

Housekeeping is an essential department of Hotel which is responsible for cleanliness, maintenance and aesthetic appeal of guest rooms, public areas and maintains clean back area. Every guest demands a clean, hygienic and pleasing ambience and housekeeping plays the most crucial role in maintaining that. Housekeeping department ensures quick and efficient preparation and cleaning of guest rooms as per the required. standards. Housekeeping co-ordinates closely with front office/ reception for room status updates, it also co-ordinates with engineering and maintenance department for any repair required in the rooms or public areas.

OBJECTIVES OF HOUSEKEEPING DEPARTMENT:

- Make sure to maintain clean, safe, comfortable, fresh, and attractive and inviting surroundings for the guest.
- Keeping the guest room ready for the new arrival and contributing in the hotel's margin of profit by selling of rooms.
- Achieving the maximum possible efficiency in making sure the care and comfort of the guest and providing maximum satisfaction by taking care of their needs.
- Making sure of high standard of cleanliness and general upkeep of all areas the guest rooms, public areas, front of the house, back of the house etc. the department is responsible for.

SUB-DEPARTMENTS OF HOUSKEEPING DEPARTMENT OF A HOTEL

The design & manpower of the housekeeping department depends on the total number of Guestrooms, Outlets, and Required Staff. The following areas of the department are the most important ones:

OFFICE OF THE EXECUTIVE HOUSEKEEPER: The administrative work of the department is carried out here.

HOUSEKEEPING CONTROL DESK: It is operational 24 hours a day. Here the housekeeping staff, is registered at the beginning and end of the shift. There are note boards, storage shelves, registers, cupboard lost and found.

LAUNDRY: Washing, ironing, dry cleaning, folding of linen etc. of staff uniform & guest clothes is done

LINEN ROOM: Here, the linen of the hotel such as bed-sheets, towels, pillow cases, etc, is stored, collected, and issued as per the various requirements.

UNIFORM ROOM: The staff uniforms are collected, stored, and distributed by this department.

TAILOR ROOM: Here, stitching and repairing of linen and uniforms take place.

HOUSKEEPING STORES: It is a storage area where the cleaning equipment and items, and guest supplies are stored.

HORTICULTURE: This department is responsible for providing flower arrangements in the hotel. This room is air conditioned with water supply, cupboards and work stations, vases, stones & flowers to fufill flower requirements.

LOST & FOUND: Any guest items left are kept along with the details of the guest who left and who found it with dates. It deals directly with the front office staff, as the guests contact here only about their missing products first.

FRONT OF THE HOUSE

Guest rooms   Swimming Pool

Hotel Lobby   Restaurants

SPA   Bars

Health Club   Tea Lounge

Beauty parlour   Shops in Hotel Lobby

Guest Elevators   Hotel Exterior

Meeting Rooms   Gardens

Banquet Hall   Fitness Centre

Public Restrooms

BACK OF THE HOUSE

Office of management   Receiving Area

Staff locker rooms   Security

Staff Elevators   Engineering & Maintenance

Storage areas   Accounts & Purchase offices

Back area Corridors

ROLE OF HOUSEKEEPIG DEPARTMENT:

- Ensures well-furnished and well-maintained guestrooms and public areas.
- Ensures excellence in housekeeping sanitation, safety, comfort and maintains overall cleanliness for guests.
- Oversees the co-ordination of and administer all housekeeping programs and projects.
- Acts as a source of contact in interdepartmental communications, vendors, professional agencies etc.
- Provides a budget, and forecasting related to housekeeping.
- To achieve the maximum efficiency in ensuring the care and comfort of guests & ensures comfortable guest stay through trained and well equipped houskeeping brigade.
- Ensures warm, friendly & reliable service from all staff to the guest.

- Ensures a high standard of cleanliness and general upkeep entire hotel as per the brand standards responsibly.
- To provide linen in rooms, restaurants, banquet halls, conference halls, health clubs etc. and maintain the required inventory.
- Provides uniforms for all the staff & maintain the required inventory.
- To manage efficiently laundering requirements of hotel linen, staff uniforms, and guests.
- To provide & maintain the floral arrangement & its upkeep & freshness and to maintain the landscaped areas of the hotel.
- To select the right vendors & ensure the quality of work is maintained.
- To co-ordinate renovation and refurnishing of the property in consultation with the approved designer by the management.
- To co-ordinate with the purchase department for the procurement of guest supplies, cleaning agents, equipment, fabrics, carpets, & aim smooth housekeeping operation & ensure guest satisfaction.
- To deal with lost & found articles.
- Carpet shampooing and its cleaning and maintainence.
- Dealing with any guest queries, complaints & requests.
  - Manpower planning/requirement
  - Safely store chemicals to avoid any accident and misuse
  - Co-ordinate with purchase for replenishments
  - Par stock levels of linen
  - Discard torn linen
  - Engage best practices to avoid any misuse of linen in any other department

DEPARTMENTS HOUSKEEPING CO-ORDINATES WITH:

1. Front Office Purchase
2. Stores
3. Personal
4. Security
5. Sales & Marketing
6. Reservations
7. Laundry
8. Maintenance
9. Food & Beverage
10. Mini Bar
11. Stores
12. Kitchen

LIST OF AMENITIES IN A HOTEL ROOM

- Sewing Kit
- Shaving Kit
- Dental Kit
- Bath Robe
- Bath Mat
- Bath Towel
- Face Towel
- Hand Towel
- Shampoo
- Conditioner
- Shower Cap
- Slippers
- Tissue Box
- Option of Pillows
- Cloth hangers
- Wardrobe
- Laundry Bag
- Laundry Slip
- Iron
- Iron Board
- Doe Rack
- Shoe Horn
- Shoe polish & brush
- Shoe shine mitt
- Slipper
- Luggage rack
- Hair Dryer
- Shower & WC
- Tea Coffee Maker
- Mini Bar/Mini Fridge
- Electronic Safe (laptop size)
- Telephone with direct dial facility
- Wi-Fi service
- Adapter on request
- Alarm Clock
- USB Port
- Smart Television with satellite channels
- Letter head & pen
- Writing pad & pencil
- Envelope
- Writing table & Chair
- Table lamp
- Compendium (A booklet that provides information about hotel and contact number of essential departments)
- Dust bins
- Room service Food & Beverage menu
- Gargle Glass

PRINCIPLES OF CLEANING

These are the basic rules to follow in any kind of cleaning activity, whatever the nature of surface or the soil.

- All soil should be removed first and then Soil should be removed without causing any harm to the surface.
- First of all the most simplest method should be tried i.e the use of mildest cleaning agen.t
- Cleaning should proceed from high to low as much as possible.
- When cleaning any area always start with the cleaner surfaces and then proceed to the dirtier surfaces so as to prevent the spread of soil & dirt to cleaner surfaces.
- While wet cleaning & polishing the floor, the housekeeping staff should walk backwards while cleaning in front of him.
- Suction cleaning should always be given preference over sweeping wherever possible.
- Sweeping should always be done before dusting and Dusting should always be done before suction cleaning.
- No delay should be done in removing the stains as delay may cause them to become permanent stains.
- The housekeeping staff should take all safety precautions while cleaning. In particular, cleaning agents and equipment's should be stacked neatly to one side.
- While the area is wet the Housekeeping staff should always display a written signnange there.
- The cleaner should start cleaning from the one end of an area and then then moves towards the exit in the end.

HOUSEKEEPING TERMINOLOGY

AMENITY: All those items which are offered/placed in a guest room at no additional cost. The items are placed for guest comfort and convenience in the guest room.

BACK TO BACK: This phrase is used to express heavy rate of check ins and check out on the same day, which means as soon as one room is made up a new guest check in.

BATH-LINEN: Includes bath towels, hand towels, face towels, and fabric bath mats.

BUFFING: Polishing for example floor is polished with a special floor polishing machine.

CLEANING SUPPLIES: Small agents & small equipment those are required in cleaning of the public areas and guest room of a hotel.

CRIB: Is a cot for babies which can be provided to guest on request

CONTINGENCY PLAN: This is a plan which is implemented incase of emergencies.

CHAMOIS LEATHER: Chamois leather is usually used for cleaning & polishing. This is effective when used wet for cleaning of windows and mirrors.

DEPARTURE ROOM: This refers to a room from which the guest has departed, paid his bills and left the hotel. Such room is also called check out or vacant room

DND: Do not disturb card is hung at the door knob, which is to inform hotel staff or any visitor that the guest does not want to be disturbed

DOUBLE LOCK: It is an occupied room which has been locked from inside and outside so that no one can enter the room

DEEP CLEANING: This term refers to employing intensive and special cleaning for public areas or guest rooms and is planned and conducted as per a schedule or for special event or requirement.

DEBRIEFING: This a briefing session which is done for the team at the end of the shift, to discuss any problem faced, information sharing or suggestions

DUVETS: These are quilts filled with feathers or synthetic fibres.

FAUCETS: Another term used for Taps.

FLOOR PANTRY: This is a room provided for housekeeping staff on each guest floor for storage of cleaning agents, equipment's, guest supplies, room linen and room attendant cart.

FOC: Free of charge/Free of cost.

FOLIAGE: Foliage is more affordable than flowers and is often used as a dark background to highlight flowers. Using foliage in flower arrangements is as a filler that creates a fuller impact without huge expense. Foliage is a collection of leaves of one of more types of plants/trees or it may also be understood as green/brown leafy material used in a flower arrangement.

GRAND MASTER KEY: This is a specially designed key which can open all locks of all a certain floor or a certain group/category in a Hotel. A grand master key may open all locks of every group

GRAVEYARD SHIFT: Night shift.

GUEST COMPENDIUM: This a directory provided in a hotel room with the objective of providing information about the hotel and aims at making the guest stay more comfortable. It is a concise yet detailed information about a hotel and its services provided either physically in the form of a booklet or digitally made available online or through an app.

GUEST REQUEST: A service or an item requested by guest.

GUEST SUPPLIES: This refers to all the items that are placed in the guest room for the comfort of the guest and are complimentary

GRA: Guestroom Attendant

HAND CADDY: It's an easy portable container that stores cleaning supplies and equipment.

HOUSKEEPING CONTROL DESK: This is one desk which provides one point of contact for all activities of housekeeping and maintains constant contact with housekeeping staff working at different locations. It also co-ordinates with front office of room status and with maintenance department for any room guest problem.

IKIBANA: Is Japanese art of flower arrangement, it aims at expressing emotions of the inner qualities of flower and other live material.

INVENTORY: Stock supplies, and other items held for future use in a hotel. For example, linen, cleaning supplies, guest amenities etc. are held in the stores as an inventory as and when required.

KEY CONTROL: A control system that requiring each staff to account for all keys during working hours.

LANDSCAPE AREA: An area where trees, shrubs, plants turf, deck, walks, ponds and so on have been used to create a natural looking scenery which is functional and visually appealing.

LINEN CHUTE: This is a narrow passage from the floor pantries of each floor for soiled linen which lands into the central place of collection in laundry.

LINEN-ROOM: Central area of the Housekeeping Department from which all uniform supplies and linen is issued.

LINT-FREE: This term refers to the fabric/cloth that do not shed lint i.e. small fibre.

LOCK OUT: When the guest room has been locked and the guest is not able to enter the room and a hotel official has to clear that.

LOG BOOK: This is an important document in housekeeping, that is used to log/write information sharing from one shift to another (writing down information ensures correct information sharing and it is essential for the next shoft to acknowledge the information received)

LUGGAGE RACK: A special designated rack provided in the guest room to place luggage is called luggage rack.

MAIDS CART: Is a housekeeping trolley that consists of guest supplies and equipment required for cleaning of guest bedroom and bathroom.

MAKE UP: Servicing of the room while a guest is registered in it.

MASTER KEY: A specially designed key which can open all locks of a certain group. For example, a master key may open all locks which are not double locked or may be master key could be for a floor etc.

MATTRESS PROTECTOR: This is the protector for a mattress, which keeps it safe from getting wet and increases the usage life of a mattress by protecting it from wearing out.

MITERING: It is a contouring method used for sheets and blankets to neatly fold and fit in the corners of the mattress that gives a smooth finish to it.

ODOUR: Odour is a strong, pervasive quality of something that is perceived by the sense of smell. It can be any pleasant or unpleasant smell inside of outdoors.

OTTOMAN: It's a comfortable sitting sofa kind but without a back.

PARLOUR: It is a sitting room which has a concealed bed

PAR STOCK/PAR NUMBER: A multiple of the standard quantity of a particular inventory item that must be on hand to support daily, routine housekeeping operations.

POTPOURRI: This is a mixture of spires, dried flower petals that provide natural fragrance pot together in a bowl. Potpourri may be placed to freshen up hotel rooms.

PREVENTIVE MAINTENANCE: This maintenance is preventive is nature that means that it is conducted in advance before the problem or breakdown takes place of furniture, fixtures, equipment or just for general upkeep in the hotel. The approach to maintain and prevent any equipment failure or pro-actively handle maintenance issue

REFURBISH: To give a fresh new look to a room by changing or redoing its furnishings, decorating it differently or even changing its carpet as well to give the room a new look

ROOM INSPECTION: The process of detailed checking of the rooms to ensure that it is clean, hygienic and all equipment's and fixtures are checked for maintenance needs.

ROOM ATTENDANT CART: It's a moveable cart with wheels used by room attendants for transporting cleaning suppliers, guest amenities & linen

ROOM STATUS REPORT: This is a report that shows overall occupancy/condition of the rooms of the hotel property. This report is essential for for both front office and housekeeping to function smoothly

ROOM STATUS DISCREPANCY: This is difference when the room status information of front office, differs from the room status information of Housekeeping

ROOM DIVISION MANAGER: This is the position which heads the front office as well as housekeeping

ROUTINE MAINTENANCE: Maintenance activities that are conducted as per general upkeep of the property and is done on a regular basis.

SANI-BINS: These are small metallic containers with lids that are kept in toilets to collect the soiled sanitary napkins.

SHOE HORN: This is a tool which is used to easily slip your foot into your shoes. It has a long handle to make it easy to use and is curved to help slip foot easily into a shoe.

SORTING: This is the process of sorting soiled linen into different categories on the basis of how badly soiled they are, coloured and white separately, whether they are to be laundered or dry cleaned as per the cloth or required cleaning method.

TURN DOWN SERVICE: This is a special service in the guest rooms in the evening whereby the room attendant enters the guest room early evening to restock the supplies, refreshes the room in terms of making the bed and prepares it for the night.

UPHOLSTERY: Fabric, textiles, paddings, springs and other materials used to decorate the furniture and to make them more aesthetic and comfortable.

VANITY UNIT: A unit that comprises of Mirror, washbasin and has flat space for amenities like soap, dental kit, brush & toothpaste and glass.

CLEANING EQUIPMENT

Cleaning equipment of the housekeeping department is broadly divided into Manual and Mechanical Equipment.

MANUAL EQUIPMENT: The equipment used to perform the tasks manually by the staff. Manual equipment is usually Brushes, mops and brooms.

BRUSHES: Brush is a type of manual equipment having major three parts Bristles, head stock and handle. Brushes are used for cleansing of various types of surfaces.

Types of brushes

1. Toilet brush
2. Carpet brush
3. Upholstery brush
4. Wall brush
5. Cloth scrubbers
6. Feather brush

BROOMS: Broom is a manual equipment having long bristles which maybe of soft or hard texture. Brooms may be soft brooms or hard brooms.

SOFT BROOM: Soft brooms have fiber which are of a soft texture and these brooms are used for cleaning smooth surfaces and meant for less dust prone areas.

HARD BROOM: Hard brooms have hard texture bristles and they are meant for rough areas and highly dust prone surfaces.

MOPS AND DUSTERS: Mops are manual equipment used for dusting of surfaces. Mops and dusters are created such that they absorb the dirt from surfaces without dispersing particles.

TYPES OF MOPS

IMPREGNATED: Impregnated dust mops are disposable floor wipes which are impregnated with a special dust absorption liquid. ... Impregnated floor mops do not dry out, bulge out, nor evaporate. Mops which may be impregnated or require impregnation before use.

KENTUCKY MOPS: Kentucky mops consist of cotton strands which are inserted into a metal.

STATIC MOPS: A mop which has polyester, acrylic or nylon strands, these are useful for large surface area cleaning.

SPONGE MOPS: Mops including sponge which are used for cleaning a hard surfaces and windows.

HOUSKEEPING EQUIPMENTS

SQUEEZEE: A mop consisting of a long handle and a wooden blade to remove excess water.

DUSTERS: Dusters are used for dusting and they are absorbent and made of cotton. They should be used in a dry state to easily dust-off particles and buff the surface.

CONTAINERS: Containers are used in the housekeeping department for carrying, collecting and transporting items from one place to other.

Types of containers:

1. Buckets
2. Dust pan and Dust bin
3. Sani bin
4. Maid's cart

BUCKETS: They are used for carrying water and other cleaning liquids. Plastic buckets are preferred by hotels as they are light weight. Buckets help in carrying water or solution during cleaning.

DUST PAN: Dust pans are used with broom to collect all the dust accumulated during cleaning process.

DUST BIN: Containers which are provided in various areas to throw in the garbage are known as dust bin.

SANI BINS: Bins which are kept in toilets for collecting the used bathroom linen.

MAIDS CART: The maids cart is the daily required equipment for the smooth functioning of housekeeping department. It is a cart having all essentials for servicing guestrooms.

MECHANICAL EQUIPMENT: Mechanical equipment is used with the help of electricity. It is essential to train the staff regarding the functioning of mechanical equipment.

VACUUM CLEANER: Vacuum cleaners are used mostly as they suit all surfaces and also are suitable to the carpeted areas. Vacuum cleaners help in removing dirt, grime and dust from a surface with the help of suction. Vacuum cleaners may be of different types like Backpack vacuum cleaner, cylindrical vacuum cleaner etc.

FLOOR SCRUBBING MACHINES: Floor scrubbing machines help in cleaning the surface with scrubbing as well as polishing it. They consist of pads which apply polish and then scrub it to give a smooth finish to the surface.

WET EXTRACTIONS SYSTEM: Wet extraction works by injecting water and suction to clean the surface. It is way better than a normal vacuum cleaner as it goes deep down the surface and plucks out the embedded soil.

SCRUBBER DRIER SWEEPER: A three in one feature used in large surfaces to sweeping, scrub and dry the areas.

TYPES OF CLEANING AGENTS

Cleaning agents are materials which may be naturally occurring or synthetic in nature used for cleaning various kinds of surfaces and materials.

MAJOR TYPES OF CLEANING AGENTS

WATER: Water is the primary cleaning agent used for cleaning surfaces.

DETERGENTS: Detergents help in cleaning by removing dirt from the surface and suspend the dirt particles.

ABRASIVES: They are used to clean out stubborn marks and stains. They scrub out the dirt and grim which detergents may not be able to.

ORGNANIC SOLVENTS: Organic solvents are basically solvents that are useful for stain removal.

DISINFECTANT: Useful for germ control in surfaces.

POLISHES: Polishes are buffing solution used for providing a smooth finish to surfaces and these finishes act as a protective layer.

GLASS CLEANERS: Cleaners used to wash glasses and remove dirt from glasses. They may be used directly or with help of dusters.

COMMONLY USED CLEANING AGENTS

BORAX: Borax is a boric acid salt, which is used to remove tea and coffee stains.

JEWELLERS ROUGE: It is used for polishing and buffing of surfaces like silver.

LINSEED OIL: Used for painting furniture and it is a byproduct of flax seeds.

PUMICE: Used as an abrasive on hard surfaces because of its porous nature.

SAWDUST: Used as an abrasive and it helps in absorbing grease and oil.

TURPENTINE: It helps to dilute paints.

VINEGAR: It is a commonly used glass cleaner.

FULLER'S EARTH: It is used to absorb grease and it is a naturally occurring cleaning agent.

METHYLATED SPIRIT: Used as a degreaser in cleaning

ACETONE: Cleans marks of grease, oil, resin, ink, permanent marker, adhesive, and paint.

CLEANING EQUIPMENTS

SANI BIN   SOFT BROOM   MAIDS CART

DUST PAN & BROOM   DUST PAN   TOILET BRUSH

WATER SQUEEZE (with handle)   KENTUCKY MOP   STATIC MOP

CARPET BRUSH   HARD BROOM   LINEN TROLLEY

HAND CADDIES   MOP WRINGER TROLLEY   CARPET VACCUM CLEANER

Customer Service

CUSTOMER SERVICE

Customer service is all about meeting the needs and desires of the customers. Customer service is the support extended by the firm both, before and after the sales to ensure a hassle free and enjoyable experience. Good customer service is prompt, attentive, knowledgeable, proactive, polite, patient, empathetic keeping the customer needs at the top of each interaction. Good customer service is critical to business success, ensuring brand loyalty one customer at a time.

WHO ARE CUSTOMERS?

Anyone who is provided with a good, product, service or idea is a customer. There are two types of customers –

- Internal Customers
- External Customers

INTERNAL CUSTOMERS: All those who are directly connected with the organization is called an internal customer. Usually, internal customer is part of the organization, like stakeholders, employees, departments or shareholders.

EXTERNAL CUSTOMER: All those who are external to the organization is called an external customer. For example, anyone buying a refrigerator, designer suit or software is a customer of the company manufacturing it

KEY TERMS IN CUSTOMER SERVICE

CUSTOMER EXPECTATION: Individual Customer expectation are created in customer's mind by many factors-their previous experience, advertisements or knowledge that they have gained about the product, service or organization. This includes everything, be it a customer, a product, service or an organization.

EXPLICIT EXPECTATIONS: These are the service standards which are clearly stated, like Dominos Pizza clearly states 30-minute delivery or free Pizza/discount (subject to T&C) similarly IBIS Hotel chain promises to solve any problem you have with the hotel room or hotel in 15 Minutes otherwise they will not charge for stay (Quality Commitment www.ibishotels.com).

An organization promises certain levels of service delivery and commits to deliver that. This could have been communicated through advertisement or brochure or a sales person. The services promised play a big role in shaping the customer expectation from the service. However, it may lead to a mismatch if the sales person or the company has over promised and fail to live up consistently to the promise made.

IMPLICIT EXPECTATIONS: These are the expectation that a customer may have developed on the basis of his personal learning from his surroundings. For example- depending on the price, he may estimate that just because a product is priced higher than its competitor it must be of better quality.

INTERPERSONAL EXPECTATIONS: This expectation is all about interaction with the service provider. Customers expect the service providers to be expert, professional, friendly courteous and with updated knowledge of the product/service they are providing

DYNAMIC EXPECTATIONS: This expectation is about how a product or service is expected to change over a period of time. The changes could be because of the changing needs of the customer, business environment or change in the organizational goals

WHAT DO CUSTOMERS EXPECT:

Quality customer service

Personalized and customized touch by the service provider

Low effort in doing business with a company

Quick resolution of any complaint

Updated & good knowledge of the service provider

Quality Product and Services that perform well

Good after sales service

BRAND PROMISE: It refers to the experience or value that each customer can expect every time they interact with an organisation. It is statement or promise communicated by an organization to its customers confirming a certain experience or value every time.

CUSTOMER DELIGHT: Customer Delight astonishes a client by surpassing their expectations and consequently making a positive enthusiastic response. This enthusiastic response prompts Word of mouth. Customer Delight legitimately influences the deals and benefits of an organization as it recognizes the organization and its items and administrations from the challenge.

PRINCIPLES OF CUSTOMER DELIGHT:

Always Be Timely.

Always Listen to Your Customers.

Give them what they need (not always what they want).

Give Customers Little Things When They Don't Expect It.

Give Customers a Point of Contact.

Give Customers Space.

Have Policies, But Always Be Flexible.

Tell Your Customers How You Will Help Them.

LOYALTY PYRAMID: The loyalty pyramid concept was introduced by David A. Aaker. The five stages are as below as customers become more faithful and loyal to the brand or a product/service. At the base of the loyalty pyramid are switchers.

SWITCHERS: No loyalty to any brand. They grab the first thing off the shelf.

HABITUAL: This person tries to buy one brand but is not at all passionate about it.

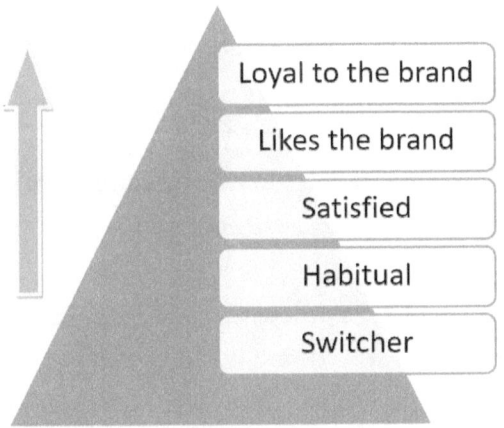

SATISFIED: These buyers are happy with the brand. But they stick with it because they don't like changes.

BRAND LIKERS: A true brand enthusiast.

LOYAL TO THE BRAND: Buyer is proud to be a part of this brand. The brand identity of the products fits so closely with the buyer's personal values and day-to-day life. Loyal custoemrs recommends the brand to others also

KEY CONCEPTS IN CUSTOMER SERVICE

CUSTOMER LIFE TIME VALUE: Customer lifetime value (CLV), represents the total amount of money a customer is expected to spend on your product and services in their life time. This helps one take decisions about how much money to invest in acquiring new customers and retaining existing ones.

CLV = average value of a purchase X number of times the customer will buy each year X average length of the customer relationship (in years)

CALCULATION of CUSTOMER LIFE TIME VALUE

- How much is your average customer sale? (1500)
- How Many Times does your average customer make a purchase from your business in a year? (12)
- Average Customer Sale x Number of Purchases in a year (1500x12)
- How many years is that customer will be your potential customer (10 Yrs)
- If your customer tells at least 10 people about the bad experience and out of that 8 stop doing business with you
- Cost Calculations {1500 x 12 x 10 (10 years) = 1,80,000}
- Customers because of Lost reputation loss= (8)
- Value of 8 lost customer 8x180000=1,44,0000.
- Total Lost Business = 1620000/-
- In the lowest Loss Business Scenario if he advocates negative feedback to only half the number estimated numbers: 1620000/2 = approx. 800000/(8 lakhs)
- APPOX Rs.8 Lakhs Loss if we lose one customer spending average 1500 per and could have been a potential customer for ten years and its effect on brand and reputation.

There is a big opportunity for Finance and front line teams to work in Sync to understand the simple fact that the entire organization has to commit to a seamless customer experience to move forward and faster, so as to be more profitable in the long run.

FCR: First-Call Resolution: Is when a customer query, problem or a question is resolved in one contact and he does not require another contact for the same.

AVERAGE HANDLING TIME: It refers to the time the call is picked up including the holding call time, talking time, during the discussion till hanging up the call. It is an important call centre metric. In the simplest terms, AHT is the average time it takes to handle a call or transaction from start to finish – from call initiation, to hold time, to talk time, and all the way through to any related tasks an agent must perform post-phone call to resolve that call.

REDEMPTION RATE: Redemption rate is the best leading indicator of whether your loyalty program is succesful or not. That's because it measures how many points have been redeemed by your members. This shows if your program is engaging enough to encourage members to return and shop more often.

REPEAT PURCHASE RATE: Repeat Purchase Rate is the percentage of customers who come back to place another order, which reflects that they found value in the last purchase and also were satisfied with the last purchase.

100% repeat purchase means every customer comes back again. 0% purchase rates would mean that no one came back to purchase again.

CRM: Customer relationship management refers to all the initiatives that an organization uses to manage its contacts and relationships, both external and internal, such as:

1. Email subscribers
2. Sales leads
3. Sales opportunities
4. Customers
5. Advocates
6. Employees

SENSORY CUSTOMER EXPERIENCE: Sensory marketing builds on the idea that bodily sensations unconsciously influence consumer behaviour. Subtle cues such as scents in a store or a signature product feel can evoke an emotional response in people. Companies build on these unconscious cognitive cues to increase brand recognition and recall, develop stronger emotional brand attachment, and influence purchases.

SEAMLESS SERVICE: Seamless service removes all potential frustration points for customers – it makes the service experience feel almost invisible to them. Customers should never have to work too hard to communicate with your company, to have their needs fulfilled, or to provide feedback.

CUSTOMER DEFECTION: The frequency with which customers stops doing business with a company is called **Defection Rate.**

The one figure every organization aims to grow is **Customer Retention Rate.**

CUSTOMER RETENTION RATE: Customer Retention refers to all the initiatives and activities that an organization implements in retaining their customers and to reduce the customer defection.

Often loyalty program, customer recognition offers etc. are part of this initiatives

Some benefits of Customer Retention:

1. It is cheaper than acquiring new customers
2. Lesser marketing cost as it leads to improved positive word of mouth
3. Loyal Customer come and buy more from you
4. Higher profitability
5. Leads to a sustainable and growing business model

REASONS WHY ORGANIZATIONS LOSE CUSTOMERS?

- Complicated process to do transactions with your company
- Having not attended the customers well
- Not having dealt satisfactorily with the customer problem
- Cheaper options available from the competitors
- A new innovative product launched in the market.
- Aiming only transactional relationship and not engaging emotionally.

The Ultimate Two Prong Business Growth Strategy:

1. **Hold on to your old customers**
2. **Make new customers**

COST OF ACQUISITION (COA): It refers to the cost of all the activities and initiatives that an organization takes to acquire new customers to purchase there good and services for example if an organization has spent USD 10000/for acquiring 10 new customers then the average cost of customer acquisition would be USD 1000/-

NET EFFORT SCORE or NET EASE SCORE:

This refers to answer around one single question:

It means, how easy is it, to do business with an organization?

It is built around the central single question from the question, and asking a rating for the same.

How easy was it for you to get the help that you wanted? The same can be answered on a scale of 1-10 (1 being easiest and 10 being extremely difficult).

CUSTOMER EFFORT SCORE (CES): it refers to that aspect of customer satisfaction measurement that focuses to measure how much effort a customer has to put in getting an issue resolved. The key question asked from the Customer is -How much effort had to put in to do business with our company or to resolve a complaint or an issue.

The response could be: Very High Effort, Very Low Effort

Low effort means happy customer and high effort means that there is a high possibility that he is unhappy and may consider taking his business to competition.

CHURN RATE: Churn Rate refers to the % at which the existing customers stop using an organizations product and services over a specified period of time.

NET PROMOTER SCORE (NPS): Was developed by Customer Loyalty Guru Fred Reichheld. Management Consultancy Bain and launched under the slogan: **"the One Number you need to grow".**

This model asks the following question- How likely is it that you would recommend company/brand X to a friend or colleague: on a scale whereby 0 is unlikely to be recommended and 10 is extremely likely to recommend.

0 1 2 3 4 5 6 7 8 9 10

Till 0–6 are Detractors

Between 7–8 are Passive and are considered Ignored in the NPS Format

Between 9 and 10 are Promoters Bain's Net Promoter Score (NPS) - the scale to measure Customer Loyalty.

For example, if we were to apply that on our above mentioned three customer categories:

PROMOTERS: The ratings by this category of customers is 9 or 10 out of ten

PASSIVES: The ratings by this category of customers is 7 or 8 out of maximum ten

DETRACTORS: The ratings by this category of customers are 0 to 6 out of maximum ten.

MYSTERY SHOPPING: Mystery Shopping is the evaluation, measurement and reporting of **customer service experience & standards** as measured by external experts who pose as customers

PHRASES CUSTOMERS LOVE TO HEAR

- I will ensure that it gets resolved.
- I absolutely agree...
- I can certainly help you...
- I will be glad to assist you....
- I completely understand the inconvenience caused to you.
- Sure sir, I will find that out for you Sir!
- Sir, I will send you an update on this latest by such and such date and time.
- Don't hang up the phone on the customer, rather wait for the customer to hang up.
- Sir, is there anything else I can help you with.
- Instead of using the words ok, replace it with certainly Sir.
- Acknowledgement! for example - Good Morning.
- What can I do for you sir?
- Have a great day sir.
- I completely understand sir.
- Thank You.
- Addressing the Customer by the name.
- "Apologies for keeping you on hold".

RESPONSE THAT CUSTOMERS HATE

1. When it takes too long to resolve an issue.
2. When Promises that are not kept.
3. Being treated rudely or treating customers with suspicion.
4. Having to check several times if a issues has been resolved.
5. Being transferred from one person to another, and having to repeat an issue several times.

THEY HATE WHEN THEY ARE TOLD

1. "That's not my job".
2. I'm surprised you haven't heard about our product.
3. Sorry, it's closing time, so I can't talk with you now.
4. Tell me your name again, and what the problem is.
5. That's against our policy.
6. That's another department.
7. To be honest Sir, I can't really do anything about this.

CUSTOMER FEEDBACK IS A GIFT!

Most of the company's feel that customer complaints are bad for business. But it is not essential that no complaint is good business. No complaints may actually mean that most of the feedbacks, received are not reaching the right ears.

Some of the reasons why Customer Feedback may not be reaching the Company Board Rooms:

a. It may reflect that no one thinks that it is important for the senior management to know about that.

b. Or it may also mean that the complaints are landing in no man's zone (i.e. complaint management is no one's responsibility and everyone is playing buck passing).

When customers complain, it means that they are trying to highlight a problem with the company's employees, processes, and policies. Rather than ignoring the complaint, it would be better for a company to acknowledge the customer's complaint, apologize for the inconvenience, and then act fast to resolve the problem.

IMPORTANCE OF CUSTOMER COMPLAINTS:

• Customer complaints can give new ideas and suggestions for new products and business lines.

• It keeps company on their toes to stay committed continuous improvement.

• The user customers are the best person to highlight "what's wrong with the product".

SOME OF THE REASONS WHY CUSTOMERS COMPLAINT?

• Low quality of products and service.

• Rude and shoddy customer service is the main reason for which customers complain and stop doing business with a company.

• Rude and untrained staff.

• Over commitment and under delivery of services and products.

• Lack of staff knowledge for product and services.

- Tossing customer from one department to another, whereby no one from the organization is ready to take ownership of the issue.
- Not keeping promises.
- Not listening to Customer feedback and customer has to keep repeating his feedback.
- Inaccessibility in connecting for after sales.
- Keeping an issue unresolved.

"DO ALL DIS-SATISFIED CUSTOMER'S ALWAYS COMPLAIN?"

The answer to that is NO. Most of the customers who are not satisfied simply walk off, without registering a complaint. The % of customers who complaint is like a tip of an ice berg whereby only a handful of them give a detailed feedback and most of them simply walk off, never to be seen again. They not only take their business elsewhere but also tell other about the poor service experience. According to research by Esteban Kolsky, 13% of unhappy customers will share their complaint with 15 or more people. Furthermore, only 1 in 26 unhappy customers complain directly to you.

"WHY MOST OF THE DIS-SATISFIED CUSTOMERS DON'T COMPAIN"?

1. They feel it's going to be a waste of their time.
2. They feel nothing will change because of their complaint, which means they lack confidence in the establishment and its team.
3. They are not sure who they should be met for registering a complaint, which means that its complex to make a complaint or register a feedback.
4. Fear of retribution: they feel, that may be challenged or heard with suspicion about the intentions and the authenticity of the complaint, hence they avoid lodging feedback.

Staying closer to Customer feedback is not only desired but is a necessity. Dis-satisfied customer's, whose complaints have not been managed, walk around affecting negatively, in-numerable prospective buyers.

STRATEGY FOR SUCCESSFUL COMPLAINT MANAGEMENT:

1. Listen patiently (with an understanding that the complaint is not aimed at an individual but a situation).
2. Do not take the complaint personally.
3. Empathize & thank the customer and confirm understanding of the Complaint.
4. Offer option of solutions or confirm timeline of issue resolution (keep promise).
5. Act promptly to resolve.
6. Confirm with the customer if the solution resolves the Complaint completely

Food Production

FOOD PRODUCTION HIERARCHY

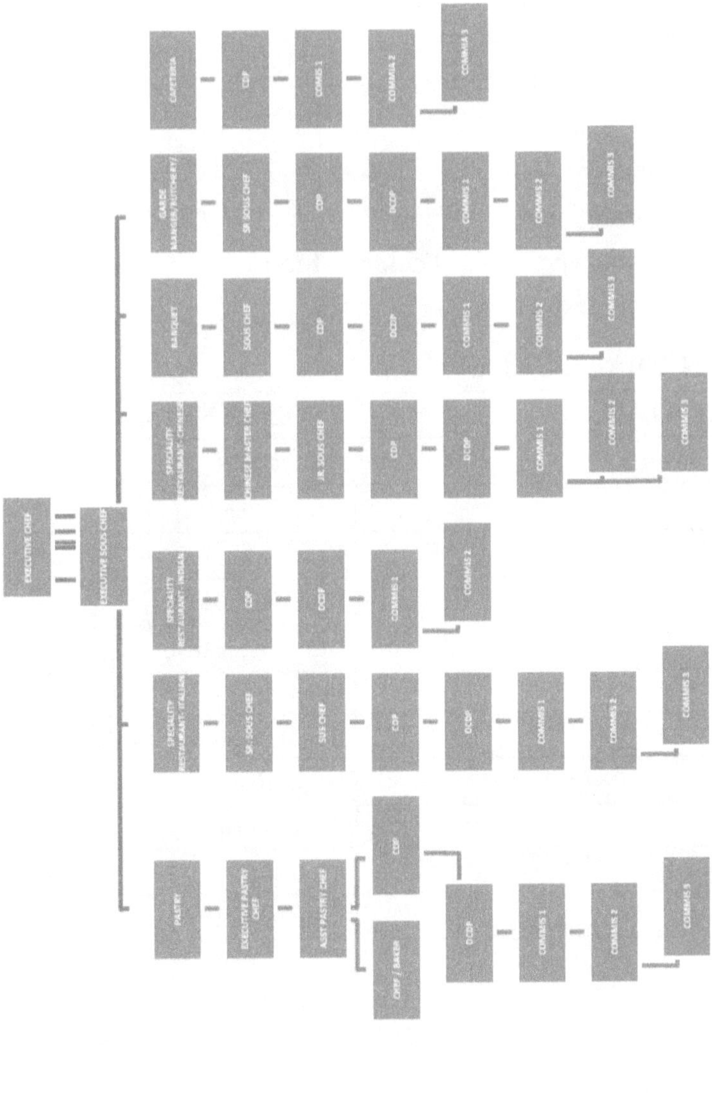

OBJECTIVES OF COOKING:

Applying heat to a food often chemically transforms it, leading to change in texture, consistency, appearance and nutritional properties

- Sterilization
- Cooking helps complex food split into simpler substances
- Makes the food more palatable
- Increases the Preservation period
- Enhancement of nutritive value
- Making food appetizing
- Makes it easy to chew
- Kills harmful bacteria
- Improves Digestibility
- Provides Variety
- Retaining nutritive value
- Retaining the original color of food
- Prevent clash of flavors

FRENCH CLASSICAL MENU

FRENCH TERM	ENGLISH TERM
Hors D'Oeuvres	Appetizers
Pôtage	Soup
Poisson	Fish
Entrée	First meat dish
Réleve	Main meat dish
Sorbet	Flavoured Ice
Rôti	Roast of games, birds or joints
Legumes	Vegetables
Entremets	Sweet Dish
Savoureux	Savoury
Dessert	Fruit/Dessert

KITCHEN DEPARTMENTS

MAIN KITCHEN: Main kitchen may have several sub sections like-Indian kitchen, continental, south Indian Tandoor. This kitchen serves primarily to coffee shop. Room service and snacks for the bar. This is a large kitchen area which caters to various food and beverage outlets

PANTRY: Pantry section is mostly responsible for tea/coffee, sandwiches, salads, juices. This section is like a service counter for all outlets.

TANDOOR SECTION: This section has tandoor and is responsible for different types of Indian breads, seekh kebabs, tandoori chicken, vegetable seekh, boti kebab etc.

BAKERY & CONFECTIONARY: This part of the kitchen is responsible for bakery items like cakes, pastries, muffins, breads, continental desserts, chocolate etc. This section makes gum paste, icing sugar, cake icing work and does all the pastry art-work. This section of kitchen is also responsible for baking & hot preparations like breads, muffins, sponge cakes, puff pastry etc. that is further used in patisserie.

BANQUET KITCHEN: This kitchen is responsible for cooking food in bulk as it caters to the banquets, conferences and large gatherings functions/events.

HALWAI SECTION: This section is responsible for Indian sweets like jalebis, rasgullas, rabri etc.

BUTCHERY: This section is responsible for the raw meat like chicken, mutton, fish, prawns, lobsters etc., these are cleaned/cut & portioned and packaged as per the specification and made ready for storage.

GARDE MANGER/COLD KITCHEN: This kitchen section is responsible for cold salads and caters to the salad requirement of various food and beverage outlets. This cold kitchen section also does mise-en-place and cold savoury items are prepared here. Cold sauces, cold starters and salads are done here

COMMISSARY: This section is responsible for storage of all green vegetables in bulk and does the mise-en-place of vegetables. Various vegetables are cleaned, trimmed, peeled and placed in refrigeration.

FRENCH NAMES FOR DIFFERENT CHEFS...

CHEF POTAGE: Soup Chef

BOUCHER: Butchery Chef

CHEF ENTREMETIER: Vegetable Chef

CHEF GARDE MANGER: Responsible for cold hors d' oeuvres

CHEF LEGUME: Legume chef

CHEF BOULANGER: Bakery Chef

CHEF PATISSERIE: Pastry Chef

CHEF GAILLARDIA: Grill Chef

GLACIER: Prepares ice cream and cold desserts

CONFISEUR: Prepares candies & petit fours

CHEF POISSOINER: Fish Chef

CHEF FRITURIER: Fry Chef

CHEF TOURNANT: Reliever spare hand

TYPES OF MENU

The different types or classes of menu are distinguished by the variations in the selections offered and by their pricing structure.

A LA CARTE MENU: An a la carte menu is a menu that provides choices within each course and in which each item is individually priced and charged. Menu items selected by the guest are cooked to order. The literal meaning of the French words a la carte is 'from the card'.

TABLE D' HOTE: A table d'hote menu is a menu which offers some (usually limited) choice and is charged at a fixed price per person for the whole menu. Table d'hote is, literally, French for 'the proprietor's (main hosts) table'. A modestly priced 'business lunch', in which 3 or 4 items only are offered in each course and the guest pays a fixed price for the whole meal, is an example of table d'hote menu. These menus are more popular for festive occasions, for e.g. Christmas, New Year Eve etc

SET MENU: A set menu is one which offers set items (one for each course) pre-arranged by the host. Set menus are utilized predominantly for functions, e.g. weddings and banquets.

CARTE DU JOUR: Carte du jour literally means 'card of the day'. It offers choices available for a particular day only. It allows the chef to offer a list of 'specials' or variations in addition to a pre-printed a la carte menu.

CYCLIC MENU: A cyclic menu is a group of menus which are rotated on a set cycle. It is a set of menus which is repeated over a period of time for example for 4 weeks. Cycle menus are usually used in the institutional sector of the industry, for e.g. hospitals, prisons on airlines and in employee cafeterias.

CONSIDERATIONS TO ACHIEVE MENU BALANCE

- Principles of digestibility
- Guests individual preferences
- Season of the year and nature of occasion
- Availability of raw ingredients
- A clear cost and pricing policy
- Nutritional value
- Flavour
- Colour
- Texture and consistency

CONSIDERATIONS TO ACHIEVE A GOOD PRESENTABLE GUEST MENU

- Use simple language so that the guest is able to understand the menu items quite easily.
- Telling the important things in the menu for items that have some religious exceptions (pork, beef), allergies (nuts, shellfish), or unique flavours.
- One should not be afraid of being a little descriptive. Use of adjectives like crunchy, juicy, fresh helps the guest paint a picture.
- The origin of the menu item and the proper method of preparation should be correctly written in the menu.

- A description of accompaniments is also important so that the guest can have a complete understanding of the full experience.
- Spellings and grammar must be proper.
- Selection of menu paper, printing ink, colour, font etc. should be appropriate and such that the printed items should be readable in the dining area in the lighting level used during meal periods.
- Overall presentation and designing of the menu should suit the theme of the restaurant.
- Maintenance of the menu cards must be ensured at all times. They should not be torn, mutilated or stained.
- Pricing should not be confusing
- Menu should be easy to order from & understand, from the guest point of vie

COOKING METHODS

- Cooking methods are classified as moist heat & dry heat.

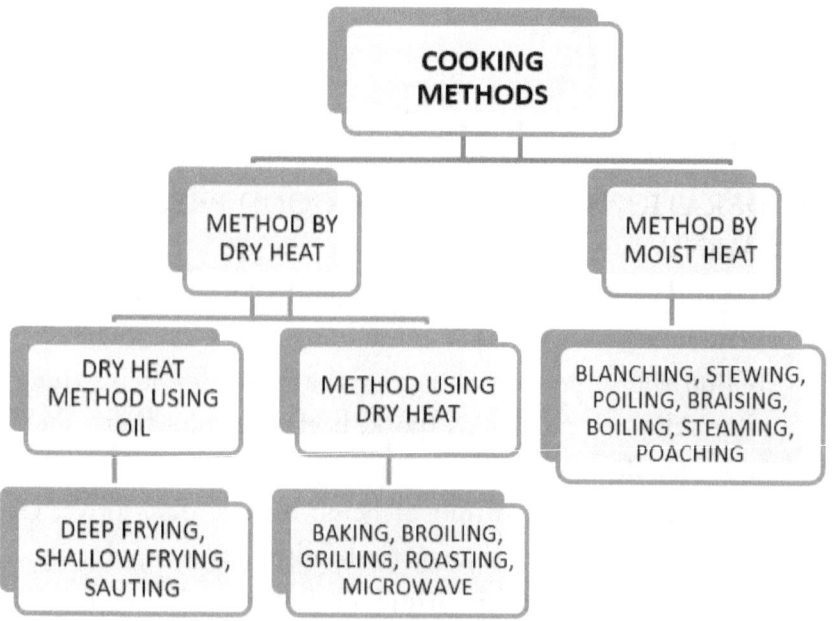

METHODS OF COOKING

SAUTEING	Foods items are placed in a heavy bottomed pan with a little hot fat and the pan with the items is shaken and flipped occasionally over the fire.
PAN-FRYING	Tender, good quality items like fish, meat and poultry are generally used for frying, as this method completes the cooking of the dish. The presentation side should always be fried first using considerably less amount of oil just enough to lubricate the pan
DEEP-FRYING	It is quick method of frying. The holding temperature range for deep fryer is 90 – 110 degree Centigrade
GRILLING	The food is placed on grill bars with sources of heat such as charcoal, coke, gas or electricity. If the source of heat is above the grill bars the equipment is called a salamander.
BROILING	Cooking by direct heat and is used synonymously with grilling. The heat source in broiling is above and in grilling is below. It is dry cooking.
ROASTING	It is usually used for cooking large pieces of meat, on a turning spit over an open fire.
BAKING	Baking is cooking of food by the action of dry heat in an oven
POACHING	Poaching is cooking gently in water which is just below boiling point. (93 – 95 degree Centigrade)
BOILING	Boiling is cooking by immersing the food in a pan of liquid, which must be kept boiling all the time i.e. quite a number of bubbles should be seen on the surface. Boiling temperature is 100 degree Centigrade.

STEAMING

```
         STEAMING
          /     \
         /       \
        ↙         ↘
     Direct      Indirect
```

STEAMING: Steaming is cooking by moist heat.

Indirect steaming is done when the food is placed in a closed pan, which is surrounded by plenty of steam from fast boiling water or in a steamer or placing the article in a perforated container or on a covered plate over a saucepan of water does **direct** steaming.

COMBINATION COOKING METHODS:

BRAISING: This is a combined method of roasting and stewing. In a pan with a tightly fit lid, braising is done to prevent evaporation, to ensure that all the juices of the food as well as any added food like ham, vegetables, herbs etc is retained.

STEWING: Stewing is gentle simmering in a small quantity of water, stock or sauce, until the cut food items are tender, and both liquid and food are served together. Stewing is a long and slow cooking method, whereby food is cut into small pieces and then cooked in minimum liquid- water-sauce or stock. Food & the cooking liquid are served together.

FRENCH GRILLING TERMS

AU BLEU	RARE, VERY UNDERDONE
SAIGNANT	UNDERDONE/MEDIUM RARE
A POINT	JUST DONE (MEDIUM)
BIENCUIT	WELL COOKED

COOKING METHODS:

Cooking methods are classified as "Moist heat" and "Dry heat"

Moist heat methods are those in which the heat is provided to the food product by water (liquid) or steam.

Dry-heat methods are those in which the heat is given without moisture, that is, by hot air hot metal, radiation or hot fat. Dry heat methods are categorised into two categories: with fat and without fat.

Different cooking methods suit different kinds of foods. The kind of cooking method selected depends on various factors - flavorus to retain, dish texture etc and also the kinf of meat that is being cooked. For example some meats are high in connecting tissues and hence tough and hence the use of moist heat. On the other hand some meats are low on connecting tissue hence the use of dry heat methods.

SAUCES

BASIC SAUCE	INGREDIENTS	DERIVATIVES
BECHAMEL OR WHITE SAUCE	Flour (90 gm) + Butter (90 gm) +Milk (1 lt) + Onion studded with clove & bay leaf (25 gm)	• MORNAY • CREAM • MUSTARD • SCOTCH EGG • ONION SAUCE
VELOUTE	Butter (90 gm) + Flour (90 gm) + Stock (1 lt) + Mushroom trimmings (25gm)	• SUPREME • CURRY SAUCE • VIN BLANC • WHITE CHAUDFROID
BROWN or ESPAGNOLE SAUCE	Fat (60 gm) + Flour (70 gm) + Tomato Puree (30 gm) + Brown Stock (1 lt) + Mirepoix (70 gm) + Herbs + Pork trimmings	• DEMI GLAZE • BERCY • MADEIRA • CHAUDFROID • DEVIL
HOLLANDAISE SAUCE	Butter (200 gm) + Egg Yolks (2) + Crushed Peppercorns (5) + Vinegar (15 ml) + Lemon juice (1/2)	• NOISETTE • BEARNAISE • MUSTARD • MALTAISE • MOUSSELINE

| TOMATO SAUCE | Flour (80 gm) + Butter (70 gm) + Bacon trimmings (40 gm) + Mirepoix (160 gm) + Bay leaf (1/2) + Garlic (1 clove) + Tomato puree (100 gm) + Tomatoes chopped (50 gm) + Brown Stock (450 ml) + Sugar (10gm) + Salt (3 gm) | • BARBECUE
• ITALIENNE
• BRETONNE
• TOMATED CHAUDFROID
• PORTUGAISE |
| MAYONNAISE | Olive Oil (1 lt) + Egg yolks (8) + French Mustard (1/4 tsp) + Vinegar (25 ml) + Lemon (1) + Seasoning | • TARTARE
• COCKTAIL
• THOUSAND ISLAND
• CHANTILLY |

CLASSIFICATION OF SOUP

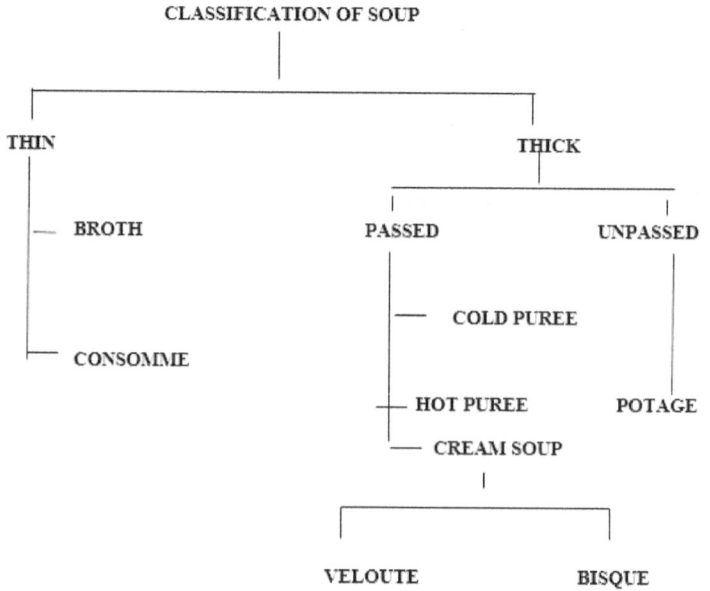

SOUP CONSISTS OF -STOCK + BODY + LIASON

BASIC SOUPS

CONSOMME	It is a strongly flavored, clarified soup and usually named after its garnish. E.g. Consommé Julienne.
BROTH	Is a clear stock and is served with solid food like diced meats, vegetables etc.
PUREE	Starchy vegetables such as leguminous plants, potatoes or cereals when pureed in soups, usually act a self-thickener's and need no further thickening agent. The cooked soup is strained and served with garnish. E.g. Crème St German.
CREAM SOUPS	They are composed of a puree of vegetables, fish, poultry or meat, thickened with béchamel sauce to give a cream finish. E.g. Cream of mushroom.
VELOUTE	These are rich creamy soups where Béchamel is replaced with veloute. E.g. Veloute Indienne.
BISQUES	These are shellfish puree soups, thickened with rice or cream.
CHOWDERS	Originated from America. They are thick heavy soups, owing their consistency to potatoes. E.g. Clam chowder.
COLD SOUPS	Chilled soups include those that are jellied with natural gelatin present in the meat stock or by addition of gelatin. E.g. Gazpacho.

INTERNATIONAL SOUPS

SOUP	ORIGIN
BOUILLABAISSE	FRANCE
FRENCH ONION SOUP	FRANCE
MULLIGATAWNY	INDIA
GAZPACHO	SPAIN
PAPRIKA	HOLLAND
MANHATTAN CLAM CHOWDER	AMERICA
COCK A LEEKIE	SCOTLAND
GREEN TURTLE SOUP	ENGLAND
MINESTRONE	ITALY
CAMARO	BRAZIL

STOCK: A stock is the soluble extract from mutton, fish, beef, or game in water.

TYPES OF STOCK: - Basically Two types of stocks

1. White
2. Brown

Importance of stocks: They are rich in nutrients, particularly proteins. They are the basic ingredients of sauces, soups and are used in cooking meats and rice.

DIFFERENT COLOUR CHOPPING BOARD ARE USED FOR:

- Red--Raw Meat
- Blue--Raw Fish.
- Yellow--Cooked Meats.
- Green--Fruits & Salad.
- Brown--Vegetables.
- White--Dairy & Bakery.

CUTS OF VEGETABLES

1.	BRUNOISE	This is a very small-diced cube, sized between 1-3 mm squares. It is often used as a garnish for consommé. Typical vegetables used are carrot, onion, turnip and celery.
2.	CHIFFONADE	Finely shredded green leafy vegetables, usually lettuce or spinach, which is used as a base, garnish or in soups.
3.	JARDINIERE	A long thin baton, about 2.5cm long and approximately 0.5cm wide x 0.5cm thick.
4.	JULIENNE	Long thin match-stick shaped pieces about 4cm in length.
5.	MACEDOINE	This is diced cube, 0.5cm (5mm) square, larger than the brunoise cut. Typical vegetables used are carrot, onion, turnip, beans and celery.
6.	MATIGNON	Thin even slices of vegetables used as a base to place meat on when roasting. Vegetables normally include carrot, onion and celery.

7.	**MIREPOIX**	A mixture of roughly chopped vegetables which are used as the base of sauces or to enhance the flavor of meat, fish and shellfish dishes. Normally onion, celery and carrot are used and these are slowly cooked in butter until they are very tender. Thyme and bay are often added.
8.	**PAYSANNE**	Paysanne cut vegetables may be either squares, triangles, circles or half rounds. In order to cut economically, the shape of the vegetable will decide which shape to choose. All are cut thinly, about 1-2 mm thick.

CUTS OF CHICKEN

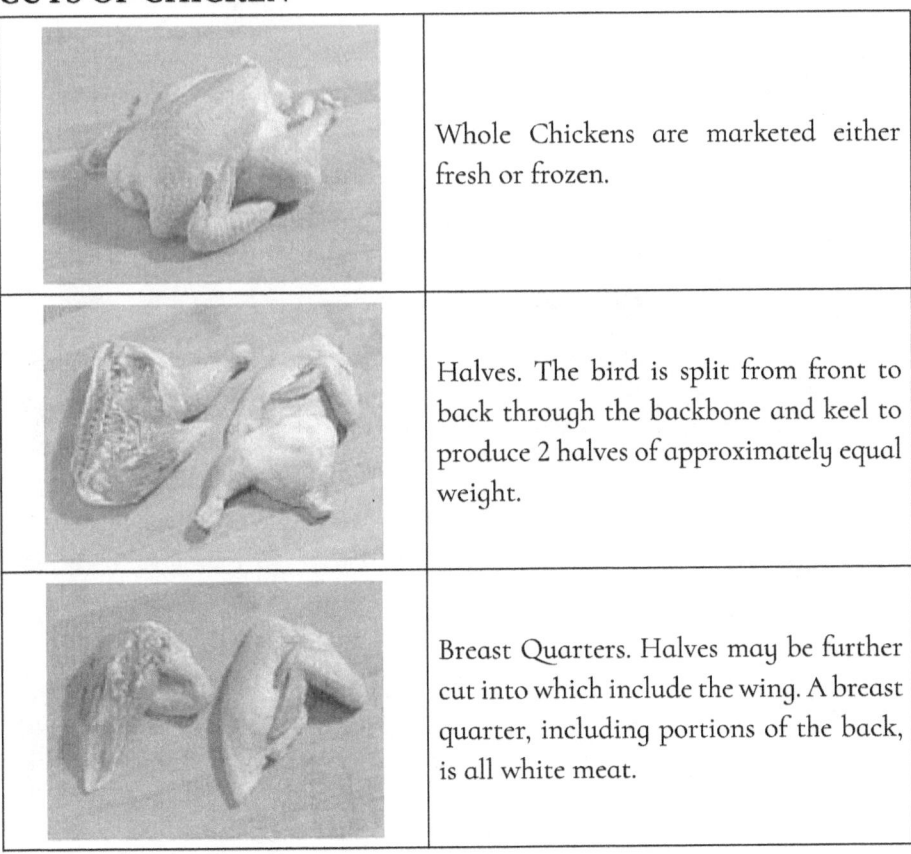

	Whole Chickens are marketed either fresh or frozen.
	Halves. The bird is split from front to back through the backbone and keel to produce 2 halves of approximately equal weight.
	Breast Quarters. Halves may be further cut into which include the wing. A breast quarter, including portions of the back, is all white meat.

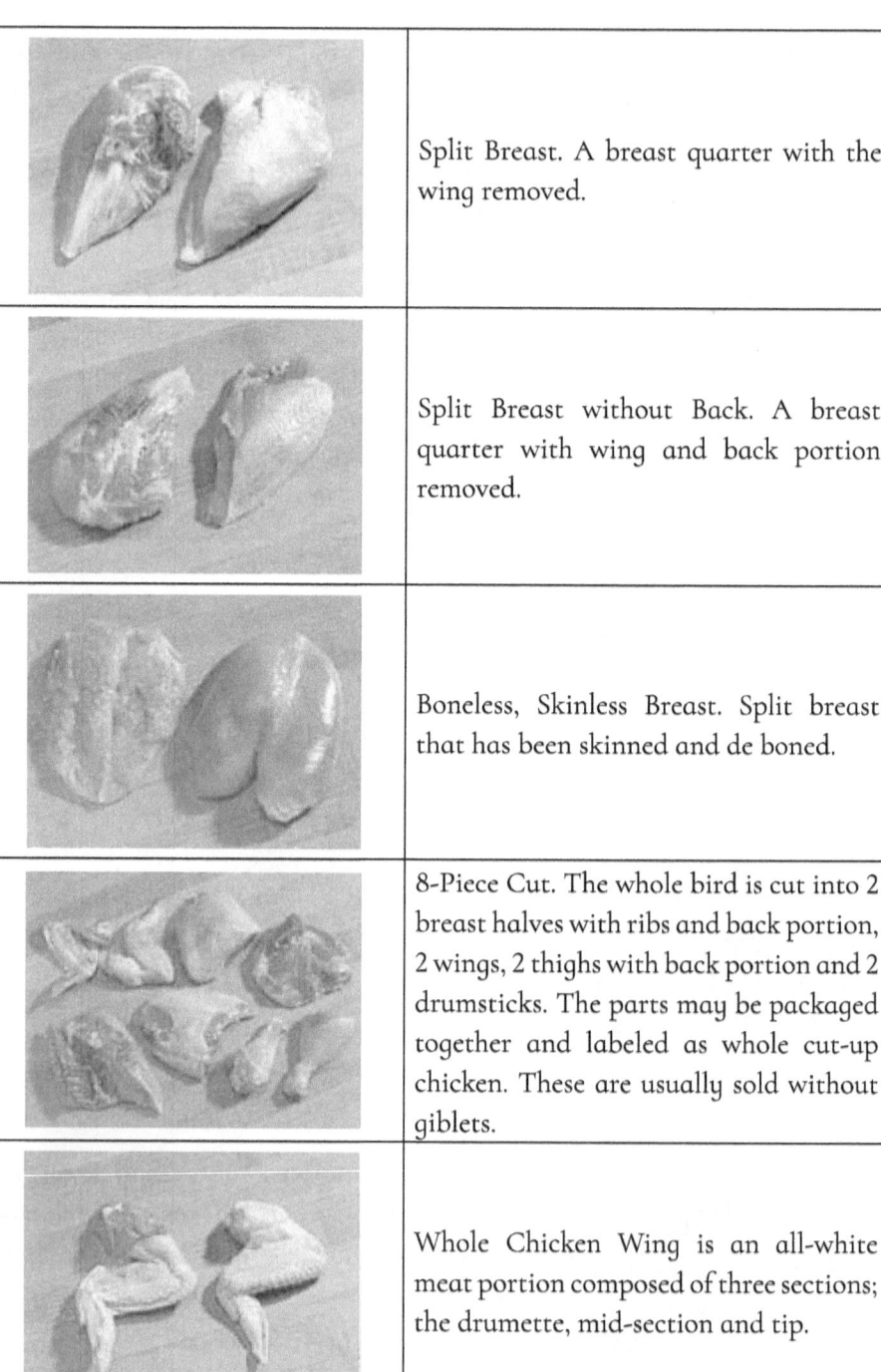

	Split Breast. A breast quarter with the wing removed.
	Split Breast without Back. A breast quarter with wing and back portion removed.
	Boneless, Skinless Breast. Split breast that has been skinned and de boned.
	8-Piece Cut. The whole bird is cut into 2 breast halves with ribs and back portion, 2 wings, 2 thighs with back portion and 2 drumsticks. The parts may be packaged together and labeled as whole cut-up chicken. These are usually sold without giblets.
	Whole Chicken Wing is an all-white meat portion composed of three sections; the drumette, mid-section and tip.

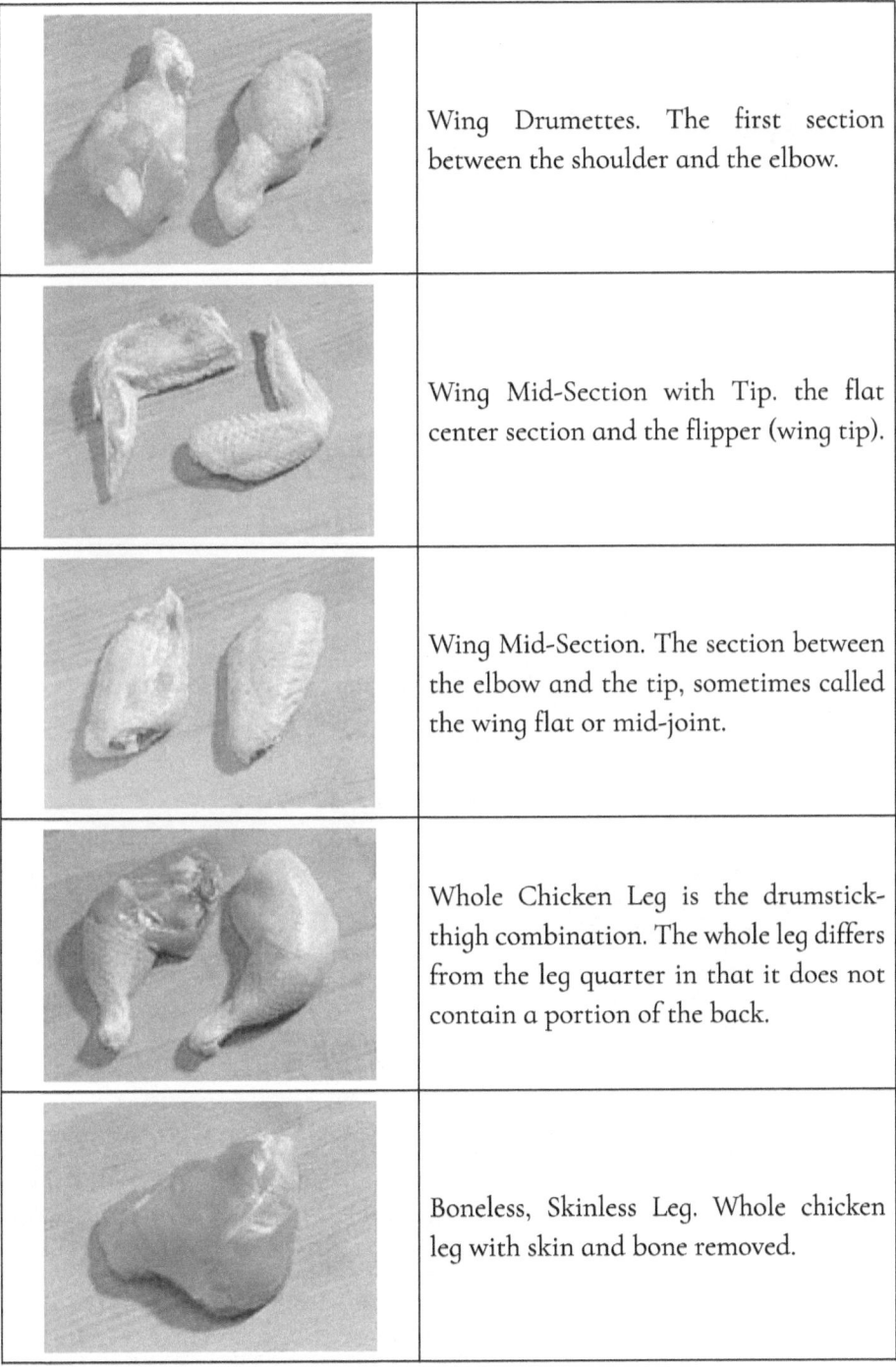

	Wing Drumettes. The first section between the shoulder and the elbow.
	Wing Mid-Section with Tip. the flat center section and the flipper (wing tip).
	Wing Mid-Section. The section between the elbow and the tip, sometimes called the wing flat or mid-joint.
	Whole Chicken Leg is the drumstick-thigh combination. The whole leg differs from the leg quarter in that it does not contain a portion of the back.
	Boneless, Skinless Leg. Whole chicken leg with skin and bone removed.

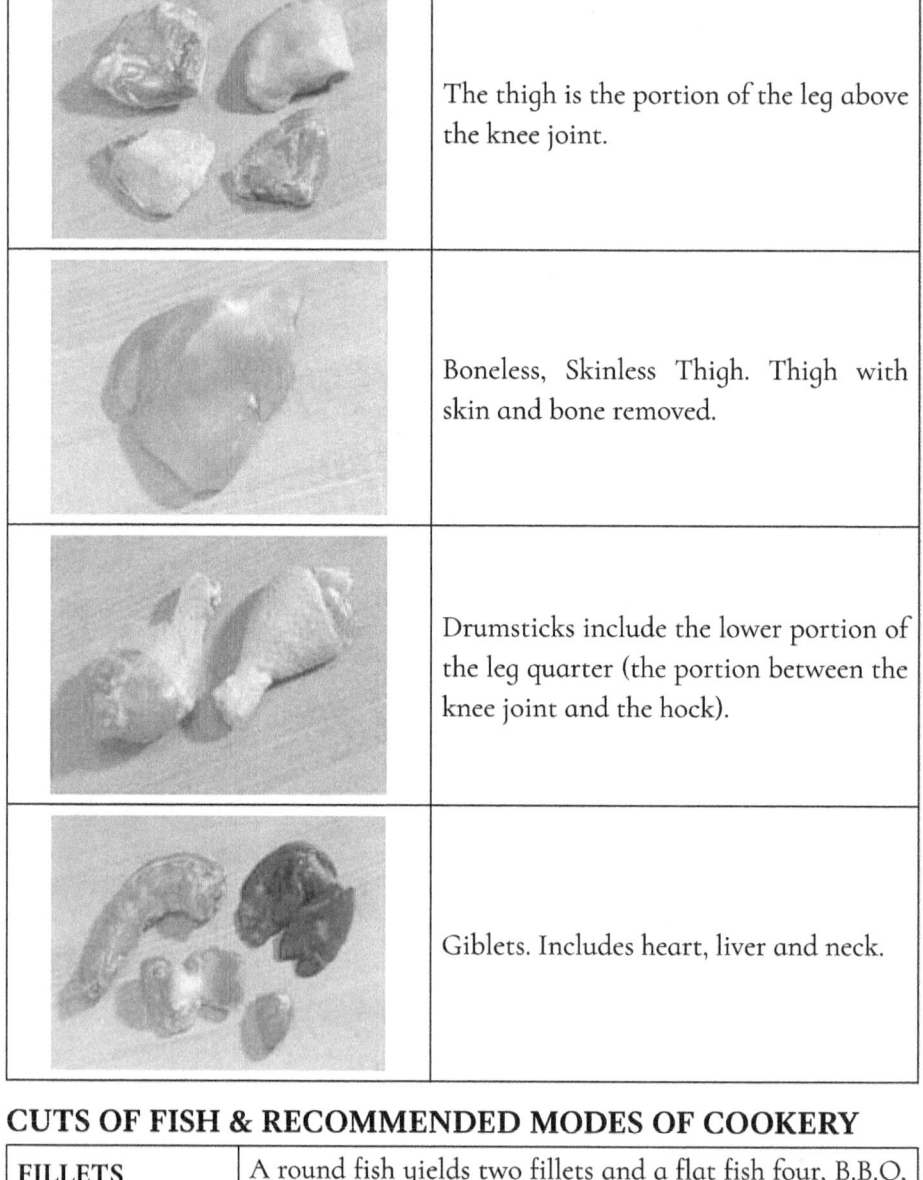

	The thigh is the portion of the leg above the knee joint.
	Boneless, Skinless Thigh. Thigh with skin and bone removed.
	Drumsticks include the lower portion of the leg quarter (the portion between the knee joint and the hock).
	Giblets. Includes heart, liver and neck.

CUTS OF FISH & RECOMMENDED MODES OF COOKERY

FILLETS	A round fish yields two fillets and a flat fish four, B.B.Q, grilled, pan fry, en papillote, poach, deep fried (with coating).
PLAITED	Also known as en tresse; fillet of fish cut lengthwise into three and plaited; Shallow fried, panéed and deep fried

DELICE	Fillet of fish neatly folded in half; poached.
PAUPIETTES	Fillet of fish, spread with a farce and rolled; poached.
GOUJONS	Strips of fillet cut 8 x .5 cm; Deep fried(with coating), stir fry.
GOUJONETTES	As for goujons but half the length; deep fried (with coating), stir-fry.
SUPREMES	Prime cuts of fillet without bone and skin; B.B.Q, grilled, pan fry, en papillote, poach, deep fried (with coating).
DARNE	A slice of round fish cut on the bone; B.B.Q, grilled, pan fry, en papillote, poach, baked
TRONCON	Slice of (large) flat fish on the bone; B.B.Q, grilled, pan fry, en papillote, poach, baked.

TYPES OF PASTA

	CAMPANELLE Flattened bell shaped pasta with frilly edge on one end.
	CAVATELLI Short, solid lengths.
	CONCHIGLIE Seashell shaped.

	FARFALLE Bow tie or butterfly shaped.
	FIORI Shaped like a flower.
	FUSILLI Three edged spiral, usually in mixed colours.
	GEMELLI Single S shaped strand, twisted in a loose spiral.
	ROTELLE Wagon wheel shaped pasta.
	ROTINI Tightly wound, 2 edged spiral.

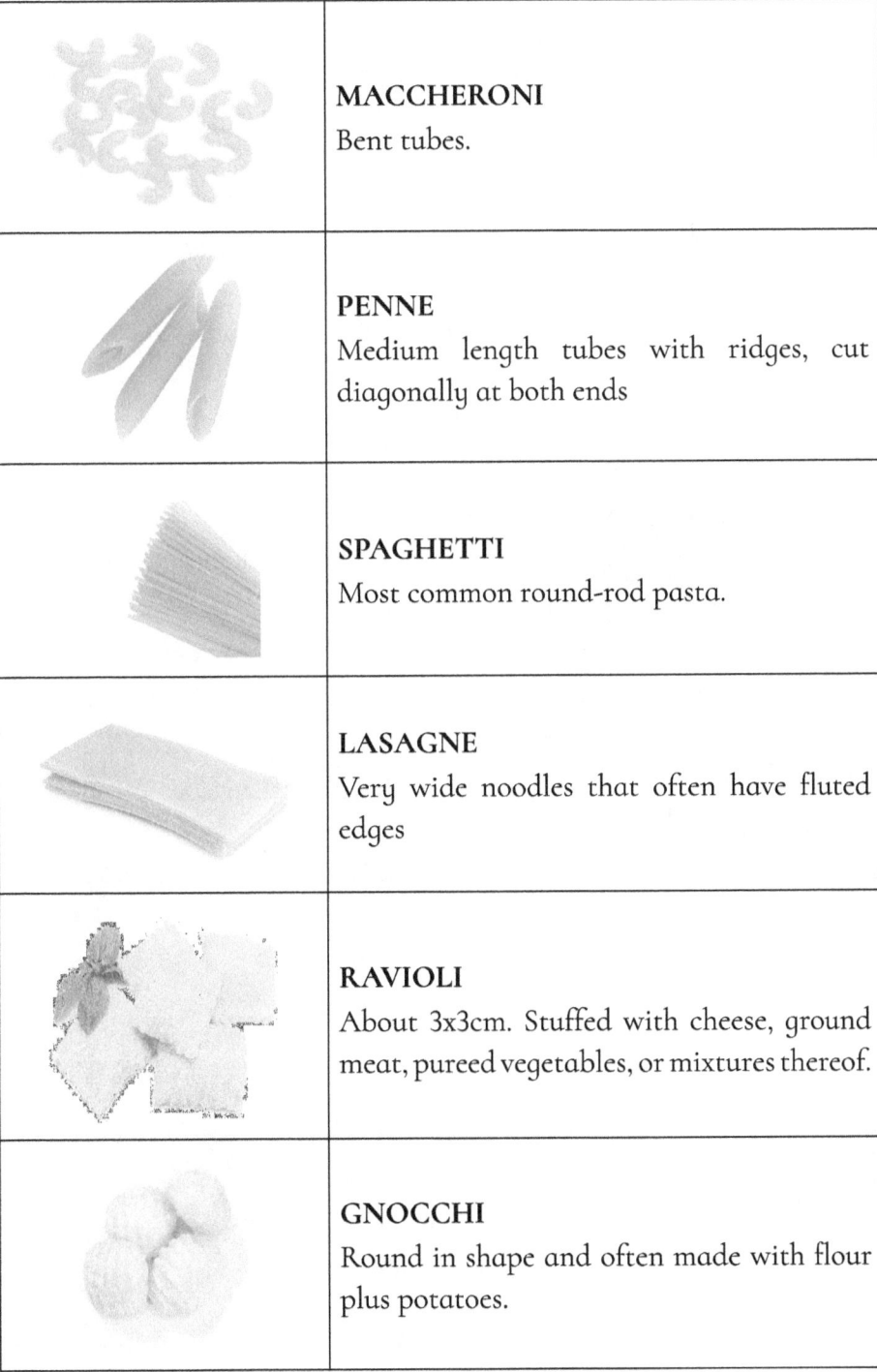

	MACCHERONI Bent tubes.
	PENNE Medium length tubes with ridges, cut diagonally at both ends
	SPAGHETTI Most common round-rod pasta.
	LASAGNE Very wide noodles that often have fluted edges
	RAVIOLI About 3x3cm. Stuffed with cheese, ground meat, pureed vegetables, or mixtures thereof.
	GNOCCHI Round in shape and often made with flour plus potatoes.

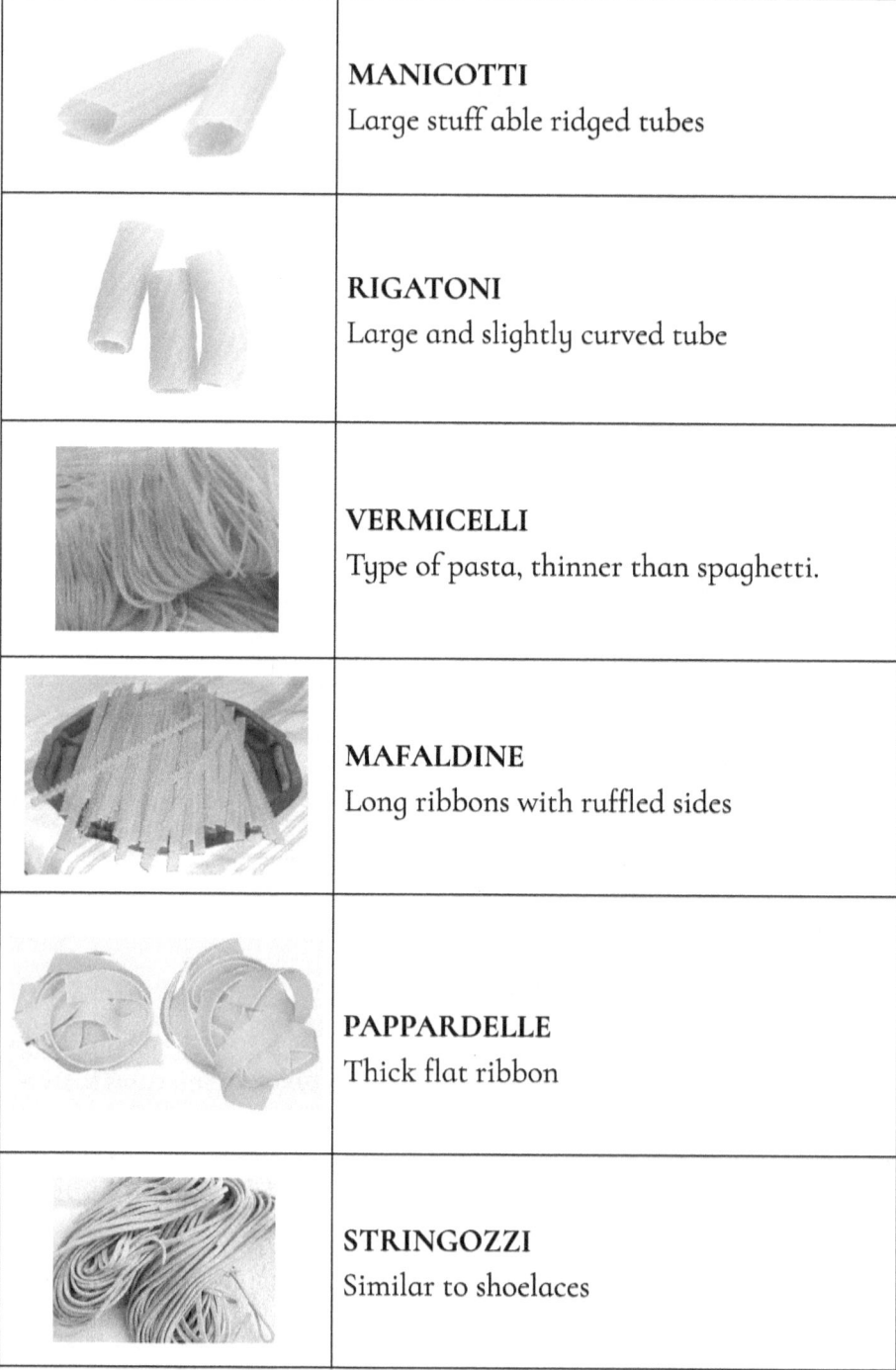

	MANICOTTI Large stuff able ridged tubes
	RIGATONI Large and slightly curved tube
	VERMICELLI Type of pasta, thinner than spaghetti.
	MAFALDINE Long ribbons with ruffled sides
	PAPPARDELLE Thick flat ribbon
	STRINGOZZI Similar to shoelaces

	RISONI Rice shaped pasta
	STELLE Small star shaped pasta
	TORTELLONI Round or rectangular, similar to ravioli. Usually stuffed with a mixture of cheese and vegetables.
	SPATZLE German egg pasta that is either round in shape or completely irregular, when hand made.

KEY TEMINOLOGY

ACCOMPANIMENT: This can be defined as those additional food items that are served with the main dish. These are flavoured food or sauces that are served with the main dish to enhance the flavour or provide contrast or balance to the main dish

AMUSE BOUCHE: Small sized savories served before the hors d'oeuvres.

ANTIPASTI: Antipasti is a plural term and antipasto is a singular term.

ANTIPASTO: Means before the Pasta or meal, so it refers to dish served before pasta may be a selection of Italian appetizers. Basically, the first course of a formal Italian meal.

APPETIZER: It is the first course in French classical menu which aims at stimulating the appetite, and is a small dish of food served before the main course.

ARRABIATA: It is a Roman sauce of garlic, tomatoes and red chilli cooked in olive oil, basil may also be used.

ASPIC: Savoury clear jelly made by simmering the bones of veal, chicken or fish meat stock & is set in a mould.

AU GRATIN: A dish that is baked with a topping of seasoned breadcrumbs and cheese.

AU JUS: It means "with juice", mostly the juices secreted by the meat.

AUBERGINE: Eggplant.

BAGEL: A Jewish bread shaped in a form of ring, by hand. It is first boiled and then baked.

BAGUETTE: Long, narrow French bread made by a lean dough.

BAIN-MARIE: Large open dish filled with hot water partly so that their contents are kept hot without over cooking.

BAKING: It is a method of cooking in which food is put in oven and cooked by dry heat.

BAVAROIS: Dessert of custard stiffened with gelatin, mixed with whipped cream, shaped in a mould & serve cold.

BECHAMEL: It is a basic mother sauce which is white in colour, made with roux (butter & refined flour), milk, cloute (onion tied with clove).

BERCY: Sauce made with white wine and shallots, served with seafood.

BEURRE: It means butter in French.

BISQUE: Thick creamy soup, usually based on seafood, e.g. Prawn bisque.

BISTRO: A small restaurant that serves moderately/simple meals in modest settings with alcohol.trem Bistor means a small restaurant , a small bar or tavern

BLACK BEAN: Salted dry soya bean available dried and bottled.

BLANC: This is a French term meaning "White".

BLANCHING: It is moist cooking method in which food is submerged in boiling water for short time to precook or partially cook the food for example-blanching tomatoes

BOEUF: Beef.

BOILING: It is moist cooking method in which food is put into water and cooked at temperature of 100 degrees Celsius.

BOKCHOY: White cabbage with fleshy white stems and light green leaves.

BON APPETIT: Enjoy your meal. Literal meaning "good appetite".

BONNE FEMME: It means simply cooked, home style; with potato.

BOUILLON: Plain un-clarified meat or vegetable broth used as stock in cooking.

BOUQUET GARNI: It is a bundle of fresh herbs such as parsley, thyme, bay leaf, peppercorns tied in muslin cloth and put to flavour soups, stews and removed before dish is served.

BRASSERIE: A French style restaurant.

BRATWURST: Uncooked highly seasoned German sausage made from pork and veal.

BRIE: Soft creamy cows'-milk cheese with soft edible crust. (Brie is a small town near Paris in France).

BRINE: Solution of salt and water used as a preservative.

BRIOCHE: Light sweet round yeast bread rolls.

BROCHETTE: Skewer on which pieces of meat etc. are cooked

BROIL: It means cooking food on direct heat.

BRUCHETTA: Baked or toasted slices of bread, oiled and sprinkled with herbs and served as an appetizer. Tomato and garlic are sometimes added.

BRUNCH: A meal that one eats in the late morning as a combination of breakfast as well as lunch.

BRUNNOISE: It is a type of vegetable cut in which vegetable is cut into fine 2mm dices, usually used for garnishing.

BUFFET: It means display of several dishes displayed on a table or sideboard from where guest serve themselves

BUSBOY: A waiter's assistant who clears tables in a restaurant.

CACCIATORA: Cooked with tomatoes, mushrooms, herbs and, usually, wine, e.g. Chicken cacciatore.

CAFÉ LATTE: White coffee made with espresso and steamed milk and has less foam than a cappuccino

CAFFEINE: Stimulant found in coffee, tea and cacao plants.

CAJUN: Cuisine developed by Creole French-speakers in Louisiana (USA). Key ingredients are Capsicum, onion, celery with plenty of peppers.

CALAMARI: Squid.

CALVADOS: Apple brandy made in Normandy (Province in N. France.)

CANAPE: Small piece of bread (usually toasted) or biscuit, garnished with caviar, cheese, pate, smoked salmon, etc. Cold canapés are usually served as savoury appetizers with drinks before a meal; hot canapés are sometimes served as entrees in the meal itself.

CANNELLONI: Form of pasta in large tubular rolls filled with cheese or meat etc. and baked.

CANTONESE: A style of Chinese cuisine. Lightly cooked fresh vegetables and meat, and sweet sauces.

CARAFE: Is traditionally a vessel/bottle with a flaring lip that holds liquid may be water, juice, alcoholic beverages.

CARAMELIZATION: It means cooking up of sugar at low heat and cook until it turns dark brown in colour.

CARBONARA: Carbonara is comprised of pancetta, egg yolks, heavy cream, garlic, and lot of freshly ground black pepper. During cooking process, a hard Italian cheese is also added

CARCASS: Body of any animal after killing or slaughtering.

CAVIAR: Fish eggs

CHAMPIGNON: Mushroom.

CHAR GRILL: Grilling with charcoal.

CHASSEUR: A sauce, cooked with white wine, shallots, mushroom and tomatoes.

CHATEAUBRIAND: Tender thick fillet steak usually served with a béarnaise sauce.

CHAUD: Hot.

CHEF: French word for "chief", usually referred to experienced cooks and kitchen managers.

CHINOIS: It is a conical wire strainer used to strain soups etc.

CHIPOLATA: Very small thin sausage in a narrow casing

CHOP SUEY: American Chinese dish consisting of meat, eggs, vegetables bound in a starch thickened sauce.

CHOUX PASTE: Cooked paste of refined flour, eggs and butter used to make pastries and desserts.

CIABATTA: Italian bread.

CITRUS FRUITS: Fruits which are tangy and sour in flavour such as orange, sweet lime and pineapples.

CLARIFIED BUTTER: In this butter is left on low heat to separate solids and then strained to get a clear butter. It has many uses in culinary.

COMPOTE: Fruit cooked or preserved in syrups

CONCASSE: It usually refers to blanched and roughly chopped tomatoes basically used in sauces.

CONSOMME: Thin clear soup made from richly flavoured stock

COOK OUT: It is a process of cooking the flour in the sauce or soup.

COOKING: It is the practice or skill of preparing food by combining, mixing, and heating ingredients. It is impacted by cooking skills and knowledge of cooking of the person cooking

COULIS: Thin puree of fruit or vegetable.

COURGETTE: Summer squash.

CREOLE: Typically, savoury dishes containing paprika, garlic and onions.

CREPE: Very thin pancakes cooked on both sides usually filled and rolled up when served.

CROSTINI: Canapé or small savoury toast served as an appetizer.

CROUTONS: It refers to small dices of toasted or fried bread used for garnishing of soups.

CRUMBING: It means covering food with dried breadcrumbs or similar things before deep frying.

CUISINE: This refers to the style, method of cooking or certain characteristic food is made which is a representation of a particular country, region or establishment

CULINARY: Culinary is the art of preparing and cooking foods. It is defined as something related to or connected with cooking.

DEMI CHEF DE PARTIE: It is a member in kitchen who is assistant to the kitchen supervisor. Also called DCDP sometimes.

DEMI GLAZE: Rich brown sauce made by reducing stock to half its original volume. Madeira, sherry or brandy is often added after the reduction.

DEMI: It means half in the French.

DEMITASSE: Very small coffee cup.

DEMOULDING: It refers to the practice of removing the bread from the mould in which it was baked.

DESSERT: Sweet course served at the end of the meal

DIM-SUM: Small savoury dumpling containing meat & cabbage wrapped in a wonton wrapper & steamed or deep fried.

DOCKING: It is art of making holes with help of fork or tool in pastry goods such as pizza base to allow steam to pass.

DOLMAS: Vine leaves stuffed with oily rice, sometimes with nuts, currants and minced lamb etc. in the rice. Served with meze.

DRAIN: It means to place the food item in strainer or colander to remove the excess water.

DREDGING: It refers to process of coating any food item with dry ingredients such as, sugar or flour.

DUMB WAITER: A small lift for carrying things, especially food and crockery between floors of a building.

EMINCE: It refers to cut the vegetables or herbs very fine or shredded fine.

EMULSIFICATION: It means dispersing one liquid into another liquid in which it is insoluble such as oil and water such as in case of mayonnaise.

EN COCOTTE: It refers to French term for the dishes served in the utensil in which it was cooked.

ENCHILADA: Fried tortilla filled with cheese and/or meat & rolled. Served with Chilli sauce and, possibly, guacamole.

ENTREMENTS: French for sweet course in French classical course.

ESPAGNOLE: It refers to brown sauce in French.

ESTOUFFADE: It means brown stock in French.

FALAFEL: Chick pea balls flavoured with spices or roll of pita bread filled with salad and hummus.

FARCE: It refers to stuffed in French.

FARINACEOUS: It refers to fourth course in French classical menu which includes starchy dishes such as pasta, rice, potato etc.

FETTUCCINE: Thin ribbons of pasta cut to a length of about 30 cm.

FILO PASTRY: A very thin unleavened dough used for making pastries such as baklava etc.

FINE DINING RESTAURANT: This kind of restaurants have full service done by waiting staff, menu has wide variety of choice, food is prepared from premium quality ingredients and they have premium pricing

FLAMBE: Food covered with spirits and set alight for a short time

FLAVONES: It refers to pigment present in the white vegetables such as potato, onions. Always cook the white vegetables in acidic medium to retain the colour.

FLORENTINE: It refers to dish made with the use of spinach.

FOCACCIA: Flat bread similar to a pizza base. Often spread with garlic-herb Butter & served warm with antipasto.

FOND DE CUISINE: Refers to kitchen stock in French.

FRANGIPANE: Custard made with ground almonds or crushed macaroons.

FRANKFURTER: Smoked beef & pork sausage usually simmered & served in a bread as a hot dog.

FRAPPE: A drink served with ice or frozen to a slushy consistency

FRENCH DRESSING: Refers to type of salad dressing made from the emulsion of three parts of vinegar to one-part oil.

FRICASSE: A dish of stewed or fried pieces of meat served in a thick white sauce.

FRITTER: Food either sweet or savoury, dipped in batter & deep fried.

FSSAI: Food Safety & Standards Authority of India

FUMET: Refers to fish stock in French.

FUNGI: A family which includes variety of mushrooms.

GALANGAL: Asian plant of ginger origin

GATEAUX: French word for cake

GAZPACHO: Cold soup of pureed tomatoes, cucumber, onions, garlic & red Pepper, often garnished with croutons. (Spanish)

GELATIN: This is a colourless flavourless & odourless food ingredient, which is obtained from, the collagen taken from animal parts. This refers to sweet & non savoury dishes

GELATO: Popular frozen dessert of Italian origin.

GIBLETS: It refers to internal organs such as liver, heart & trimmings taken from the poultry or chicken.

GLUTEN: A protein obtained when the refined flour is kneaded with water.

GNOCHHI: Small pasta dumplings made from potato or semolina.

GRATINATING: It refers to covering the dish with sauce, breadcrumbs, cheese and then gratinate or cook in salamander to give colour.

GUERIDON TROLLEY: Moveable trolley from which food is carved, flambed, prepared or served

HACCP: Hazard Analysis Critical Control Point. It is a management system in which food safety is assessed

HALAL: Slaughter.

HASH BROWN: Shredded pan fried potatoes.

HOI SIN SAUCE: Sweet & spicy sauce made of Soya beans, garlic & spices & served as condiments, esp. with Peking duck & pork dishes. (China)

HOLLAINDAISE: It is a warm yellow mother sauce made from emulsion of egg yolks, vinegar and clarified butter.

HORS D' OEUVRES: It refers to small savoury appetizers served as the first course of a meal.

INFUSION: It refers to liquid obtained after steeping the food such as coffee, tea etc.

JAGGERY: A non-centrifugal cane sugar consumed in Asia.

JARDINIERE: Is a cooking term that refers to cut of vegetables into thick battons like thick stick or finger shape

JULIENNES: It refers to a kind of vegetable cut in which food item is cut into thin strips of 1mm x 1mm x 25mm.

KUNAFA: A sugar-soaked pastry which is common in Arabic countries

LAKSA: Spicy seafood soup with rice noodles. (Singapore).

LARDING: It means to inserting of pork fat into meat with the help of larding needle to keep the meat moist.

LASAGNA: An Italian dish made of layers of thin flat pasta altering with fillings

MACAROON: Small almond flavoured cake or biscuit.

MELBA TOAST: Melba toast is a dry, crisp and thinly sliced toast, which is served with soup/sald and may be topped with melted cheese.

MENU: It refers to list of dishes priced separately which gives the brief details to the guest about the dishes.

MERINGUE: Egg white whipped with sugar & baked.

MEZE/MEZZE: Assortment of cold hors d'oeuvre, often almost a meal in itself

MIS-EN-PLACE: It is term which is very common in kitchen which means basic preparation in advance to save the time at the time of service.

MISO: Paste made from fermented tofu, used to make miso-shiru (Jap/ soup)

NASI GORENG: Fried rice with chicken or prawns, shredded omelette, onions, spices.

NOISSETE: A small round & tender cut of meat

NORI: Kind of seaweed, dried & pressed into thin sheets. Used as an edible Wrapping for Sushi.

OFFAL: Heart and other organs of an animal used as food. This refers to the internal organs excluding muscles and bones and is not indicative of edible organs always

PAVLOVA: Soft meringue cake filled with cream & topped with fruit.

PEACH MELBA: Dessert of peaches with raspberry sauce and vanilla ice cream.

PESTO: Sauce made by blending basil, parmesan cheese, pine nuts, garlic and olive oil.

PETIT FOUR: Small fancy cake or biscuit. Varieties are: Plain petit-fours, fresh petit-fours, savoury petit-fours which are served with aperitifs.

PILAF: Another word for pilau. Middle eastern rice dish.

PITA(Greek): Flat round double-layered bread which can be cut open & filled.

POACHING: It is a moist cooking method in which food is gently simmered in the liquid in which there is no movement of liquid at temperature of 93-95 degree Celsius.

POISSON; It refers to fish in French.

POT ROAST: A method whereby a piece of meat is cooked slowly in a covered dish.

PUDDING: Soft food item of ingredients mixed in flour & usually steamed or baked, e.g. bread & butter pudding, Christmas pudding. The sweet or dessert course of a meal.

PUNCH: A blend of fruit juices, sugar and water.

QSR: Quick service restaurants, they serve fast food, limited menu and has a take away options and has an informal service approach.

QUICHE: Open pie or flan, filled with savoury custard holding other ingredients.

RATATOUILLE: Vegetable stew containing tomatoes, onions, eggplant, capsicums, & Zucchini, flavoured with garlic & ground pepper.

RAVIOLI: Type of pasta shaped as envelops.

RELISH: Condiment, sauce, or pickle, usually eaten with plain food.

RICOTTA: (Italy): White, moist, light cheese made mostly from the whey of milk.

ROULADE: A dish cooked in a form of roll.

ROUX: a mixture of fat and flour used in making sauces.

SABAYON: Mixture of egg yolks, white wine, & sugar whipped together to form a rich foamy dessert usually served just warm.

SALAMANDAR: Those kitchen devices that are used for overhead grilling, toasting, and browning of grating dishes & to give finishing touches to a dish rather than cooking them

SALSA: Salsa translates into sauce. Salsa is about serving a variety of sauces on table at room temperature and goes well with tacos and mexican food.

SUSHI: Means it is sour, which has to do with vinegar rice & often includes raw fish. Raw fish may not always be an essential ingredient

SASHIMI: Its a japanese raw fish delicacy or sometimes a thinly sliced meat that is often consumed with soy sauce.

SATAY: Small pieces of meat grilled on a skewer and served with a spicy sauce that contains peanuts.

SHALLOT: Small brown onion much used in French cookery to flavour sauces.

SHITAKE: Type of mushroom from Japan and China.

SMOOTHIE: Beverage of blended fruit mixed with yoghurt & honey.

SORBET: A frozen dessert made from sugar sweetened water with flavouring.

SOUFFLE: Sweet or savoury sauce mixture to which beaten egg whites have been Added which cause it to raised once baked. Usually served hot. But can be served cold also, e.g. Fruit soufflé, cheese soufflé, etc.

STIR FRY: Dish cooked rapidly over high heat while stirring briskly with very little oil

STRUDEL: Dessert of thin pastry rolled up round a fruit filling and baked.

TAGLIATELLE: Long ribbons of pasta curled around one another.

TARTAR SAUCE: The sauce is named after the Tartar tribe. It is a cold sauce that goes well with fried fish, and consists of mayonnaise mixed with chopped onions and gherkins and capers

TEMPURA: (Japan): Strips of fish, shelled prawns, or vegetables fried in a light batter and served very hot, usually with daikon radish.

TEPPANYAKI: Meat, fish and vegetable fried/grilled at the table.

TERIYAKI: Teriyaki means teri means lustre and yaki means grilled or boiled. It also refers to a japanese dish that consists of fish or meat which is marinated in soya sauce and grilled.

TIRA-MISU: (Italy): It is a coffee flavoured Italian dessert

TOFU: (Japan): Highly nutritious curd made from Soya beans.

TORTE: (Germany): Rice cake made in layers, sandwiched together with cream & Covered with chocolates, fruits, or nuts.

TORTILLA: (Mexico): Flat round pancake made of maize served hot & usually filled meat or beans and a sauce.

VESTE BLANC: French word for white chef's coat.

VINAIGRETTE: A mixture of oil, vinegar and various herbs etc. usually used to add flavours to the salad.

VINDALOO: Very hot S. Indian curry, spiced & flavoured with vinegar.

WASABI: A horseradish plant.

WOK: A large thin pan shaped like a bowl used for cooking Chinese food.

WON TON: A small round dumpling with a savoury filling usually eaten boiled in a soup.

YUM CHA: Traditional chinese brunch that involves tea with dim sums.

POPULAR BAKERY PRODUCTS

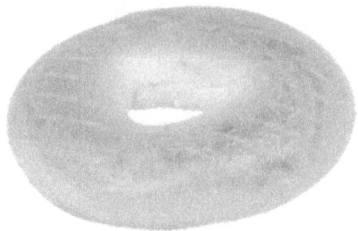

CROISSANT   BAGEL   MUFFIN

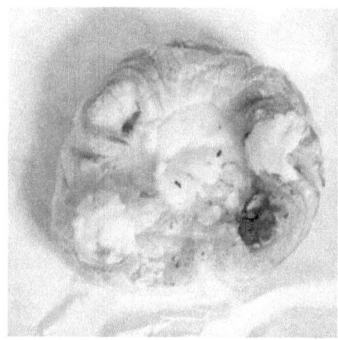

DANISH PASTRY   CUP CAKE

DOUGHNUT   PRETZEL   FOCACCIA BREAD

MACARON   BAKED ALASKA

BAGUETTE BREAD APPLE PIE A LA MODE

SWISS ROLL FRENCH BREAD LOAF FRUIT TART

CHOCOLATE MOUSSE BAKLAVA

KITCHEN STEWARDING

Kitchen stewarding department plays an important role in the functioning of both food production and food & beverage service departments. Though the operations of the kitchen stewarding department are mainly in the back area, it is still one of the most important departments. This department ensures smooth flow of kitchen & restaurants, bar & banquets in a very big way.

Kitchen Stewarding is headed by Executive Kitchen Steward who reports to the food and beverage service manager. Several shift supervisors work under the Executive Kitchen Steward and each of them are responsible for carrying out the assigned tasks. Each supervisor has a team of utility workers who have to be trained and supervised effectively to ensure that they do the jobs assigned to them properly.

SOME KEY TASKS PERFORMED BY KITCHEN STEWARDING ARE:

- Waste Disposal.
- Pots & pans washing.
- Cleaning & Maintaining Kitchen equipment.
- Deep Cleaning of Kitchens regularly.
- Pest Control.
- Ensuring Hygiene & cleanliness of kitchens.
- Managing Inventory of cutlery, crockery, glass ware.
- Re-ordering of cutlery, crockery, glassware, pots & pans.
- Replenishing glassware, cutlery, crockery etc for all restaurants, bars & banquets.
- Provide & stock fuels.
- Manage Gas Bank.

BEVERAGES

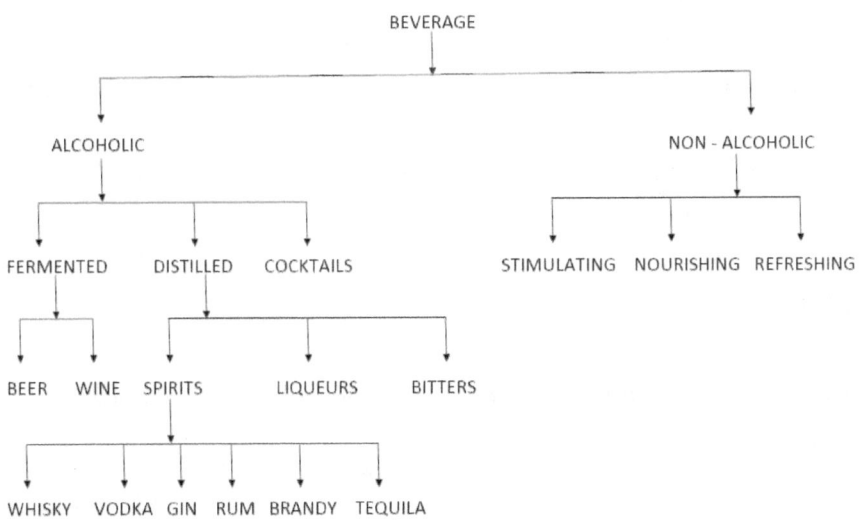

BEVERAGES: Any liquid that can quench the thirst are called beverage. Beverage is any kind of liquid. Water, tea, coffee, milk, juice, beer and any kind of drinks item are classified as a beverage product. It is a liquid that is intended for human consumption.

NON-ALCOHOLIC BEVERAGES: Non alcoholic beverages are drinks that do not have an intoxicating agent in them and they may be sweet corbonated beverages like aerated drinks, mineral water, squash, smoothies, juices, shakes or juices etc. These drinks do not have any alcohol % in them.

ALCOHOLIC BEVERAGES: These refers to beverages which contains ethyl alcohol or ethanol as an intoxicating agent. Such beverages are produced by adding fermentation of yeast into products like grapes, grains, barkey, fruits, sugarcane or rice. Some examples of Alcoholic beverages are Wine, Champagne, Beer, Whiskey, Brandy, Aperitif, Digestive, Liqueur, Spirits, Sake, Rice Wine and Cocktails.

PROOF

The word proof came into existence when certain early distillers started demonstrating the strength of their products by mixing it with gun powder and igniting it

If it failed to ignite it was considered to be extremely weak

It it exploded and got burned out immediately then it was considered to be too strong

If it burned steady displaying a blue flame it was proved to be suitable for drinking and hence the start of the word "Proof"

So, 100% proof was for consumption, which meant that it had 50% alcohol, anything under that was called under proof (UP) and anything above that was called over proof (OP)

Spirit bottles now a days show both alcoholic content & proof

ABV stands for alcohol by volume

So for example 45% abv meant 90 % proof

To understand three scales of one must understand the following

1. One sikes scale the absolute alcohol is rated as 175
2. On Gay Lussac scale the absolute alcohol is rated as 100
3. On American scale, the absolute alcohol is rated as 200

KEY TERMINOLOGY

AFTER TASTE: It is the flavour that continues to stay in your mouth after you swallow the wine. The length of the after taste is one of the most important indicator of wine quality

AGING: It is activity of maturing of the wines in wood casks or barrels.

AROMA: The primary smell of a wine, consisting of the odour of the grape juice, the fermentation process, and of the oak barrels in which the wine was made/aged

BALANCE: The ratio of a wine's important components, including fruitiness, sweetness, acidity and alcoholic strength. A balanced wine displays a unison of components, whereby no single element dominates

BODY: The body of a wine indicates the fullness & total mouth feel of a wine. A light-bodied wine would be have mild flavour, while full-bodied wines will have a concentrated flavour. Light-bodied wines give a feel somewhat like water in mouth and full-bodied wines are heavier and feel like milk density

BOUQUET: Deep & complex aromas that develop with age is known as bouquet. They are because of the process of fermentation, processing and aging, and mostly develop after bottling.

CLOSED: Not very aromatic, due to recent bottling or due to the particular stage of the wine development.

CORKED: Corky or Contaminated by a faulty cork which gives the wine a cardboard smell. Bad corks can be a major problem, as they can ruin otherwise good wine bottle. Appox 2 to 5 bottles out of 100 are affected by bad corks.

CORKY WINE: When the wine is stored incorrectly, i.e when the the wine does not touch the cork, in this case it may possible that the wine become corky

CRISP: Refreshing wine with balanced acidity.

DECANTING: The process of decanting means pouring a wine from the bottle into another container slowly without disturbing the sediments of the wine at the bottom of the bottle

EARTHY: Wines with distinctive soil character or seem like a rustic wine which could be the key reason behind its complexity

FINISH: The final taste left in the moth after one has swallowed the wine. Wines differ in finish i.e some have long or short finishes.

FIRM: This reflects a wines structure and texture which may be because of its acidity, this term is about expression or description of a wines structure or how a wine feels in the mouth

FLABBY: A flabby wine lacks balance and is low in acidity and is a negative term to express a wine quality. It also means that the taste of the wine is not enjoyable.

FRUITY: Being a fruity wine is indicative of a wines taste or smell that may resemble a fruit

GRIP: When a wine has a firm, tactile finish.

HARD: Too tannic or acidic; often a characteristic of wine that indicates that it requires more time in bottle.

JAMMY: Slightly cooked flavours of jam rather than fresh fruit, often a characteristic of red wines from hot climates.

LEAN: When a wine lacks in flesh and body. This may not necessarily be a negative comment, as some types of wines are lean by nature.

LEES: Solid residue, mostly dead yeast cells, grape pulp, skin etc., that is left in the cask after the wine has been drawn off. Many wines are deliberately kept on their lees for an extended period of time to enrich their texture and add complexity to it

MIDDLE PALATE: This refers to the the part of the tasting experience between the nose of the wine and its finish. The impact of a wine in the mouth.

MULLED WINE: This is served hot or warm and is also called spiced wine. This beverage is made with red wine along with various mulling spices and often raisins.

MOUTH FEEL: The physical impression & texture of a wine in the mouth

NOSE: The aroma or bouquet of a wine.

OAKY SMELL: Flavour/ aroma of the oak cask in which the wine was vinified /aged. Oaks impact may be elements such elements as vanilla, clove, cinnamon, cedar, smoke, toast, bourbon and coffee.

OXIDIZED: Wjen a wine turns stale due to excessive exposure to air. An oxidized white wine may have a darker or even brown colour.

POWERFUL: Generally high in alcohol

SHARP: Unpleasantly bitter/ sharp.

SOFT: Low in tannin and/or acidity.

SPRITZ: The flavour or taste of carbon dioxide on the tongue generally found in young, light white wines.

SWEET: Term that is not just applied to those wines with significant residual sugar but also to those that shows outstanding richness

TANNIN: Tannin is substance that is mouth drying as well as bitter, that is found in the skins and stocks of grapes as well as in wood barrels. Tannin is an important ingredient and act as a preservative

ULLAGE: Loss of wine or spirit from a cask or bottle due to evaporation or leakage

VDT (Vine de table): table wine, or the basic wines, not of very high quality but commonly used for every day purpose.

WINE MAKING TERMS

ACIDIFICATION: The addition of acid during fermentation, to increase the acidity of a wine.This is required when the grapes are harvested too ripe and they produce wines with low acidity and high pH value . Acidification stabilizes a wine.

ACIDITY: The acids in a wine provides liveliness, longevity and balance to a wine. Too much acid makes a wine sour or sharp taste on the palate, while too little results in a flabby, shapeless wine. If Tannin may be identified as the spine of a wine, and in that case acidity is its nervous system.

BARREL OR CASK: Most of the world's greatest wines are aged in barrels, usually made from oak. A barrel is a hollow cylindrical container which is bulging in the centre and is longer than it is wide and is often made of white oakwood

CHAPTALIZATION: The process of addition of sugar during fermentation to increase a wine's alcoholic strength is called chapatalization

FERMENTATION: The process of converting grape juice into wine through the action of yeasts present in the juice, which turns sugar into alcohol.

FILTRATION: This is a technique used by wine makers to clarify the wine and aims to remove its sediments and haze. This method also prevents wine from appearing cloudy and also its prevents the wine from re fermenting in bottle

LEES: This term is used for the solid residue that remains in the cask after the wine has been drawn off (which refers to dead yeast/grape pulp/ pips & skins.) Sometimes white wines and some reds are kept on their lees for sometime, with the aim to protect them from oxidation and also to enrich their textures and add complexity.

MUST: This refers to the freshly crushed grape juice that may contain skin, seeds and stems of the fruit.

RACKING: the process of transfer of the wine from one cask to another to separate it from its lees.

SEDIMENT: Solid matter also called as little crystals or wine diamonds deposited in a bottle during the course of the maturation process.

SULPHUR: The most common disinfectant for wine. Sulphur in wines serve two purpose: It prevents wines from reacting with oxygen and it also inhibits the growth of bacteria and wild yeasts in grape juice and wine

Most winemakers feel that it is nearly impossible to produce stable wine without judicious use of sulphur products at one or more stages of vinification: just after the harvest to thwart fermentation by the wrong yeasts, in the cellar to prevent microbial spoilage and oxidation and at the time of bottling to protect the wine against exposure to air. But as a general rule, the amount of sulphur used in the production of fine wine has never been lower than it is today.

TANNIN: A substance found in skin, pips & stalks of grapes & in wood barrels which is bitter & mouth-drying substance. Tannin acts as a preservative and is thus an important component if the wine in the aging of wines Tannin are often sharp & harsh in a young wine, but are observed to soften as the wine ages in the bottle.

YEAST: It is one of the key element, that differentiate wine from grape juice. Yeasts converts sugars of wine grapes into carbon dioxide and alcohol by the process of fermentation. Certain wild yeasts are naturally present on grape skins, however cultivated yeasts are mostly used to control fermentation more carefully.

WHISKY: Scotland Name whiskey comes from the old Gaelic Language of Scotland- UISGEBEATHA (Pronounced as WHISKEH'BA) The term Uisgebeatha means WATER OF LIFE

There are three varieties of whiskey

Malt Whisky

Grain whisky

Blended whisky

Malt Whisky: Made from best barley which is allowed to germinate so as to convert starch of the grain into sugar. After the conversion the grain is called Green Malt which is heated over furnace(fire) fired by Peat. The smoke when passes through drying green malt gives it a smoky flavour, this process of drying takes two days. Whiskey is distilled two times in pot stills Malt whiskey takes 8 -15 years to mature however legally can be sold only after three years.

Grain Whisky: This whisky is made from different grains such as corn, wheat or rye. Many Canadian and American whiskeys are called grain whiskeys.

Blended Whisky: This product is obtained by blending different types of whiskeys together. They are ideally blended in ratio of of 50:50 of malt and grain whiskies, by increasing the malt content the better the quality can be achieved

OTHER WHISKIES

Irish Whiskey: Produced in Ireland, whereby the distiller uses a mixture of malted and unmalted grain in the mash, added to this is the third distillation and this results in a softer & a very refined product.

Canadian Whiskey: Different grains are used like Rye, Corn and Malted barley to produce this product. Distillation is by continuous still, all whiskies must spend a minimum of three years in cask Canadian whiskies are sold as 10,12 and 18 years of old.

American Whiskey:

BOURBON is made in Kentucky and made from a minimum 51% Corn Mash and malted barley. Some may contain little Rye as well. The main character of Bourbon whiskey comes from the new but Charred American oak cask. There are two styles of bourbon i.e Sweet Mash which uses fresh yeast and Sour Mash uses old yeast from a previous brew

GIN: A flavoured alcoholic beverage, i. e Gin is produced by re-distilling high proof spirit with juniper berries and few other flavouring agents. It was initially believed that juniper berries contained an aromatic oil that offered diuretic properties that could cure various ailments of kideney and bladder but not found to be true. A British soldier introduced Gin to England when he carrier from Netherlands a sample of Juniper flavoured spirit named Dutch Courage. The Dutch called it Genièvre (French word for juniper) & an England it was named as Gin.

VODKA: Vodka is a clear distilled alcoholic beverage, it is colourless, odourless, flavourless unaged spirit, which comprises primarily of water and ethanol but may carry some impurities or flavours.

Vodka can be made from any ingredient that can be fermented to make alcohol but most popularly produced from potatoes, sugar, beet molasses and cereal grain. Vodka is defined as a neutral spirt without any distinctive aroma, taste or colour.

RUM: Rum is an alcoholic beverage made by fermenting and distilling byproducts of sugar cane, i.e. molasses or sugar cane juice. The climate and the soil impacts the final rum taste, that is the reason that the run produced from molasses in Barbados is very different in taste than a rum that is made from Dominican molasses. White rums are distilled in stainless steel casks giving a straight forward rum experience. Often caramel is added to aged rums to correct its colour or sometimes may be darken it to give it an older look. Rum with cola is of the most favourite way of consuming rum worldwide

TEQUILA: Tequila is a fermented & distilled alcoholic beverage made from the blue agave plant, which is produced in an area of Mexico known as Tequila. When produced outside these geographical limits, it is called mescal. Blue Agave grows best on red lava soil. Agave Azul grows naturally in southwest Mexico because of the unique combination of altitude, soil conditions, humidity, annual rainfall, average temperature and exposure to the sun. It takes up to 8 - 12 years for a Blue Agave plant to mature. Tequila is best served cold and straight in a shot glass. A popular & unique way to consume it is - season your tongue with citrus and salt by first squeezing a wedge of lime and then pouring salt on the back of the hand and licking it everytime. Tequila is then gulped straight carrying the seasoning with it.

COGNAC: Cognac is made from certain specified grape varieties-ugni blanc. Cognac must be made in Cognac region in France to be called a cognac while brandy can be made in any part of the world. Cognac features amongst the oldest spirits of the world and is ingredient of various classic cocktails. Cognac is an expensive drink as it accounts for only 1% of the worlds spirits by volume as it has an extremely limited production as they are barrel aged for much much longer time making it an exclusive and expensive drink

Cognac is best served neat and during dinner and best served in cognac snifter

These are:

V.S. (Very Special)

V.S.O.P. (Very Superior Old Pale)

X.O. (Extra Old)

ARMAGNAC: Cognac and Armagnac are both French brandies & are made from white wine grapes. Cognac is made from Ugnia Blanc grapes and Armagnac is made from Folle Blanche, Colombard and Baco Blanc. The two are manufactured by different process -Cognac goes through two rounds of distillation in pot stills and on the other hand Armagnac only goes through one in a column still. This difference in process completely changes the end product.

WHISKY: Whiskey is a dark distilled spirit which is made from variety of grains-barkey-corn-rye & wheat. The word whiskey comes from gaelic uisge – which means water of life. Whisky is one of the most popular alcoholic beverages which is created from the distillation of grain based products. The color of the whisky comes from the oak wood casks and from the little amount of caramel. Whisky can be aged only in wooden casks and it can survive in the bottle for 100 years without any change in its colour. A whisky bottle once opened can remain good for five years. The spelling of WHISKEY is used by Irish and Americans and WHISKY spellings are used in Scotland & Canada

TYPES OF WHISKY

SINGLE MALT WHISKY– It must be made from 100% malted barley & distilled from a single distillery by pot still distillation process

BLENDED MALT WHISKY –It is a blend of single malt scotch whiskies from more or a minimum of two distilleries

BLENDED GRAIN WHISKY – a mixture of grain whiskies from atleast two different distilleries

BLENDED SCOTCH: It is a blend of single malt & single grain scotch whiskies

BLENDED WHISKY– It is a mixture of malt and grain whisky, usually from different distilleries. By law, to be allowed to be called Scotch Whisky it has to be matured in Scotland in oak casks for at least 3 years Bottled whisky may be a mixture of casks of any age over 3 years Bottles do not have to have an age statement, but if there is one, the age on the label must be the age of the youngest whisky in the mix in completed years A whisky aged 3 years and 364 days is legally still 3 years old

SCOTCH WHISKEY: For any whisky to be scotch whiskey

It must have been produced at a distillery in Scotland from water & malted barley

The spirit must be matured in a warehouse in Scotland inside an oak cask for a minimum of 3 years

SINGLE MALT: A single-malt scotch whisky is a product of a single distillery & not the product of a single batch or a single barrel, but a single distillery. A single-malt Lagavulin may contain whiskies from different barrels produced at the Lagavulin distillery, but it must contain only whiskies produced at Lagavulin.

DIFFERENCE BETWEEN SINGLE MALT & BLENDED WHISKY: Single Malt Scotch Whisky is also a blend, though it's a blend of malt whisky produced only from one distillery and word single means single place of origin however Blended Scotch Whisky is a blend of grain as well as malt whisky from multiple distilleries.

LIQUEUR: Liqueurs is an alcoholic drink which comprises of distilled spirits & are flavoured and sweetened by sugar, fruits, herbs etc. The term liqueur originates from the Latin word LIQUIFACERE, which means to dissolve (which refers to flavouring materials dissolved in the spirit). Monk Benedictine of France produced first the liqueur in the year 1575 and the first bottled liqueur was by Bols in Holland. A lady by the name Catherine di Medici started the tradition of liqueur after meals as a Digestif. Most liqueurs range between 15% to 55% alcohol by bolume

LIQUEURS COMPRISE OF:

BASE SPIRIT- Every liqueur starts with a base, which is often a neutral spirit, although any kind of spirit can be used.

FLAVOURING AGENTS- The preparation of liqueur involves the infusing of the flavour from the flavouring agent into the spirit.

SWEETENING AGENTS- After the flavour has been set, the liqueur is sweetened mostly by sugar syrup. In the next step the liqueur is then diluted with water to the desired proof. Liqueurs are not aged but they require a resting period after every step of production process.

CORDIAL: Cordial is used to describe a tonic, syrup, or non-alcoholic drink that is often sweet, but many people also consider the term to describe any type of liqueur that has a low alcohol content, or even a medicinal beverage. Cordials are described as non-alcoholic, syrupy drink such as a lime cordial or elderflower cordial.

APERITIF: Aperitif word originated from the Latin word Aperitivers means- to open up. In this context, it is to open up the appetite for the future courses to come. These are alcoholic beverages that can stimulate the appetite. Two Categories of Aperitifs -Spirit Based/Bitters and Wine Based. Some popular spirit-based aperitifs are:

CAMPARI: It is a bitter orange and herb flavoured liqueur produced in Italy. This is red in colour and Herbs and bitter orange rind are steeped in neutral alcohol.

JAGERMEISTER: This unique flavoured product is made from from 50 herbs like liquorice, aniseed, juniper berries, poppy seeds and saffron steeped in neutral alcohol. It is best served after meals in an old-fashioned glass

VERMOUTH: It is of German origin & is an aromatised wine which is fortified. Ingredients in this are aromatic herbs, sugar and alcohol. The base wine is ordinary wine, which is fortified with Mistelle. Mistelle is comprises of-unfermented grape juice and brandy in the ratio of one part of brandy and four parts of grape juice.

LILLET: Lillet, both red and white, is dry and full-bodied. Best way to serve this is chilled from a refrigerator -on the rocks with a twist of lemon, slice of orange or a splash of soda.

BEER: Beer is a fermented, alcoholic beverage which is flavoured with hops and is made from barley, wheat, rice and other grains. The main ingredients used in brewing beer are Grains, Hops, Yeast, Water and Sugar. Head in a beer is the name for the foam on top of your beer. This is the most widely consumed alcoholic drink on our planet. Yeast converts sugar into alcohol, hops gives it the flavour and it also give it a bitterness that balances the sweetness of the malt, the starch source that gives it the strength and flavour is malt and also provides the fermentable material

TYPES OF BEERS LAGER: The generic name for any bottom fermenting beer is Lager. Lager came from the German word "Lagern" (to store) & is used for this type of beer because they are stored for long time at low temperature. Lager traditionally was stored in cellars or caves for completion of fermentation process. They are bright gold to yellow in colour can be medium to light in body and are carbonated. This Beer is made with bottom fermenting yeast. Lager is fermented at lower temperatures (45 to 55 °F/7 to 13 °C) and this process takes longer to ferment than ales. Since the fermentation is at a low temperatures, the yeast byproducts are reduced and results in a crisp beer Pilsners and bock are examples of lager beers

ALE: A term that is used for fermenting beer but originally produced in Britain with defining character of top fermentation with 4% v/v. It is of a darker colour than lager beer with more hops and aroma, and little carbonation. Ale is generally bitter to taste with a slight tanginess. Ales are beers made with top fermenting yeast & are fermented between 68-75°F (20-24°C).

IPA- INDIA PALE ALE: A Strong heavily hopped beer brewed in Britain. The recipe was designed to withstand long sea voyages to distant parts of the British Empire, like India.

BOCK: A very strong lager traditionally brewed in winter to celebrate the coming of spring and are full bodied, malty and well hopped.

BROWN ALE: A British-style, flavoured with roasted caramel malt & top-fermented beer & lightly hopped

DRY BEER: In the late 80's, Asahi Brewery of Japan refined a brewing process that fermented virtually all the sugars in their beer. Described as having less aftertaste, it actually had almost no taste at all. It sold well, though, so major breweries around the world began brewing "Dry Beers" of their own.

WITBIER: Belgian style"white" beer. It is a cloudy wheat beer which is spiced with coriander and orange peel.

STOUT: This is a dark, top-fermented beer with varieties like dry stout, oatmeal stout etc

BITTER: This is a British style of pale ale that has variety of colour from gold to dark amber. The alcoholic strength is from 3% to 5.5% alcohol by volume.

LAMBIC: This type of beer brewed in the Pajottenland region of Belgium. Different types of lambic beers include gueuze, kriek lambic and framboise

DUNKEL: Dunkles, is a word used for different type of dark German lager. German word- Dunkel means dark. Dunkel beers range in color from amber to dark reddish brown. They are have a unique smooth malty flavor.

PALE ALE: is a kind of ale, a top-fermented beer made with predominantly pale malt. The higher proportion of pale malts results in a lighter colour. The term first appeared around 1703 for beers made from malts dried with high-carbon coke, which resulted in a lighter colour than other beers popular at that time.

PORTER: This style of beer was developed in London. It is wellhopped and dark in colour because of use of brown malt.

LAMBIC: A traditionally Belgian brew that is sour. It is usually fruit flavored (peach, raspberry, cassis, cherry) and fermented with wild yeast several bacteria.

DRAUGHT (DRAFT) BEER: These beers are not pasteurised because many people think that pasteurisation kills the authentic taste of beer. These beers are served straight from the container & should be kept refrigerated.

WINE: According to the wine and spirit association of Great Britain, wine is defined as an alcoholic beverage obtained from the juice of freshly gathered grapes, the fermentation of which must have been carried out in the district of its origin, as per the local tradition and customs. Egyptian records as old as dating from 2500 BC refer to the use of grapes for winemaking. The first wines may have originated in the Middle East. There are many references to wine in the Old Testament.

TYPE OF WINES:

TABLE WINES- Also called still or natural wines, table wines are made from juice that is pressed from the grape. The juice is allowed to ferment naturally, sometimes with the addition of controlled amounts of sugar and yeast. These wines are further classified on the basis of their colour.

>Red wine - Made from black grape
>White wine - Made from white grape
>Rose wine - Made from black grape

SPARKLING WINES- These wines contain carbon dioxide. Sparkling wines go through a double fermentation, the second of which takes place in the bottle.

FORTIFIED WINES- These wines receive an extra dosage of alcohol, usually a grape brandy, at some point in their production. The alcohol content of fortified wines is higher than that of table wines, ranging from 14 to 23 percent.

AROMATISED WINE- These are the wines which are fortified and flavoured with some herbs. Vermouth, for example, is an aromatic wine, to which herbs have been added.

Different types of wines are paired with different types of foods and are served on different occasions in different courses of the menu.

CHAMPAGNE: Champagne is a sparkling wine produced, harvested and processed in a specific part of the province of champagne, originating from certain noble varieties of grapes fermented naturally inside the bottle, in accordance with the rules laid down by the French government. The principals of these rules are: Only the following three varieties of grapes can be used

a) Pinot Noir (black) b) Pinot Meunier (black) c) Chardonnay (white)

Wines to be prepared at locations meant only for champagne wine.

Natural process known as METHODE CHAMPENOISE to be used

LIQUEUR CHART

LIQUEUR	FLAVOUR
Abrotine	Apricot
Absinthe	Anise flavour
Advocate	Egg, Sugar
Amaretto	Almond flavour
Anisette	Aniseed
Arrack	Herbs, Sap of palm trees
Bailey's Irish Cream	Honey, Chocolate, Cream
Benedictine DOM	Herbs
Calvados	Apple

Campari	Bitter orange aperitif
Chartreuse	Herbs/Plants
Cherry Brandy	Cherry
Cointreau	Orange
Crème de bananes	Creamy banana flavour
Crème de cacao	Chocolate/Vanilla
Crème de Casis	Creamy black currant flavour
Crème de Framboise	Creamy raspberry flavour
Crème de Menthe	Mint leaf infused liqueur
Curacao	Orange flavour
Drambuie	Heather, Honey, Herbs
Fernet Branca	Bitter menthol/eucalyptus flavoured
Galliano	Smooth spicy liqueur with vanilla and anise flavour
Glayva	Honey, Almonds, Herbs, Spices
Grand Marnier	Orange flavoured cognac based
Jägermeister	Blend of citrus, liquorice, even saffron and spice
Kahlua	Coffee
Kirsch	Cherry
Kummel	Caraway Seeds
Malibu	Coconut flavoured
Maraschino	Maraschino Cherry
Midori	Melon flavoured

Parfait Amour	Violets, Lemon peel, Spices
Patron XO Café	Tequila based liqueur with roasted coffee flavour
Peach Liqueur	Brandy based peach flavoured
Sambuca	Flavoured with anise , herbal spice that gives flavour of adsinthe and black liquorice
Schnapps	Comes in many flavours- cinnamon, apple, peppermint
Slivovitz	Plum
Southern Comfort	Peaches, Oranges
Strega (The Witch)	Herbs, Bark, Fruit
Tia Maria	Coffee
Triple sec	Orange flavoured
Van De Hum	Tangerine

BEVERAGES & WHAT THEY GO WELL WITH:

	Straight	On the rocks	Water	Soda	Coke	Tonic	Lemonade	Orange juice	P/A Juice
Deluxe Scotches	#	#	#	#					
Premium Scotches	#	#	#	#					
Regular Scotches	#	#	#	#					
Single Malts	#	#	#	#					
American Whisky	#	#			#				
IMFL Whisky	#	#	#	#					

Dark Rum			Rarely recommended			#			
White Rum						#			
Gin				#		#			
				With lime juice/ cordial					
Vodka		#		#	NA	#	#	#	
Tequila	#								
Cognac	#	#	Hot water						
Liqueurs	#	#							
Kahlua	#	#							
Sambuca (coffee bean and flame)	#	#							
Aperitifs									
Campari		#		#				#	
Pernod			#						
Pimm's No.1(gin based)						#	#		

SOME POPULAR COCKTAILS

Sn.	Base	Name	Composition	Method
1.	Gin	Dry martini	60 ml. Gin 1 dash of vermouth	Stir in cocktail glass
2.		Gimlet	60 ml. Gin 30 ml. Lime-cordial	Shake, Champagne saucer
3.		Pink Lady	60 ml. Gin Grenadine syrup Egg white, FR lime	Shake, ice cubes Champagne saucer
4.		Singapore Sling	45 ml. Gin 15 ml. Cherry liqueur 10 ml. sugar syrup Soda	Stir, hiball glass, top with soda

5.		Gibson	60 ml. Gin 1 dash dry vermouth	Stir cocktail glass
6.		Tomcollins	60 ml. Gin 15 ml. Fresh lime 15 ml. Sugar syrup soda to fill	Stir Collins glass
7.		Ginfizz	60 ml. Gin 20 ml. Fresh lime juice 20 ml. Sugar syrup 1 tsp egg white	Shake, fizz with soda, Collins glass
8.	Vodka	Black Russian	30 ml. Vodka 30 ml. Coffee liqueur	Shake, cocktail glass
9.		Screw Driver	60 ml. Vodka 10 ml. Fresh lime 150 ml. Orange juice	Stir hi-ball
10.		Bloody Mary	60 ml. Vodka 1 dash tobasco 3 dash Worcestershire sauce 30 ml. Fresh lime tomato juice to fill	Stir, roly poly
11.	Rum	Planters punch	60 ml. Dark rum 80 ml. Pineapple juice 40 ml. Orange juice 10 ml. Fresh lime Grenadine Syrup	Stir, then float rum, hi-ball
12.		Daiquiri	45 ml. Clear rum Sugar Syrup 10 ml. Fresh lime	Shake, champagne saucer(Different flavours can be Created like strawberry, banana, kiwi)
13.	Whisky	Whisky sour	60 ml. Whisky 15 ml. Lime juice 10 ml. Sugar syrup 1 tsp egg white	Shake, parfait glass
14.		Manhattan	45 ml. Rye Whiskey 15 ml. sweet vermouth 1 dash angostura bitter	Stir cocktail glass

15.		Rob Roy	45 ml. Scotch 15 ml. Sweet Vermouth 1 dash angoustra bitter	Stir, cocktail glass
16.		Whisky old fashioned	60 ml. Whisky 2 dash angoustra bitter 1 cube sugar 30 ml. Soda	Mix sugar, bitters, soda, ice cubes, top with whisky soda on side roly poly
17.	Brandy	Side car	45 ml. Ind brandy 15 ml. Cointreau 10 ml. Lime juice	Shake, champagne saucer
18.		Brandy Alexander	45 ml. Ind brandy 15 crème de cacao 15 ml. Fresh cream	Shake, cocktail glass
19.		Grasshopper	30 ml. Ind brandy 15 ml. Crème de methe green 15 ml. Fresh cream 15 ml. Cacao white	Shake, ice cubes in a shaker Cocktail glass
20.	Tequilla	Margarita	45 ml. Tequila 15 ml. Clear orange liqueur cointreau 10 ml. Fresh lime	Shake with ice cubes Champagne saucer

COCKTAIL

A cocktail is an alcoholic beverage consisting of a spirit/several spirts with other ingredients like some other juices, flavourings etc. in a definite proportion. In other words, it is a combination of spirits, at times also wines, flavourings, sweeteners and sometimes addition of juices, soda, lemonade, tonic water, etc

PARTS OF A COCKTAIL

BASE – Base is the fundamental ingredient, usually a spirit. The type of spirit added to the cocktail determines the type of cocktail like gin cocktail, rum cocktail etc.

MODIFIER – Modifier soothes the sharpness of the liquor and adds character to the flavour.

FLAVOURING AGENT – It includes liqueurs, cordials etc. A modifier can also be used as a flavouring agent.

COLOURING AGENT – These are liqueurs which impart colour to the cocktail. For example, Blue Curaçao, Grenadine, Khus Syrup etc.

MIXER – It is the non-alcoholic part of the cocktail, which dilutes the drink & also lowers the alcohol by volume. They also enhance the overall flavour and may also make drinks to be more sour, sweeter of more savory

GARNISH – It enhances the eye appeal of the cocktail. It may include a twist of lemon or any fruit etc.

MOCKTAIL

It can be defined as a potable, non-alcoholic mixed drink with refreshing, thirst quenching, nourishing and stimulating characteristics which consists of mix of fruit juices or soft drinks or other non-alcoholic flavours.

PARTS OF MOCKTAIL

BASE – It is basically the fundamental ingredient and has a defined effect on the Mocktail. It could be a juice or a combination of two or more juices.

MODIFYING AGENT – These help in modifying the flavour of the mocktail. It may include soda, cream, ice cream, soft drinks, sugar syrup, egg or lemon juice etc.

FLAVOURING/COLOURING AGENTS – These provide a distinct flavour as well as colour to the mocktail. They include squashes, cordials and fruit syrups like grenadine syrup, blue curaçao, khus syrup, mint syrup, ginger syrup, guava syrup, kiwi syrup, strawberry syrup etc.

ADDITIVES – These are added to enhance the flavour or taste of the mocktail. They include Tabasco sauce, Worcestershire sauce, salt, sugar, ginger ale, nuts etc.

GARNISH – It is a part that is used to enhance the eye appeal of the mocktail. As far as possible it is generally edible, usually a fruit that is also an ingredient of the drink.

ICE – It is important to use ice properly to make a chilled mocktail. It should be taken care that the ice should not be warm; otherwise the resulting drinks will be weak and diluted

DIFFERENCE BETWEEN COCKTAIL AND MOCKTAIL

BASIS	COCKTAIL	MOCKTAIL
Alcoholic content Preparation Taste Price Government regulation	It has alcoholic content. Preparation needs some conventional methods. Cocktail has sour or bitter taste. The price of cocktail is costlier than mocktail. Age limit to consumers.	It does not have any alcoholic content. No conventional method is required can be prepared by anyone. Mocktails are sweeter. Mocktails are usually cheaper than cocktail. No age limit required.

DIFFRENCE BETWEEN COGNAC AND ARMAGNAC

BASIS	COGNAC	ARMAGNAC
Region Grape varieties Distillation process	Produced in cognac region of France. Produced with Ugni Blanc grapes. Distilled through pot still method.	Produced in Armagnac region of France. Armagnac uses three additional grape varietals: Folle blanche, Colombard, and Baco Blanc. Distilled through patent still method.

DIFFERENCE BETWEEN SPARKLING WINE AND CHAMPAGNE

SPARKLING WINE	CHAMPAGNE
Sparkling wine are so called because it has significant level of Carbon Dioxide which makes it fizz.	Champagne are sparkling wine but can only be called Champagne if it comes from the Champagne region in northern France.

DIFFERENCE BETWEEN LIQUOR AND LIQUEUR

LIQUOR	LIQUEUR
Liquor are spirits with bitter taste and less sweetened with liqueur. Produced by fermentation and distillation method Yeast-based fermentation of a liquid brewed to have fermentable sugars is necessary.	Liqueur are sweetened and flavoured spirit. Produced by infusion or maceration method A spirit base is necessary for the preparation of liqueur.
Liquor are spirits with bitter taste and less sweetened with liqueur. Produced by fermentation and distillation method. Yeast-based fermentation of a liquid brewed to have fermentable sugars is necessary.	Liqueur are sweetened and flavoured spirit. Produced by infusion or maceration method. A spirit base is necessary for the preparation of liqueur.

CLASSIFICATION OF WINE

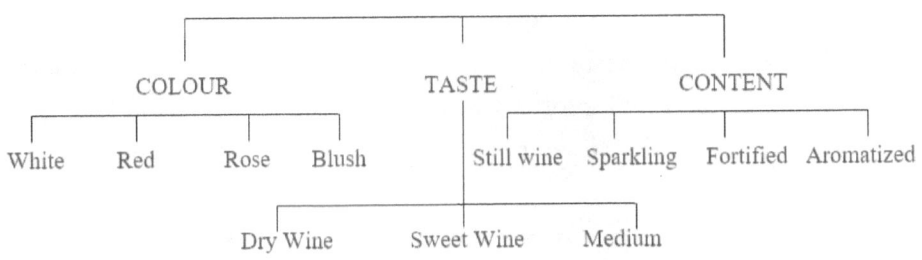

WINE: Wine is the alcoholic beverage obtained from fermentation of freshly gathered grapes. The fermentation takes place in the district of origin, according to local tradition and practice.

Wine Regions

France	Italy	Spain
Bordeaux	Piedmont	Rioja
Loire	Veneto	Jerez
Champagne	Lombardy	Toro
Alsace	Liguria	Rueda
Burgundy	Tuscany	Malaga
Beaujolais	Abruzzi	Alella
Cotes du rhone	Sicily	Velencia
Gascony	Marches	Penedes
Jura	Valle D'aosta	La mancha
Savoie	Trentino	Almansa

WHAT IS VDP AND VDT

VDP-Vin de Pays are the country wines. This French wine law was introduced in year 1960. The wine coming under this category are made from the approved grapes of the particular region and also guarantees the minimum alcoholic content and the minimum area of production.

VDT-Vin de Table is the basic wine laws of France. It applies to approximately 40% of the total wine production in France. It does not restrict on grape varieties used. The labels of these wines are not allowed to display the area of production. These wines are sold in carafe or in glasses in café and named as carafe wine.

FULL BODY WINE: Body refers to the texture of wine in the mouth. These could be a red wine or a white wine. A full body wine has rich, complex & well-rounded flavour that lingers in the mouth. Alcohol % over 13.5% by volume

Example of full body white wine- Cabernet & French Bordeaux.

Example of full body red wine- Chardonnay & Sauvignon Blanc.

MEDIUM BODY WINE: Medium body wines fall somewhere in between full body and light body wines. Alcohol % of 12.5 to 13.5% by volume.

LIGHT BODY WINE: Light bodied wines have a lean & delicate nature, this is because they have light viscosity and consistency and have lightness of water which does not necessarily mean thin. Example of a light body wine is Riesling, Pinot noir, sauvignon blanc. Alcohol % at or below 12.5% by volume.

WHAT IS A VINTAGE WINE?

A vintage wine is a wine produced from grapes that were primarily grown and harvested in one specified year. These wines have same quality as that of port wine.

WHAT IS APPELLATION CONTROLLE

Appellation Controlee or Appellation d' Origine Controlee (AOC) is one of the French wine laws enforced by the Institute National des Appellation d' Origine (INAO) which maintain the highest quality standards while manufacturing of wines.

It guarantees the following:

- Production area
- Grape varieties
- Different viticulture methods such as pruning, density of planting etc.
- The maximum production (i.e number of hectolitre per hectare)
- The minimum alcoholic content
- Various vinification method-blending, ageing etc.

TYPES OF WINES

TYPES OF WINE	ALCOHOLIC CONTENT	SERVING TEMPERATURE
Sparkling Wines 1) Champagne 2) Vin Mousseux 3) Sparkling wines from other countries	9-15 % abv	4.5 to 10 degrees
Still Wines Red White 3) Rose	9-15 % abv	15.5 to 18 degrees 10 to 12.5 degrees
Organic wines	9-15 5 abv	12 to 16.5 degrees
Vin doux natural	17% abv	15 to 18 degrees
Fortified wines 1)Sherry 2)Port 3) Madeira 4) Marsala	15-22 % abv 15-18 % abv 18-22 % abv 18 % abv 18 % abv	4.5 to 9.5 degrees 15.5 to 18 degrees 8 to 12.5 degrees 4.5 to 9.5 degrees
Aromatized wines Vermouth Dubonnet St Raphael Pineau de Charente	14-55 % abv 14.7 5 abv 14.8 %abv 17% abv	15.5 to 18 degrees

STILL WINES: (Alcoholic percentage between 9-12 % by volume).

RED WINE: Being fermented in contact with grape juice skins from which wine gets the colour Normally dry wines.

WHITE WINE: Usually produced from white grapes, but grape juice is usually fermented away from the skins. Normally dry to sweet.

ROSE: Made in three ways- from black grapes fermented on skins for about 48 hrs; by mixing red and white wines together: or by pressing grapes so that some colour is extracted.

SPARKLING WINES:

- Champagne
- Effervescent wines made outside the champagne region are known as vin mousseux or sparkling wines.
- Semi-sparkling wines are known by the term pettilant.

SWEETNESS IN SPARKLING WINES:

French term	English Term	Quantity of Sugar
Extra brut	Very dry	Up to 6 g
Brut	Very dry	Less than 15 g
Extra sec	Dry	12 to 20 g
Sec	Slightly sweet	17 to 35 g
Demi sec	Sweetest	35 to 50 g

ORGANIC WINES:

These are the wines also known as green or environmentally friendly wines, are made from grapes without the aid of artificial insecticides fertilizers.

Alcohol-free, de-alcoholised and low alcohol wines

Alcohol free – Maximum 0.05% alcohol

De-alcoholised -Maximum 0.50% alcohol

Low alcohol- Maximum of 1.25% alcohol

VIN DOUX NATURALS: These are the sweet wines that had their fermentation muted by the addition of alcohol in order to retain their natural sweetness, Muting takes place when alcohol level reaches between 5 % and 8% by volume. They have the alcohol strength of about 17.5 by volume.

FORTIFIED WINES: (Within The EU They are known as Liqueurs wines or vins de liqueurs)

The addition of wine distillate (brandy or neutral spirit) to a wine to increase the alcoholic content. This stabilizes the wine

E.g. Port, Sherry, Madeira, Marsala.

AROMATIZED WINES: These Are flavoured and fortified wines

E.g. Vermouth, Punt d mes, Dubonnet, st Raphael, Lillet.

DESSERT WINES: The Dessert wine can be defined as any wine that can possess in excess of 2% residual sugar with an alcoholic content between 5% and 21% by volume.

For the great dessert wines, the grapes are left on the vine until the regular harvest has ended. This concentrates sugar in the grapes.

In certain fine wine regions, and in the best years they may be affected by *Botrytis cinerea,* or noble rot, this causes the skins to break, so much of the liquid in the grapes evaporates, concentrating the sugar further.

Some of the Dessert wines are fortified and some not fortified, some sparkling and some still.

FORTIFIED DESSERT WINES: There are many types and styles of fortified wines. All involves the addition of grape spirits to still wine to increase the alcoholic strength above 15%.

Many add the spirit before the wine is finished fermenting, leaving a high % of residual sugar, making a sweet, and fortified wine (i.e. Port). Others add sweetening agent during the process to effect a change in the residual sugar content if desired (i.e. Sherry).

WINE BOTTLE SIZES:

Name	Bottle size
Quarter bottle(pony)	18.7 cl
Half Bottle	37.5 cl
Bottle	75 cl
Magnum(2 bottles)	1.5 Litres
Jeroboam(4 bottles)	3 litres
Rehoboam(6 bottles)	4.5 litres
Methuselah(8 bottles)	6 litres
Salmanazar(12 bottles)	9 litres
Balthazar (16 bottles)	12 litres
Nebuchadnezzar(20 bottles)	15 litres

GRAPE VARIETIES

Black	White
Cabernet sauvignon	Semillion
Pinot Noir	Sauvignon blanc
Gamay	Chardonnay
Sangoviese	Riesling
Grenache	Palomino

WHITE GRAPES:

CHENIN BLANC – Naturally high acidity. Used for still wines, from dry to sweet, sparkling wines and some of the longest living white wines.

COLOMBARD – Grown in Cognac and Armagnac regions. Used for light, crisp, fruity wines.

GEWURZTRAMINER – Yellow gold, full bodied, low in acid, slightly oily in texture. Grown in Germany, Alsace, Austria, Italy.

MUSCAT – It is the only grape to produce wine with the same aroma as the grape itself. Grown in Cyprus, France, Germany, Portugal, Australia, Spain.

PINOT BLANC – Produces soft, rounded wines with a hint of aroma. Grown in France, Germany, Italy.

SEMILLON – Golden skinned, used to make dry and sweet white wines, notably in France and Australia.

PALOMINO – Best known for use in the manufacture of sherry. Widely grown in Spain and South Africa.

VERDELHO – Grown throughout Portugal. Gives its name to one of the four main types of Madeira wine.

SYLVANER – Grown in central Europe and Germany. Highly acidic and early ripening variety.

CLAIRETTE – Provides flaccid wines that generally needs blending with other varieties. Grown in France.

RED GRAPES:

BARBERA – Highly acidic. Basically from Piedmont, grown in California.

CABERNET FRANC – A light variety with less tannin, ripens early. Produces medium bodied, soft, leafy flavoured wines.

GAMAY – Famous for wine Beaujolais. Produces rather dull red wines.

GRENACHE – has signature raspberry or white pepper flavour. Gives high alcohol, pallid wines. Grown in Australia and California.

MALBEC – Grown in Argentina. Produces full, richly fruity, spicy red wines with flavours of mulberries and blackberries. Better known for harder, leaner, high acidic wines.

MERLOT – Is softer, less acidic, more plummy with blackcurrant flavour. Grown in Bordeaux, Pomelo, Washington State, California.

NEBBIOLO – Predominantly associated with Piedmont region of Italy. Produces lightly coloured red wines that turn brick orange as they age.

TEMPRANILLO – Used to produce full bodied red wines. Native of Spain.

ZINFANDEL – Produces a robust red wine. Has high sugar content.

PETIT VERDOT – Used in classic Bordeaux blends. Ripens much later than the other varieties. Added in small amounts to add colour, tannin and flavour.

FACTORS AFFECTING QUALITY OF WINE:

SOIL: The aroma of the wine is influenced by the acids or the traces of minerals present in the soil because of the different grapes are grown in different types of soil.

GRAPE VARIETY: Grape play an important role in determining the type of wine to be produced because different variety of grapes has different aroma and other features.

CLIMATE: Climate plays an ideal role in the grape cultivation. The average temperature is 14 degrees C. The average yearly temperature should not be below 10 degrees C. The grape gets damaged from excess of sun shine, hail storm, wind, frost, rain etc.

VITICULTURE: This is the most important and every step of viticulture (ploughing, pruning, weeding, spraying, harvesting etc. is done in a particular month of every year considering the weather. The delay in schedule influences the character of wine.

VINIFICATION: This means the method of making wine. The process such as pressing, fermentation, type of yeast, maturation containers etc. determine the character of wine.

AGEING: Ageing also play a important role in wine making. The longer the wine matured, the mellower and smoother will be the wine, taking the flavour of vanillin from the wood.

STORING: Wines should be stored at appropriate temperature and in the rooms free from direct sunlight and vibration.

STORAGE OF WINES

1. Wines should be stored in Cellars.
2. The cellar should have an even temperature.
3. It must be free of vibrations, strong sunlight or humidity.
4. The temperature maintained in the cellar must be around 15°C.
5. Wines must be stored horizontally so that the cork remains moist and does not dry out, allowing air in the bottle.
6. White wines must not be stored for very long time in cold rooms or refrigerators.
7. White wine stock should be rotated in such a way that the wine kept for longest, should be served first.
8. Sparkling wines should not be stored too long.
9. Prolonged shaking and disturbances also spoil the wine.
10. The bottle of wine should be re-corked as soon as a glass has been poured.
11. Once the wine bottle is opened, it should be consumed as soon as possible.

KEY TERMINOLOGY

AFTER TASTE: It is the flavour that lingers in your mouth after you swallow the wine. The length of the after taste is perhaps the single, most reliable indicator of wine quality.

AGING: It is the maturation of the wines in wood casks or barrels.

AROMA: The primary smell of a wine, consisting of the odour of the grape juice itself, of the fermentation process, and, of the oak barrels in which the wine was made or aged.

AUSTERE: Tough, dry and often due to a severe tannic structure or simply to the extreme youth of a wine.

BALANCE: The ratio of a wine's key components, including fruitiness, sweetness, acidity, tannin and alcoholic strength. A balanced wine shows a harmony of components, whereby one single elements does not dominates.

BODY: The body of a wine indicates the fullness, weight and concentration and total mouth feel of a wine. A light-bodied wine would be having less concentrated flavours, while full-bodied wines are notably more concentrated. Light-bodied wines give a feel similar to water in mouth and full-bodied wines gives a feel like milk as far as heaviness.

BOUQUET: The complex and deep aromas that develop with age is known as bouquet. They are attributed to the process of fermentation, processing and aging, and largely develop after bottling.

CLOSED: Not especially aromatic, becasue of recent bottling or to the particular stage of the wine's development.

CORKED: Corky or Contaminated by a tainted cork which gives the wine a cardboard smell. Bad corks are a major problem, as they can ruin otherwise sound bottles.

CORKY WINE: In case the wine is stored incorrectly, whereby the wine does not touch the cork, in this case it may possible that the wine become corky or spoiled.

CRISP: Refreshing wine with sound acidity.

DECANTING: The process of decanting means pouring a wine from the bottle into another container slowly without disturbing the sediments of the wine at the bottom of the bottle.

EARTHY: Can be a component of complexity deriving from the wine's distinctive soil character.

EXTRACT: Essentially the minerals and other trace elements in a wine; sugar-free dry extract is everything in a wine except water, sugar, acids and alcohol. High extract often gives wine a dusty, tactile impression of density.

FAT: Rich wine has a mature fruit character, aroma and taste. It also has a balance acidity.

FINISH: The final taste left of wine after you swallow. Wines can be said to have long or short finishes.

FIRM: Perceptibly tannic and/or acidic, in a positive way.

FLABBY: Lacking acidity and therefore lacking shape.

FRUITY: Being a fruity wine means a wines taste/smell that resembles a fruit

GRIP: An emphatically firm, tactile finish.

HARD: Too tannic or acidic; that means wine that needs more time in bottle.

HOT: Noticeably alcoholic.

JAMMY: Slightly cooked flavours of jam rather than fresh fruit, this refers to red wines from hot climates.

LEAN: Lacking flesh and body. Some types of wines are lean by nature.

LEES: Solid residue, mostly dead yeast cells, grape pulp, skin etc., that remains in the cask after the wine has been drawn off. Many wines are kept on their lees for a period of time to enrich their texture and add complexity.

MIDDLE PALATE: The part of the tasting experience between the nose of the wine and its finish. The impact of a wine in the mouth.

MULLED WINE: This is served hot or warm and is also called spiced wine. This beverage is made with red wine along with various mulling spices and often raisins.

MOUTH FEEL: The physical impression of a wine; its texture.

NOSE: The aroma or bouquet of a wine.

OAKY SMELL: Taste of the oak cask in which the wine was aged. Oak flavours can include such elements as vanilla, clove, cinnamon, cedar, smoke, toast, bourbon and coffee.

OXIDIZED: Developing a tired or stale taste due to excessive exposure to air. An oxidized white wine may have a darker or even brown colour.

POWERFUL: Generally high in alcohol.

SHARP: Unpleasantly bitter or hard-edged.

SOFT: Low in tannin and/or acidity.

SPRITZ: The faint prickle on the tongue of carbon dioxide generally found in young, light white wines.

SWEET: A term applied not just to wine with significant residual sugar but also to those that shows outstanding richness and rightness.

TANNIN: Tannin is bitter, mouth drying substance found in the skins and stocks of grapes as well as in wood barrels. Tannin acts as a preservative and is an important component.

ULLAGE: Loss of wine or spirit from a cask or bottle due to evaporation or leakage

VDT (Vine de table): table wine, or the basic wines, not of very high quality but commonly used for every day purpose.

WINE MAKING TERMS

ACIDIFICATION: The addition of acid (usually tartaric) during fermentation, frequently necessary in hot climates where grapes tend to overripe and become deficient in acidity, thereby losing freshness.

ACIDITY: The acids in a wine (principally tartaric, malic, citric and lactic) provides liveliness, longevity and balance: too much leaves a sour or sharp taste on the palate, while too little results in a flabby, shapeless wine. If tannin is the spine of a wine, then acidity is its nervous system.

BARREL OR CASK: Most of the world's greatest wines are at least partially aged in barrels, usually made from oak. A barrique is the standard Bordeaux barrel, holding 225 litres or the equivalent of about

300 bottles of wine. But casks may be as large as 100 hectolitres (i.e., 10,000 litres) or more.

CHAPTALIZATION: The process of adding of sugar during fermentation to increase a wine's alcoholic strength.

FERMENTATION: The conversion of grape juice into wine through the action of yeasts present in the juice, which turn sugar into alcohol. This alcoholic fermentation is also known as primary fermentation.

FILTRATION: A method of clarifying and stabilizing wine to give it a pleasingly lucid colour and to remove yeasts, bacteria or other solid matter that might otherwise spoil the wine after it has been bottled. Excessive filtration, like excessive fining, can strip a wine of aroma, body, texture and length.

FINING: A method of clarifying wine by pouring a coagulant (such as egg whites) on top and letting it settle to the bottom. In general, a fining agent is allowed to fall through the wine, while in filtration, the wine is passed through a filter.

LEES: Solid residue (mostly dead yeast cells and grape pulp, pips and skins) that remains in the cask after the wine has been drawn off. Many white wines and some reds are kept on their lees for a period of time to protect them from oxidation, enrich their textures and add complexity. Wines protected by lees contact can often be made with less sulphur addition, but careful technique is essential to ensure that off aromas don't develop.

MUST: Grape juice not yet have fermented or in the process of being fermented into wine.

RACKING: Transferring the wine from one cask to another to separate it from its lees.

SEDIMENT: Solid matter deposited in a bottle during the course of the maturation process. Sediment is generally a sign that the wine was not excessively filtered prior to bottling.

SULPHUR: The most common disinfectant for wine. Most winemakers feel that it is nearly impossible to produce stable wine without judicious use of sulphur products at one or more stages of vinification: just after the harvest to thwart fermentation by the wrong yeasts, in the cellar to prevent microbial spoilage and oxidation and at the time of bottling to protect the wine against exposure to air. But as a general rule, the amount of sulphur used in the production of fine wine has never been lower than it is today.

TANNIN: A bitter, mouth-drying substance found in the skins, stalks and pips of the grapes--as well as in wood barrels. Tannin acts as a preservative and is thus an important component if the wine is to be aged over a long period. Tannins are frequently harsh in a young wine, but gradually soften or dissipate as the wine ages in the bottle.

YEAST: The various microorganisms that cause fermentation. Wild yeasts are naturally present on grape skins, but cultivated yeasts are generally used to control fermentation more carefully.

BAR EQUIPMENTS

PEG MEASURER   LEMON SQUEEZER   BAR SPOON

COCKTAIL SHAKER   WINE STAND   ICE CUBE TONG

MUDDLER   POURER   WINE OPENER

SPEED RAIL   SPEED RAIL   HOWTHORNE STRAINER

BOSTON SHAKER   ICE SHOVEL   SALT & SUGAR RIMMER TRAY

BARTENDING TERMINOLOGY

ABSINTHE: This green alcohol is notorious for various rumours regarding its aftereffects. It is considered to have a hallucinatory effect that accompanies the intoxication.

ALE: This is warm, top fermented version of beer, which gives it a higher sugar content.

APERITIFF: This is a drink that is usually served with a meal, to trigger the taste palette.

BITTERS: Added as a mixer in many a drink, this is a herbal alcoholic essence that is extracted from a mixture of the Gentiana flower and other herbs.

BLEND: A drink that is mixed in an electric blender.

BLENDED MALT: Refers to Scotch that is made from a mixture of a couple of different malts that is taken from different distilleries.

BOSTON SHAKER: The glass which is used to build a drink and is later covered with a shaker to mix the drinks is known as the Boston Shaker.

BOURBON: An American form of whiskey that is made from distilling a mash of at least 51% corn, with the rest being either malted barley, wheat or rye. The distilled liquor is stored for at least 2 years in charred white oak barrels, giving it a distinct smoky flavour.

BRANDY: A spirit distilled from primarily grapes, but also fermented fruit mashes, such as apples, peaches, and plums. Most brandies are barrel-aged, however, some are bottled clear and un-aged, such as grappa.

CAMPARI: An Italian liqueur, known for its red colour and bittersweet flavour marked by underlying flavours of cherry, clove, orange peel, cinnamon & cascarilla.

CARBONATION: The process of making effervescent wine by adding carbon dioxide to it

CASK: A cask is another name for the wooden barrels used to store spirits. Sometimes charred, casks can impart unique flavours such as smoke, vanilla and caramel into the spirits it's storing.

CHASER: A chaser is a mixer that is generally consumed after taking a shooter, shot, or a neat drink. Chaser is a drink of a different kind that is taken immediately after a strong or a weak drink.

CIDER: It is a beverage made of apple juice

COBBLER: Drink poured over crushed ice in a tall glass. These may be sweetened with sugar or liqueur and may be decorated with a fruit or a sprig of mint.

COGNAC: Cognac is a French brandy made in the Cognac region from ugni blanc grapes. Cognac must be aged at least two years in oak barrels.

COOLER: A mixture of soda, ginger ale, a lemon twist, and spirit that is served in a tall Collins glass. It could also be an alcoholic beverage with fruit essences flavours. Example Breezers, Wild berry Cooler, Smirnoff Ice.

CORDIAL: These are sweetened distilled spirits , that are dessert like. for example chocolate or cream spirits. this is also used to describe non alcoholic syrupy contents like lime cordial etc.

CURAÇAO: Named after a Caribbean island where bitter oranges are grown, Curaçao is a liqueur flavoured with the dried peel of the citrus fruit.

DAIQUIRI: The main ingredients of a daiquiri is rum, citrus fruit and sugar or any other sweetner

DIGESTIF: This is a drink served after a meal, and is the sweeter counterpart of an apéritif.

DIRTY: This means adding olive juice to a martini which makes it dirty, more the olive juice dirtier the martini.

DISTILLATION: The process of making a spirit pure, where the fermented product is heated to separate the alcohol from the water. Distillation typically takes place in a pot still or a column still.

DRY: Dry in bartending would mean "Go Easy in the" So if order a dry martini, you will then be served a drink where the quantity of Vermouth is reduced. If you're talking about wine, dry wines are less sweet. And if you're talking about champagne, then it means the opposite, i.e., it tends to be sweeter than a normal champagne.

ENERGY DRINK: Energy drinks claim to enhance performance and boost energy. They usually contain ingredients like caffeine, sugar, taurine, ginseng and other proprietary ingredients.

EGGNOG: A classic drink containing a combination of eggs beaten with cream or milk, sugar, and a liquor such as brandy, rum, or bourbon.

ETHYL ALCOHOL: Also known as grain alcohol, ethyl alcohol is the intoxicating addition/product in any spirit, wine or beer.

FERMENTATION: The process of converting sugar into to alcohol and carbon dioxide by using various agents such as yeast or bacteria.

FORTIFICATION: The process of manufacturing fortified wine by the addition of some spirit.

GARNISH: Salt, sugar, mint, citrus wedges, and other ingredients that is used to add character or style or may be ornament a drink to make it look great, in visual as well as taste.

GRENADINE: A thick, bright-red syrup that is traditionally made from pomegranates. This cocktail syrup is non-alcoholic.

IRISH WHISKEY: Irish whiskey are those which are made on the island of ireland. Irish Whiskey is often triple distilled from blend of unmalted & malted barley and is aged for 3 years in wooden casks.

KIRSCH: Spirit distilled from blackberries. It has subtle flavour of cherry and bitter almond taste

KOSHER SALT: The Kosher salt has a larger grain which makes kosher salt the most commonly used salt when garnishing the rim of a drink.

LIQUEUR: Liqueurs are strong sweet alcoholic flavourful spirits that are generally consumed after meal! they oftne have additional flavour of a fruit, sugar, herbs, spices etc.

LIQUOR: A distilled spirit, which has a higher alcohol content than that of beer or wine.

MARGARITA: It's a Mexican cocktail that consists of tequilla, orange liqueur and lime juice often served with a salt on the rim of the glass. This drink is served straight up, on the rocks as well as blended with ice

MIXER: A non-alcoholic ingredient in a cocktail or mixed drink, typically a soda or juice.

MUDDLE: To crush ingredients with a muddler, for example for mojito (mint leaves) to extract various oils.

NEAT: Neat order at the bar counter would mean a guest is asking for a shot straight from the bottle, means no ice.

NIGHTCAP: When you're down and out of it, and you plan to call it a day, the final drink you have like a wine or other liquor, before you hit the sack is known as a nightcap!

NOSE: The aroma of wine.

POUSSE-CAFÉ: A layered drink consisting on successive cordial layers, creating a rainbow-like effect.

PICK-ME-UP: A drink designed to relieve the effects of overindulgence in alcohol.

PROOF: In American standard for measuring the alcohol content in a distilled spirit or liqueur. The proof is double the percentage of alcohol so 40% alcohol equals 80-proof.

RUM: Rum is a alcoholic beverage that is distilled from a fermented cane product - sugarcane juices or molasses.

RYE: A whiskey typically produced in America or Canada, distilled from a mash containing a minimum of 51% rye, with the rest being a mix of wheat, corn and malted barley.

SAKE: Japanese rice wine.

SANGRIA: It's a wine-based cocktail that contains wine, triple sec, orange juice and fruit. It has many variations, by using different juices.

SCHNAPPS: A clear alcohol often flavoured with fruit and spices.

SCOTCH: A whisky produced in Scotland from malted barley and aged for three years in oak barrels. Most scotch has a distinct smoky flavour from drying the malt with a peat fire.

SHANDY: Beer with Sprite or 7Up.

SHERRY: Made in the Jerez de la Frontera district of Spain, sherry is a fortified wine. There are two types of sherry, dry and sweet, the latter being a dessert wine.

SHOOTER: A shooter may be a layered drink or a neat shot of alcohol that is meant to be consumed in a single gulp.

SHOT: A shot is one serving of any spirit that is served in a shot glass and consumed neat in one gulp in a single move.

SINGLE MALT: Malt whiskey or scotch made at a single distillery and not blended with any other malt.

TEQUILA: A spirit produced in the Jalisco state of Mexico from the Weber Blue Agave. Tequila is clear or golden and is often served in mixed drinks or as a shot with salt and lime.

TODDY: It's a sweetened liquor, served hot, often spiced

TONIC WATER: A bitter carbonated drink made with quinine and sugar. It is often used as a mixer with gin and vodka.

TRIPLE SEC: A sweet, orange-flavoured liqueur made from brandy and orange peels. It is often used as a mixer in cocktails like the margarita or Long Island Iced Tea.

TWIST: The rind of lemon which is peeled by using a lemon zest, and creating a lemon twist which is long and thin

VERMOUTH: A fortified wine flavoured with aromatic herbs. There are two styles of Vermouth, sweet or dry, and it is often used in famous cocktails like the martini.

VIRGIN: Refers to non-alcoholic drinks. Cocktails with alcohol for example Virgin Mary, Virgin Pina Colada

VODKA: A clear spirit of Russian origin made primarily from grains, but can also be made from potatoes, fruits, or sugars. Vodka is typically distilled and then bottled un-aged at 80-proof or higher.

WHISKY/WHISKEY: A broad drink category for spirits distilled from the fermented mash of corn, rye, barley or wheat. The USA and Ireland spell whiskey with an "ey", whereas in Scotland and Canada, the extra "e" is omitted.

ZOMBIE: A drink containing a mixture of different rums and citrus juices.

TYPES OF COFFEES

COLD COFFEE: This coffee is a blend of coffee, milk and sugar and is served cold

CAFÉ FRAPPE: Frappe refers to iced blend drink, may be shaken or blended. Served cold often with whipped cream and a topping

FRAPPUCCINO: This is a Starbucks trademark product and only they are allowed to sell that

DE-CAFFEINATED COFFEE: Also called as Decaf in short form. This coffee is made from coffee beans from which 97% of the caffeine is reomed.

TYPES OF COFFEE

FILTER COFFE: This is a unique south Indian variation to coffee, which is stronger and is made with specially brewed powder. It is made in south Indian coffee filter which has two cylindrical vessels. The top vessel is used for perforation while the lower filter collects brewed coffee made by adding water to the roasted coffee powder. Boiling milk may be added depending on how strong is your coffee requirement

ICED COFFEE: It is made from simple brewed coffee that has been cooled and poured over ice. Served in Tom Collins filled with ice, add filter coffee, and serve sugar syrup separately along with fresh cream.

INSTANT COFFEE: Ready to make coffee mix packet & just add that to boiling water

IRISH COFFEE: Irish coffee is made of four ingredients – coffee, Irish whiskey, sugar and whipped cream and is served in Irish coffee mug

RUSSIAN COFFEE: Russian coffee include Vodka, rich espresso and cream and sometimes gentle topping with cream & sugar to taste.

ALCOHOLIC CONTENT

- Vodka | ABV: 40-95%
- Gin | ABV: 36-50%
- Rum | ABV: 36-50%
- Whiskey | ABV: 36-50%
- Tequila | ABV: 50-51%
- Liqueurs | ABV: 15%
- Fortified Wine | ABV: 16-24%
- Unfortified Wine | ABV: 14-16%
- Beer | ABV: 4-8%
- Malt Beverage | ABV: 15%

Food & Beverage Service

QUALITIES OF A HOSPITALITY PROFESSIONAL

COMMUNICATION SKILLS & ABILITY TO LISTEN: Not only they should have excellent communication skills but they should be expert listeners and pay complete attention to what guest is saying to understand customers' requirements better and in one time

PERSONAL HYGIENE: They must follow all aspects of personal hygiene and presentation by dressing up as per the prescribed standards and uniforms

CONFIDENCE: It's a key personality trait of service providers as it builds customers confidence in the service provider

ENTHUSIASM TO SERVE: They should feel enthusiastic and cheerful towards serving and fulfilling the needs of the customers

JOB KNOWLEDGE: they should be well aware of their job title and job responsibilities and empowerments to perform effectively

PRODUCT KNOWLEDGE: Should have good knowledge about the products and services that they are serving so that they can share information with the customers and make them feel assured and answer any customer queries satisfactorily

CUSTOMER FOCUS: They should stay focused towards customer that they are serving so that they are able to anticipate there needs and fulfill them timely and effectively.

EMPATHY: They should be able to think like customers or put themselves into the shoes of the customer to understand him and his requirements better

ANTICIPATION SKILLS: By anticipating guest requirements a service provider can effortlessly surpass guest satisfaction and achieve wow/ customer delight

CULTURAL AWARENESS: By understanding different cultures, a service provider is best equipped to serve for example by greeting them in their traditional way, by informing them dishes from their cuisine etc can be a big differentiator in providing excellent services

TEAM PLAYER: A service provider must be a team player, as for providing or rendering and service or product they have to co-ordinate with different departments hence it is essential for a seamless service to ensure great teamwork

STRONG WORK ETHICS: The service providers must be ethical to earn the trust of the organization, their colleagues, guests and their supervisors so that they are fully empowered to conduct and serve guests. To be punctual, to be honest, to be transparent, to be organized, to work with dedication and commitment are some of key traits

ADAPTABLE & FLEXIBLE: Service providers have to often work in during odd timings of work schedule, working in different work environments makes adaptability and essential feature of service providers. They often have to deal with various guests from across the world with different expectations, which is very demanding to meet hence service providers must be flexible in their service approach

RESOURCEFUL: While serving various customers often service providers come across unusual guest requests and circumstances, which service providers can handle only if they are resourceful and adapt quickly in understanding the guest needs and find a way to fulfill that to the best of their abilities

BRAND AMBASSADORS: The service providers must display the values of the organization as they are the key representation of their brand/organization

GROWTH MINDSET: Growth mindset is all about the ability to learn new skills. Service professionals must be open to learn new skills to upgrade themselves and stay competitive

ABILITY TO DO SERVICE RECOVERY: Incase a service or a product that is served is not acceptable to the guest, the service professionals must be able to find a solution and ensure that customer complaints are resolved effectively and timely.

ABILTIY TO WITH STAND PRESSURE: The service professionals must have the ability to h stand work pressure and handle effectively customer feedback and customer complaints and provide effective earliest possible solutions.

TYPES OF FOOD & BEVERAGE OUTLETS		
COMMERCIAL	INDUSTRIAL	WELFARE
Hotels	Cafeteria	Old Age Homes
Restaurants	Canteens	Prisons
Pubs	Packed Food Outlets	Orphanage
Kiosks	Tiffins	Destitute Homes
Drive Ins	Air Catering	Religious Places
Event Management	Railway Catering	Disaster Catering
Fast Food	Hospital	
Tea Lounge	Institution Catering	
Bar		
QSR		
Fine Dining		
Upscale Dining		

TYPES OF SERVICE

AMERICAN SERVICE: American service is a pre-plated service which means that the food is served onto the guest's plate in the kitchen itself and brought to the guest. The portion is predetermined by the kitchen and the accompaniments served with the dish balances the entire presentation in terms of nutrition and color. This type of service is common in a coffee shop where service is required to be fast.

CAROUSEL: The carousel is a circular counter that revolves to display the food items. The carousel is fitted in such a way that the one side is always inside the kitchen and other side is in the service area. As the carousel revolves the counter is filled up from the kitchen and guests selects the food as it revolves.

CARVERY: Carvery is a type of assisted service. This service method includes both table service and self-service. Some parts of the service are done by the waiter at the table and some parts of the service is done guests themselves.

COUNTER SERVICE: Counter service sometimes called cafeteria service. The guests come in line, collect their food from the counter and seat at the table to have the food. Food may be grouped together such as cold and hot, or main course and desserts etc. In some places the guests also have to clear the empty plates and cutleries after having the food.

DRIVE THRU: The customer drives the vehicle to the counter and orders and collects the food and leaves the counter

DRIVE-IN -SERVICE: The guests order the food from the vehicle parked at designated areas and service is done at the vehicle. The food is placed on trays that are clipped in the door or steering wheel.

ECHELON: In echelon service the counters are arranged in such a way that it provides better view of the foods and arranged in angular way.

ENGLISH SERVICE: English service is often referred to as "Host Service" or "Silver service". The food is brought on platters by the waiter and is served by them ising spoon and fork into customers plate. The waiter then portions the food and serves to the guest plate.

FOOD COURTS: Food courts include series of individual counters where customer may either order and eat, or buy from a number of counters and eat in separate eating area.

FRENCH SERVICE: It is a very personalized service. Individual portioned food is brought from the kitchen in dishes and slavers which are placed directly on the table. The plates are kept near the dish and the guests help themselves.

GUERIDON SERVICE: This is a service done from the gueridon trolley. The cooking is done at the gueridon trolley place near the guest table and service is done at the guest table. The waiter plays an important role as he is required to fillet, carve, flambé and prepare the food with showmanship.

KIOSKS: A small structure which is open from one or more than one side and vends merchandise like food, beverages or newspapers.

LOUNGE SERVICE: In lounge service the food and beverage is served at the lounge area of a hotel.

ROOM SERVICE: In room service the service of food and beverages are done in the guest room. The food is taken to the guest room in a tray or room service trolley.

RUSSIAN SERVICE: Table is laid with food for guests and presentation is done elaborately. Guests help themselves. This is an elaborate silver service much on the line of French service. Display and presentation are the major part of this service. Some parts of the service such as carving and portioning etc. are done by the waiter.

SELF SERVICE: In the self-service the service is done by customer themselves. The guests collect the food from the counters and then he/she may sit at the table or stand at high table to have the food.

TABLE SERVICE: It is a type of service. Table service is the service done at the table, where the guests are seated. In the table service either service personnel or waiter serves the food to the guests or the guests help themselves.

TAKE AWAY: The food order is placed at a counter and the food is collected from the same counter and take the food away from the premises for consumption.

TRAY SERVICE: In the tray service the food and beverages are brought in a tray and given to guests. Such services are seen in hospitals, guest rooms etc.

VENDING MACHINE: The customer inserts the value of the food item displayed in the vending machine and selects the food by pressing a knob. The vending machine dispenses the selected food. The vending machine can dispense hot or cold food.

TYPES OF BANQUET SET UPS

OVAL BOARDROOM

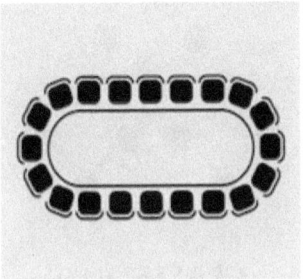

U-SHAPED BOARDROOM

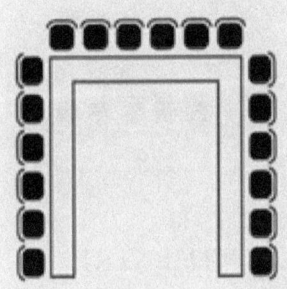

ROUND 8'S OR 10'S

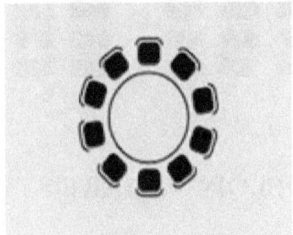

BOARDROOM

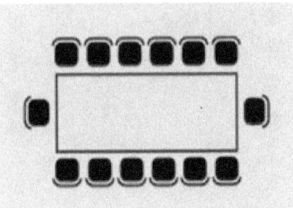

INFORMAL BOARDROOM

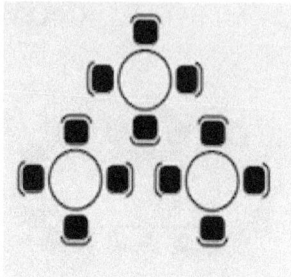

CLASSROOM

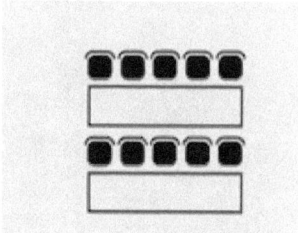

THEATRE

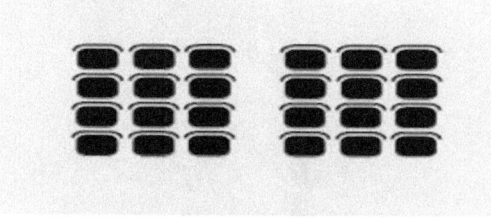

HOLLOW SQUARE STYLE

CRESCENT HALF ROUNDS

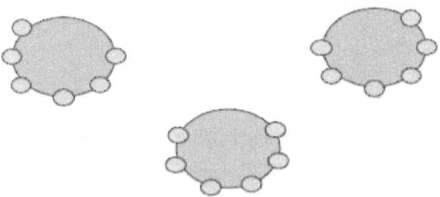

TYPES OF BUFFET

BRUNCH BUFFET: Is a late morning meal whereby lunch and breakfast are combined together. Brunch is often combined with alcoholic beverage often champagne/sparkling wine/cocktails. The brunch buffet comprises of standard breakfast and lunch dishes. There is a wide display of hot and cold dishes. It may have breakfast dishes from juice, fresh fruits, cereals with milk, breakfast meat, fish, eggs to order with live stations, variety of breads and breakfast beverages. The lunch sections have cold sections including meat, pâté, galantines and also a variety of hot meats, vegetable dishes with a selection of desserts.

FORK BUFFET: This is also known as standing buffet or occasion buffet. Here the guest is offered a meal which can be easily eaten with fork while standing holding a plate and a drink. A few chairs are available. It is offered at informal events and has an advantage of accommodating more guests in a less space.

FORMAL BUFFET: In this type of buffet, tables and chairs are laid out with covers. The first course and coffee is served and the guest has to help himself for the main course and dessert.

FINGER BUFFET: In a finger buffet bite size food items are offered for which no cutlery is required. Fancy cocktail sticks are provided to the guests to pick the food. The main object is to allow conversations, mingling and provide an informal atmosphere. These buffets are particularly useful in pre-dinner or pre-lunch cocktails.

RESTAURANT BUFFET: To encourage more sales during the lunch hours, some restaurants also offer lunch buffets along with the a la carte menu. There is a lavish spread of buffet reasonable priced to attract locals. The success of these lunch buffets encouraged the management to come up with breakfast buffets too. These buffets may also have various live counters, cheese bars etc.

DISPLAY BUFFET: These buffets present one particular item which may be a house dessert or a wine. The idea is to promote the particular item so it is mostly displayed in the lobby area or at the restaurant entrance.

REGIONAL/ETHNIC BUFFET: Regional and ethnic buffet is the one in which foods of a particular city, state or country can be offered along with matching décor. One can create ethnic look by giving various props and lightings etc.

SERVICE SEQEUNCE IN FOOD & BEVERAGE OUTLETS
BAR

Greeting guest (as per time of the day)

↓

Anticipating/confirming the no. of pax

↓

Asking for preference of seating & assist in seating guest

↓

Presenting the beverage menu

↓

Gratis (complimentary) with cocktail napkin to be served

↓

Taking beverage order

↓

Feed in Billing

↓

Serving drinks as per order (as specified)

↓

Snacks to be served from the platter (silver service)

↓

Repeat drinks to be asked when the glass is one-third full

↓

Presenting the bill when the guest asks for it

↓

Asking for guest comments on the comment cards on his experience

↓

Bid warm farewell to the guest and thank for visiting

COFFEE SHOP SERVICE SEQUENCE

Greet and escort the guest (offer two options of seating areas)

↓

Seat the guest

↓

Ascertain mineral water or regular water and serve accordingly

↓

Beverage menu offered

↓

Beverage order picked up from dispense bar and served

↓

Offer a la carte menu or Buffet

↓

Order taking, up selling/suggestive selling

↓

Feed the order in the billing software

|

↓ ↓

A LA CARTE	**BUFFET**
↓	↓
Bread picked up from Bain Marie kept on wooden platter alongside cheese dip & served	Bread picked-up from Bain Marie kept on wooden platter alongside cheese dip & served
↓	↓

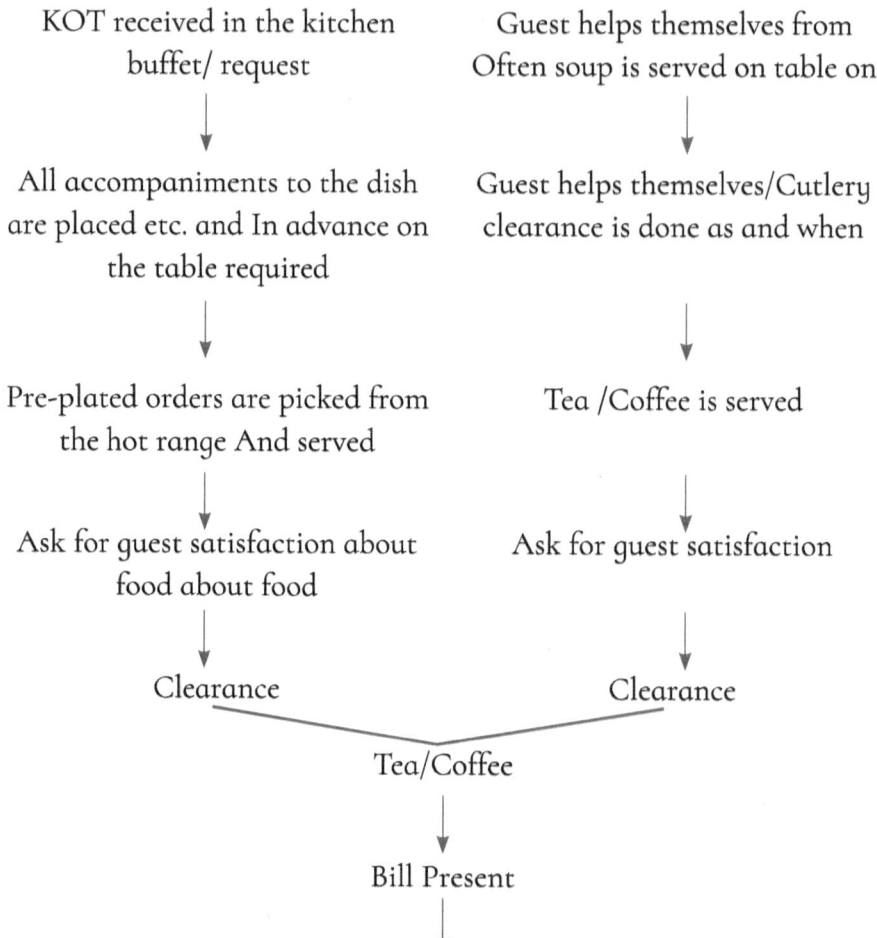

KOT received in the kitchen buffet/ request

↓

All accompaniments to the dish are placed etc. and In advance on the table required

↓

Pre-plated orders are picked from the hot range And served

↓

Ask for guest satisfaction about food about food

↓

Clearance

Guest helps themselves from Often soup is served on table on

↓

Guest helps themselves/Cutlery clearance is done as and when

↓

Tea /Coffee is served

↓

Ask for guest satisfaction

↓

Clearance

Tea/Coffee

↓

Bill Present

↓

Settle payments and provide guest check copy and thank the guest

ROOM SERVICE

Room orders are taken by the order taker. Guest is informed about the appox. delivery time of the order.

↓

Order is fed in the system and kitchen gets there copy and also dispense bar if there is any beverage order

↓

Copy of the KOT is handed over to the steward to make arrangements for the order

↓

Steward lays the trolley in case of hot food order and tray otherwise

↓

Accompaniments and cutlery crockery is set on the trolley as per specifications and then he proceeds towards the respective kitchen for order pick up and straight away places the hot food order in the hot case.

↓

He carries the order to the room through service lift and serves the order as per guest requirement

↓

Brings down the clearance to the dish washing area and soiled linen is kept back in the room service area

SERVICE OF WINE
ESSENTIALS FOR SERVING WHITE WINE

White Wine must be served chilled @10 to 12 degrees °C.

Equipment required Wine bucjet, wine stand, wine opener & wine napkin

A proper glass would make wine taste better – so choose an appropriate glass

Serve the host small sip to approve the wine for taste and temperature

Ensure that ladies on the table are served first and host the last

Ensure all class are spotless and clean and not chipped in anyway

Promptly refill the glass when level is below 10% of the glass

Slowly pour the standard wine pour (3 oz.) into the center of the glass until it's around one-third full

To serve another bottle, enquire from the host if it should be served in fresh glasses

WHITE WINE SERVICE

Carry the bottle to the guest table in a clean wine bucket filled with ½ ice and 1/3Water. Wipe the water as you take out the wine to show the wine label to the guest

Announce the name of the wine/vintage and on confirmation ask if you may open and serve the wine

Place the wine in the ice bucket at 45degrees and open the wine with the wine opener. Ensure to cut the seal on the neck of the wine, with the knife in the cockscrew opener

Put the removed seal in your pocket and close the knife and use the cockscrew to open the wine. Unscrew the cork and put it into your pocket

Offer the host to taste the wine and pour small sip into the glass for his approval

Before serving show the label to the guest, ensure the wine is held with the wine napkin at the back

Serve the ladies first and then the person on the left hand side of the host

Pour equal portion of wine in everyone's glass and serve the host in the end, and ask the host if another bottle is to be served

SMART TIPS DURING WINE OPENING

Avoid Dripping the wine during service, which happens due to slow twisting action of the server to catch the last drops from dripping. Use of a clean cloth can prevent any such drops escape

Do not cut the foil from the lip but from below the lip

Do not twist the bottles while taking out cork, but rather twist the cork

Popping up of the cork should be easy and with a little sound

THUMB RULE FOR SERVICE WINE (TEMPERATURE)

Red Wine: Room temperature

Sparkling/Champagnes: Best Served Chilled

White Wine: Best Served Cold

Affordable wines, may be served little on the chilled side as this will cover up for any off aroma

ESSENTIALS FOR SERVING RED WINE

Mostly red wines taste better when decanted

Decanting of a red wine allows wines to breathe and it also helps to separate sediments that have formed during aging

Slowly pour the standard wine pour (4 oz.) into the centre of the glass until it's around half full.

RED WINE SERVICE

Announce the name of the wine/vintage and on confirmation ask if you may open and serve the wine

Open the wine with the wine opener. Ensure to cut the seal on the neck of the wine, with the knife in the cockscrew opener

Put the removed seal in your pocket and close the knife and use the cockscrew to open the wine. Unscrew the cork and put it into your pocket

Offer the host to taste the wine and pour little sip into the glass for his approval

Before serving show the label to the guest, ensure the wine is held with the wine napkin at the back

Serve the ladies first and then the person on the left-hand side of the host

Pour equal portion of wine in everyone's glass (or serve till the half mark of the glass)

Serve the host in the end, and ask the host if another bottle is to be served

TYPES OF CUTLERY

Baby Spoon   Butter Knife   Coffee Spoon   Fish Fork

Ham Fork   Roast Fork   Sugar Spoon

Dessert Spoon   Dessert Fork   Ice Cream Spoon

Oyster Fork   Olive Spoon   Salad Spoon & Fork

Fruit Spoon   Table Spoon Table Fork & Table Knife

Pastry Fork   Pastry Tong

FOOD & BEVERAGE TERMINOLOGY

ABC: ABC stands for Ashtray, Budvase and Cruet. ABC is kept at the center of the table while laying the cover.

ABOYER: Aboyer aids the communication between the kitchen and restaurant. He receives the food order from the service staff and announces the order to the kitchen. Aboyer is responsible for hot plate section of the pantry.

BACK OF THE HOUSE: Back of the house is the ancillary area of the restaurant, where all the supporting service is carried out. Some of the back of the house sections are pantry, dishwashing, hot plate, still room etc.

BAIN MARIE: Bain Marie is equipment that holds the Food hot. The equipment contains cylindrical drum, which is heated with water. Bain Marie is usually used in Hot Plate section of the pantry.

BARKER: Barker is another term for Aboyer. Barker is the person who communicates between service and kitchen and help to pick up the food in time. Usually the order taken by the waiter is handed over to the Barker.

BONE CHINA: It is a white translucent ceramic material made from kaolin, china clay and bone ash. It is used in restaurant to serve various dishes.

BRIEFING: Briefing is done prior to the opening of the restaurant. In the briefing the senior most staff gives instructions to the junior staff with regard to availability of dishes, special items of the day, and also some training & any other specific instructions for the evening operation.

BUFFET: Buffet is a type of assisted service, where food and beverage is displayed at counters. Waiter assists at the counters to take the food from the counters or the guest help themselves.

BURNISHING MACHINE: This is a revolving drum like container using for cleaning silver ware, with safety shield attached to it. The burnishing machines are attached with ball bearing to run that effectively. Soap power is used to clean the silver ware hygienically.

CAROUSEL: Carousel is a circular counter that revolves to display the food items. The carousel is fitted in such a way that the one side is always inside the kitchen and other side is in the service area. As the carousel revolves the counter is filled up from the kitchen and guests selects the food as it revolves.

CHAFING DISH: It is a hollowware used to keep the food warm usually in buffet service. Chafing dish has a water container, which is the base, food container and place for fuel. Using the fuel, the water is heated up and in turn the food is heated up with the hot water.

COVER: Cover is the space on the table allotted for table-wares to the guest to consume his/her meal. The size of the cover is 24 inch * 18 inch.

CUTLERY: Cutlery is the term denotes all the cutting implements such as knives. Cutlery can be made of EPNS or stainless steel.

DUMMY WAITER: Dummy waiter is another term for side board. it is a restaurant furniture and used to keep all the serving equipment's for a meal session

GUERIDON TROLLEY: It is a mobile trolley from which the gueridon service is done.

HOSTESS: Hostess is a member of restaurant brigade. Duty of hostess includes taking restaurant reservation and receiving them at the door, welcoming guest and assisting them with seating.

MAITRE D'HOTEL: Maitre d'hotel is the Supervisor of a F&B outlet. He looks after the day to day operations of a food service outlet.

MENU: Menu is a list of food and/or beverage than can be served to a guest at a price. It helps guests to select what they would like to eat and/or drink. It is a document that controls and directs an outlet's operation and is considered the prime selling instrument.

MISE-EN-PLACE: Mise-en-place means "putting in place" and the term denotes to the preparation of a work place for ultimate smooth service. To ensure that the restaurant is ready for service the waiter makes sure that this station has been efficiently prepared for service.

MISE-EN-SCENE: It means prepare the environment of the outlet before service. Mise-en-scene includes preparing the restaurant welcoming, create ambience with regard to cleanliness, furniture setting and temperature.

NAPKIN: Napkin is restaurant linen. Napkin is used to decorate the table using various folds and also used to keep on the lap of the guest to protect their clothes during service.

SALESMANSHIP: Salesmanship is the process to persuade guests to buy goods and services. The food and beverage service personnel are technical salesman, hence they should have a thorough knowledge of the proper presentation and service of all the food and beverage served in the establishment. Salesmanship is an art of one to communication between a seller and a buyer, whereby the seller persuades the buyer to make a purchase.

SOMMELIER: Sommelier is the French term for wine waiter. He is responsible for the service of all alcoholic drinks during the service of meals, and is also a sales person. He requires to have a thorough knowledge of beverages and wines as food accompaniments.

TABLEWARE: Table ware is a type of restaurant equipment's used to keep on the table. Table ware includes flatware, cutlery and hollowware. Table ware is made either EPNS or stainless steel.

TRANCHEUR: Trancheur is the French term for carver. His responsibility is to carve the meat joints in front of the guest and serve to them.

GLASSWARE

(Pictures Courtesy: Ocean Glass Public Co Ltd, Thailand)

Champagne flute   Champagne Saucer   Margarita

Beer Goblet   Beer Mug   Beer Mug

Brandy Balloon   Martini Glass

Liqueur   Sherry   Shot Glass

Irish Coffee   Red Wine   White Wine

High Ball   Tom Collins   Carafe

Banana Split   Hurricane

Cost Control

COST CONTROL

FOOD CYCLE

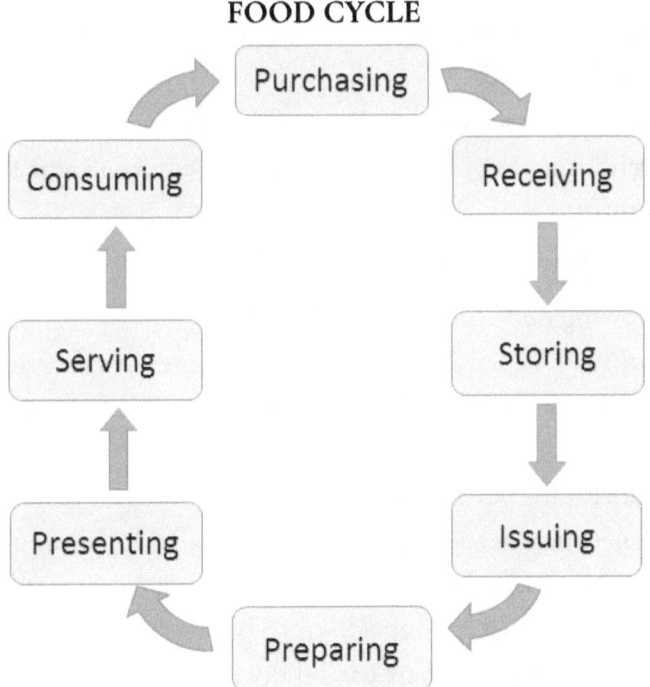

ESSENCE OF COST CONTROL: Minimizing the expenses of the company, without compromising the quality, of the product (service/food) that the customer receives.

APPROACHES TO COST CONTROL: Pre-Operational Control, During Operations Control Post-Operational Control.

AREAS WHERE COSTS CAN BE CONTROLLED IN THE F&B DEPTT.

- PURCHASING
- RECEIVING
- STORING & ISSUING
- PRODUCTION
- SALES

COST CONTROL AT PURCHASING

- Designing Standard Purchase Specifications (SPS)
- Selection of a Suitable Supplier, (well negotiated prices for the quality required)
- Adopting prescribed Methods of Purchasing
- Purchasing at the Right Time, Right Quality, Right Place, Right Quantity

COST CONTROL AT RECEIVING

- Following an Inspection Procedure
- Quality – As per SPS (Standard Purchase Specification)
- Items to be received as per the unit specified (Numbers, Liters, Grams etc.)
- Quantity (as per the order placed)
- Temperature as specified in the purchase order/standard purchase specifications
- Wrong & substitute items (Not to be received)
- Items close to pass their use-by date (Not to be received)
- Damaged or broken cartons (Not to be received)
  - Delivery to be received at Designated Areas at Specific Dates & Specific Time by Trained Staff
  - Limited Access to Receiving Area
  - Discourage frequent product delivery after the closing of receiving department (unless it is an emergency requirement)

- Auditing - Invoices with the Purchase Order & Daily Receiving Record

COST CONTROL AT STORING

- Appropriate Facilities & Equipment's
- Storing items at the required Temperature
- Cross check the physical quantity received from receiving with the accompanied document
- Cross verify regularly physical stock in various stores with the stocks being shown in the Bin Cards/inventory management software
- Storage of items in prescribed Containers/shelves
- Maintaining hygiene & Cleanliness in storage areas
- Fixing Definite Locations of items for easy access & easy physical verification
- Rotation of Stocks and application of LIFO & FIFO
- Availability According to Use
- Keep a track of items close to expiry to avoid loss of inventory
- Cross check the unit in which the items are received matches with the details mentioned in the purchase order
- Security of the items in stores by keeping stocks under lock & key

COST CONTROL AT ISSUING

- Adopting specific issuing procedures for as per the policies and procedures of the organization.
- Issues of goods should always be against the approved requisition and never without it
- Ensure the approval is done by the approved authority as per the policy of issue for that department
- Requisitions should be marked separately for groceries, perishables, engineering etc etc
- All issued quantities should be update in the inventory management software/bin card at all times

- Never issue items which are not mentioned in the requisitions, the issue should always be matching with the requisitions (including number for items and its units)

COST CONTROL AT FOOD PRODUCTION

- Watch out for the yield
- Volume forecasting
- Portion-Sales Analysis
- Popularity Ratio
- Portion- Sales History
- Occupancy of the Hotel (helps in forecasting)
- Special Events in town (helps in forecasting)
- Weather (helps in forecasting)
- Season of the Year (take advantage of seasonal fruits/vegetables)
- Holidays/Public Holidays or week-ends(helps in forecasting)

TECHNIQUES OF COST CONTROL DURING PRODUCTION

- Follow- Standard Recipe
- Follow -Standard Portion Size
- Follow standard Yield

COST CONTROL AT SALES

- Billing Procedures: Cash & Credit Sales
- Cashier's Sales Summary Report: Sales Mix, Popular & Non-Popular Items, Changes in Customer's Interests
- Portion Control & Correct Service
- Suitable Pricing Methods
- Market Oriented Pricing
- Cost Oriented Pricing

COST CONTROL TERMINOLOGY:

IKT: INTER KITCHEN TRANSFER: This is a document must be supported whenever there is transfer of food from one kitchen to another This document must be a support document for any food movement/

transfer between kitchens, as this documents also transfers the cost from one kitchen to another for the transferred items

IBT: INTER BAR TRANSFER: This is a document must be supported whenever there is transfer of beverages from one bar to another This document must be a support document for any beverage movement/ transfer between bars, as this documents also transfers the cost from one bar to another for the transferred items

YIELD: This term is often used in culinary, which refers to how much of the edible, finished or processed product is achieved, which involves deduction of the wastages & losses that may occur during preparation and cooking. In short yield is the edible or the usable part of the raw material por food which is obtained after the process of preparation & cooking has been performed

EP: EDIBLE PART

AP: AS PURCHASED

YIELD TEST: There is a considerable difference between cost or products (AP & EP). The state in which the food products/raw material are purchased, and the weight that forms the edible part are very different. Hence it is crucial that this difference must be accounted for while establishing selling prices as well as while establishing the standard recipes. It becomes necessary to conduct yield tests to achieve the actual cost of Edible Portion. In short yield test is a process to compute the actual cost of a product that experiences weight/volume, loss during pre-preparation & during cooking

$$\text{TOTAL YIELD\%} = \frac{\text{Remaining Weight}}{\text{Original Weight}} \times 100$$

IMPORTANCE OF YIELD TEST:

For establishing purchase specifications

For establishing the selling prices of dishes in the menu

To establish control standards and measure yield against that

In decision making of purchasing i.e in what form a particular item should be purchased

This also helps in establishing standard recipes & prices

This is also helpful in establishing ordering levels and purchase quantities

To provide guidelines of receiving for receiving department

YIELD PERCENTAGE

$$\text{Yield\%} = \frac{\text{Number of portions x Unit portion size}}{\text{Purchase Quantity}} \text{ X } 100$$

BUTCHERS YIELD TEST: This process helps ascertain the true value/quality of meat, fish & poultry. This is a useful tool to establish the actual cost of the EP-edible portion, and hence in comparisons and decision making while purchasing (to decide in which form meat, fish or poultry should be purchased either buy whole, or boneless etc) Yield testing is a technique to find the number of edible portions are produced after performing trimming, cutting, butchering, fat trimming, deboning or removal of inedible or unnecessary & useless parts removal.

UNDERSTANDING FRAUDS IN FOOD & BEVERAGES

- Frauds are the pilferages where lot of mental work is exercised to have some personal benefits from the organization's assets.
- It causes loss of revenue to a greater extent
- It encourages anarchy and poor discipline
- It impacts the work culture in an extremely negative way
- It negatively impacts the brand image in the market [place

FRAUDS IN BAR

1. **Order Filled but Not Rung Up:** In this case, the bartender delivers the drink as requested by the customer, but never rings it up on the cash register and simply pockets the sale. Manager's vigilance is critical here to ensure that no drink is served until it is rung up in the cash register.

2. **Bringing in Extra Product:** In this case, the bartender sells the product that he or she has brought in and pockets the sale. Bottle stamps or markings help in preventing this type of theft since non marked bottles can be easily detected.

3. **Over and Under Pouring:** When the bartender under-pours, he may be making up for drinks they have given away or sold but may not have rung up. When the bartender over-pours, he may be doing so for their friends or for extra tips this activity may yield.

4. **Dilution of Product:** It is often called as "watering the drinks". This method involves adding water to the product in order to make up for the spirits that have been either stolen or given away. Detection of this theft is rather difficult. Periodic sampling of a known proof alcohol against bar stock by a knowledgeable person may be the only defense.

5. **Product Theft:** Alcohol is highly desirable product. So, its theft is always a possibility. This is especially true in an area where the bartender has access to both, product inventory and exit. Proper control as well as strict rules restricting the access is the only way.

6. **Product Substitution:** If the bartender substitutes less expensive liquor for the call brand, he may be pocketing the difference in price between the two items. This has the effect of shortchanging the customer who has paid a premium for something he did not receive.

7. **Adulteration:** An experienced barman can adulterate the drinks such as sherry or liqueur with cheaper types of drinks, making a profit on the sale which he will pocket. A keen eye on part of the controller, when sampling, will be an important defense against frauds of this nature.

8. **Mixing Drinks:** Mixing expensive drinks with cheaper ones, especially when mixing cocktails, could produce additional revenue which could be skimmed off by the barman.

FRAUDS IN KITCHEN

1. **Eating by the staff:** A few people think that a staff member helping himself to food in the kitchen is technically not a fault.

But, if a certain number of portions to be sold at profit are required from a certain quantity of prepared food, then the staff is not only frauding the management of the cost, but also the profit it should have yielded when sold.

2. **Pilfering:** Fruits, eggs, packaged food are items could easily be put in shopping bags or handbags and carried out. Locker rooms for staff should be outside the kitchen and no bags allowed inside the kitchen. Anyone attempting to carry items out on their person should be easily visible to vigilant supervisor.

PRECAUTIONS

1. Receiving goods directly into the kitchen should be in hands of a responsible member of staff who should check the goods carefully.

2. Goods from the stores or cellars on requisition should be checked against the copy of requisition in the kitchen. Quantities should be weighed and numbers checked.

3. Regular spot checks should be made on portion size served to the customers. By serving small portions, a surplus can be built up to be either eaten by staff or carried out.

4. Pre portion packs, such as butter, jam and sauces are easily carried out. These should be counted and a check kept on their issue.

5. Keep all storage areas locked and secure.

6. Issue food only with proper authorization and management approval.

7. Monitor the use of carryovers.

8. Do not allow food to be prepared unless a guest checks is pre-rung with the appropriate order.

9. Maintain an active inventory management system.

10. Ensure that all food received is signed for by the appropriate receiving clerks.

11. Do not pay suppliers for food products, without an appropriate receiving clerk.

12. Do not use petty cash to pay for food items unless a receipt and the product can be produced.

13. Conduct periodic physical inventories of all level A, B and C products

14. Do not allow employees to remove food from the premises without management's specific approval.

LIST OF FRAUDS

- Substitutions
- Dilution of merchandise
- Short pouring
- Theft of merchandise
- Complementary drinks
- Return of merchandise issued to private parties
- Customers
- Intentional omission of items.
- Reusing of checks
- Pocketing checks or reusing unauthorized checks
- Overcharging
- Falsification of tips or other charges
- Cashier changes the total of check after collection
- Cashier keeps the money and pockets, destroys a check
- Cashier bunches sales, split –rings, under rings
- Cashier gives incorrect changes
- Cashier performs incorrect addition
- Cashier falsifies pay out or adds item to complimentary checks and removes them from other checks
- Rings sales using other cashier's code.

REMEDY:

- Increased supervision
- Using Mystery Shopper to audit the service providers and service standards
- Increased Spot Checks by Food & Beverage Controller
- Pin-pricking of bottles
- Examination of labels of empty bottles
- System of secret coding of stock while supplying from cellar
- Using friends in bar to reveal malpractices in bar
- Having a Cost Budget for Purchasing

Food and Beverage Management

FOOD & BEVERAGE MANAGEMENT

OVERVIEW: Food and Beverage Management is a complex function as it has various aspects to it. It involves planning, setting goals and objectives, taking decisions, staying competitive in product & pricing, assigning tasks to teams and individuals. It is also about controlling revenue pilferages and wastages and setting up control procedures and policies for food and beverages. This also includes maintaining a great working environment where team members feel valued and motivated & provide consistent great service to guests. This subject also includes reviewing and measuring performance against the budget and drafting and implementing long and short-term strategies. Daily reports reflect the sales mix and daily feedbacks reflect what customers have to say about your services and products and people. All this is required & reviewed in food and beverage management and appropriate action plans are drafted to stay on top of all areas.

FUNCTIONS OF FOOD & BEVERAGE MANAGEMENT

Menu Planning

Menu Merchandising

Menu Engineering

Food & Beverage cost control

Policies & procedures

Budgeting & Forecasting

Establishing Standards for product & process

Identify purchase products for food and beverages

Ensuring smooth operations of food & beverage outlets

Maintaining hygiene & cleanliness

Measuring the performance against the budget

CRM-Customer Relationship Management

Taking corrective actions in case of deviations from the goals & objectives

Customer experience & customer satisfaction

Customer Complaint Management

Review Customer Feedback & manage Service recovery as and when required

WHAT IS A MENU: A menu is a list of dishes (food/beverages) that are available for sale in a food service outlet or that can be served at a meal

WHAT IS MENU PLANNING: Is the process of decision making resulting in what is to be served in any given meal period-breakfast, lunch, dinner, brunch etc.

FUNCTIONS OF A MENU:

- Menu makes the first impression on the guest
- Introduces the establishment to the guest
- Helps the kitchen department to order raw material in accordance with the menu
- Informs the guest about the offerings and its pricing
- It also informs the guest about the accompaniments and cooking method used
- It often presents dishes in a logical order making it easier for the guest to choose course or a dish
- Offers choices available for the customer
- It promotes certain dishes by highlighting them as Chefs special

FACTORS TO BE CONSIDERED WHILE PLANNING A MENU:

- Type of establishment
- Pricing strategy
- To take into account the food preference of the customer
- Type of service style
- Religion, tradition & cultural patterns

- Equipment and kitchen personnel capability & competency
- Seasonal & local fresh fruits & vegetables use in the menu
- Kind of clientele
- Concept & philosophy of the business
- Operational hours of the establishment
- Extent of Use of convenience food
- Nutritional needs
- To create a balanced menu in terms of flavors, colors, texture & method of cooking used
- Type of event
- Capability of staff & equipment
- Pricing of the menu, keeping in view the cost
- Availability & seasonality of supplies

COMMON MENU DESIGN MISTAKES:

- Creating an extremely small menu, giving customers very few options to choose from
- Using small font to write the menu
- Missing to provide some description of the dishes
- Use of complex words and expressions making it difficult for guests to interpret dishes
- Having complex design on the background of the menu paper making it difficult to read
- Missing to mention some crucial policies and practices
- Missing out to offer chefs choice or customization to some extent for any guest allergies
- Leaving some blank pages in the menu

MENU MERCHANDISING: Refers to any technique used to stimulate sales within the Food and Beverage facility. The efficient menu merchandised will affect the popularity of the food and beverage facilities. Menu is the key tool through which offerings of Food & beverages are sold by a restaurant establishment. A Restaurant may have the best of the Chef creating the best dishes but if we can't sell them, the restaurant will not make profit. To effectively sell & advertise restaurant items to a customer once he is in your store effectively through a menu resulting in sales is called menu merchandising.

Menu Design in Style-

Menu should be Presentable and well-designed as it makes the first impression on the guest.

Use Images to tempt the guest to order certain items.

Provide Interesting description of dishes.

Use font size which is easy to read.

Menu must be neat clean and never torn or worn out.

It should be easy to read in terms of the text, simplicty of language and not overpowering background that makes reading it difficult.

Easy to navigate and locate items and information required for ordering.

Avoid creating a monotonous menu.

KEY ASPECTS FOR EFFECTIVE MENU MERCHANDISING

Menu should be clean and not torn & dirty

Font size and color should be easily legible (keeping in view the level of light/dim light of the restaurant)

Menu items should be well segregated veg together, non- vegetarian, separate, health conscious together & kid's menu at one place. Wines & cocktails separated from food.

Have tempting images or pictures of dishes, drinks and desserts.

Mark Chef special with a special icon to encourage customers to order Chef's special dishes more.

Use of tent cards promoting for example – dish of the day, dessert or may be a beverage offer.

Use of poster showcasing, a food festival or a promotional offer.

Offer free samples of the dishes/drinks

Create combo offers at an offer price tempting guests for value price meals combinations

IMPACT OF COLOUR ON MENU DESIGN

Green colour implies that the food is fresh

Orange stimulates the appetite

Red encourages to take action

LEARN TO KNOW THE CUSTOMER EYE MOVEMENT IN THE MENU:

We tend to order mostly from the top two items of each category, that is the reason the restaurant owners place there most profitable items there, though some people tend to order from the bottom rows as well. The restaurant owners by placing the most expensive dishes at the top gain the following effect on the customers: Customer Psychology: having looked at the most expensive dishes customers feel that t we are getting a great bargain as they scroll down the menu for low priced dishes

UNDERSTANDING HOW CUSTOMER EYE MOVE ON THE MENU

The customers look at the centre of the menu and then to the top right corner and then to the top left corner. These are the sweet spots to place your most profitable and popular items that you would want to promote and sell more

TIPS FOR MENU MERCHANDISING

Price is a major influence while ordering that is some restaurant price like Rs99/to give an effect that customer is getting a great deal

A great description can sell any dish, try connecting with nostalgia or a story or a tradition

Give good amount of description/information about a drink, wine or a dish this empowers a customer to order

Engage in story telling about the restaurant that creates credibility and authenticity

MENU ENGINEERING

Menu engineering determines the contribution margin & popularity of dishes in the menu and helps in redesigning the menu. It helps in achieving improved strategy to earn more profit.

It is the study of profitability and popularity of various dishes that feature in a menu. It is also about how to feature and place the dishes to have maximum impact on the customers to have a desired outcome. The process of menu engineering helps F&B managers to ascertain, the best performer and worst performing dishes. It's a process to figure out what's working in the menu and what items are not working out, and how to take corrective actions to maximise profitability and improved overall results.

Focuses on the following aspects-

1. Customer Demand- How many customers visited the establishment and their overall feedback
2. Menu Mix-Analyze the dishes ordered by guests and figure out what are their favorite dishes and what is that they are not ordering
3. Each dish individual contribution to the overall profits as compared to the other dishes

PURPOSE OF MENU ENGINEERING:

- Identify which dishes are popular and which dishes are not being ordered
- Helps identify the menu dishes to be taken off from the menu and replace them with more interesting dishes which customers have a demand for
- Helps design a more effective & profitable menu
- Helps review recipe's and menu portion sizes and tune then better as per guest's demands
- Helps review which items are underpriced or over-priced & take corrective measures.

WHAT IS A STANDARD RECIPE?

A standard recipe is one which has been tried several times by a service operator/chef and has produced same good results when a standard set of procedure is repeated with similar specification of ingredients/raw material with use of similar equipment.

STANDARD RECIPE

It is a written document which tells how a dish is to be prepared and aims to achieve consistent results. It specifies the ingredients their weights and measures method of cooking, portion size garnishes and presentation, accompaniments, cost etc. It is extremely advantageous to add the final picture of the Dish and display it in the kitchen to keep standards consistent

STANDARD RECIPE COMPRISES OF:

- Menu Item Name
- Portion Size
- Recipe for how many portions
- Ingredients with quantities & quality specifications
- Garnishing
- Step by Step process of preparation
- Cooking temperature
- Time to prepare
- Picture of the finished dish
- Serving temperature
- Plating
- Equipment & utensils to be used
- Cost per unit of each ingredient
- Calculated cost of the recipe/per portion cost
- Costing done last date

ADVANTAGES OF STANDARD RECIPE:

- Consistent quality results every time
- Standard Portion Size

- Better Portion control
- Consistent Guest Experience
- Better control & forecasting of Food Cost & profitability
- Ease of ordering & receiving department of raw material

Recipe Name: _____   Recipe Number: _____

Section (Grains, Entrees, etc.): _____   Yield: _____

Meal Pattern Contributions: _____   Serving Size: _____

Ingredients	50 Seryings Weight	50 Servings Measure	100 Servings Weight	100 Servings Measure	___ Servings Weight	___ Servings Measure
.						

Procedure:

OBJECTIVES OF STANDARD RECIPE:

1. To determine the quantity and quality of ingredient to be used.
2. To obtain the yield obtainable from a recipe.
3. To determine the cost per portion.
4. To determine the nutritional value.
5. To facilitate portion control.
6. It helps in costing of dishes, pricing menus for the banquet.
7. It helps in uniform quality and taste.
8. Require less supervision.
9. Less training is required for a newly appointed employee.
10. Establishes food cost control.

FOOD & BEVERAGE MANAGEMENT CONCEPTS

SOP-Standard Operating Procedure: SOP is the written documented methods of doing various routine & repeated activities in a hotel. SOP's ensure consistency & quality in products, process & services.

SOP may be upgraded from time to time as better & new ways of doing jobs are discovered, however any change in the SOP requires approval by the management and new trainings are conducted before new SOP is established.

BRAND STANDARD: Brand standards are those essential elements of hotels that ensure consistent service & experience to the customers across different properties of same brand. It defines the core values, the mission & vision of the business. It is a set of guidelines & business principles which guide the business the way it is to be operated. It is that thread that keeps the brand essence together in spite of its presence at various locations. For example, the same logo, color, font size, design of stores, business tagline, standardized guest experience, standardized service standards, room designs, features and facilities and even consistencies in policies and procedures.

IMPORTANCE OF BRAND STANDARDS: For customers to receive consistent experience it is essential that brand standards be followed which result in fulfilling the brand promise that the customers expect from a brand. Brand standard ensure that customers receive the service experience which they expect from that brand. It helps provide a consistent experience across various Hotels. Consistent service & positioning leads higher customer confidence in the Brand that develops customer loyalty. Brand standards strict following helps become easily recognizable amongst the competition.

Consistent standards & well communicated policies create a better perceived brand value.

Since the business ethics, values & mission is clearly defined to external as well as internal customers it gives focus to business giving it a competitive advantage.

CUSTOMER SERVICE AUDIT: This audit aims at uncovering some of the aspects of customer service which require improvement or change as they are identified as pain points from the customer's point of view. The identified points when improved upon leads to higher customer satisfaction

PURPOSE OF CUSTOMER SERVICE AUDIT: The purpose of a brand audit is to ascertain how the business is performing in the eyes of the customers. It offers the following benefits:

- Helps you to determine the positioning of your business and to plan corrective strategies
- Empowers to discover the strengths and weaknesses of your business.
- Guides to align your offerings more accurately with the expectations of customers.
- The audit uncovers various negative & positive practices which create customer perceptions & helps design imporved customer experience.
- To audit the restaurants to ensure standard operating procedures are followed.
- This helps to uncover any inconsistencies in service standards that might prevent Customer satisfaction.
- To evaluate and judge the quality of the services provided, facilities offered and product choice to our customers, thus providing a consistent service with-in the Hotel.
- To ensure that first time customer, return to patronize the restaurant again.
- Convert this customer into a loyalist who in turn will sell the restaurant to others.
- This helps increasing business which will in turn increase the profitability.

MENU SALES SUMMARY: Is a detailed summary of menu items sold, this statement which is software generated shows:

1. Quantity/Unit of each dish sold,
2. Unit value,
3. Total amount of each dish sold

4. Can also be taken out meal period wise

5. Also shows the amount contribution of each item to the total sales also called as Contribution factor

POPULARITY INDEX (PI): This reflects the popularity of a dish in the menu as compared to the other dishes. This is achieved by the following formula-

Number of portions sold of a dish/total portions sold (including all dishes)

This helps the restaurant manager understand which dish is selling the most and gaining popularity and repeated guest orders.

EVENT MANAGEMENT

EVENT MANAGEMENT: Events in the hospitality industry include weddings, business meetings, celebration dinners and fundraisers. The event planner, owner of a hotel, banquet room manager or restaurant owner all strive to make these events a success from the client's, guests' and his own point of view. **Event Management has following three Steps in Planning**

PRE-EVENT   EVENT DAY   POST EVENT

PRE-EVENT

- Proposal
- Budget
- Identify Income and Expenditure
  - Venue selection
  - Target Audience/Guest Size
- Target Audience Status
- Target Audience Convenience
- Climatic Conditions
- Venue History

- Venue Services
- Venue Fees
- Venue Inspection
- Amount of Work Required
- Lighting
- Entertainment
- Negotiation & contracts with different vendors
- Seating arrangement
- Contingency Plan
- Security arrangement
- Legal permissions etc required for the event
- Marketing Plan (as per the contractual scope of work)

EVENT DAY

Briefing of the team

Duty allocation

Communication amongst all during the entire event

Checklist to be used for all assigned jobs

POST EVENT REPORT

EVENT EVALUATION: Event evaluation is necessary to make you and your team more efficient and effective, the next time you organise an event. It is necessary to find out the mistakes and learn from them. Steps involved in writing the evaluation

STEP 1. Determine the extent to which and advertising objectives have been achieved.

STEP 2. Get feedback from clients and target audience

STEP 3 Document a complete post event report to learn from & to get better

KEY FOCUS OF EVENT MANAGEMENT

GUEST SATISFACTION: In hospitality industry, the first priority is the satisfaction of the client, the person who booked the event and is paying for it. The event must go as planned, with the amenities as per clients expectations, such as the number of tables and chairs, floral arrangements, food, drinks and entertainment. Any problems must be solved quickly providing seamless experience. A successful event leads to the future opportunities for additional business from the client.

GUEST EXPERIENCE: Those attending the function have different expectations from the event. Their experience depends on the quality of the food, friendliness of the staff and the overall look & feel of the venue. A successful event has good food served at the correct temperature. The service is friendly but not over attentive. Any special requests within reason are handled quickly and politely. For example, if a guest is a strict vegetarian and the meal includes meat, but arranging an additional vegetable doesn't take much time or effort. A guest at a successful event will refer new business or tell others what a great time he had.

PROFITABILITY: Events cannot be profitable if they are not well planned and all expected and unexpected cost are not accounted for and anticipated in advance. Events are all about detailed planning and planning for contingencies and creating, memorable experiences. To achieve sustainable profitable event company one must focus on an exceptional guest exprience and delivering quality service and product. It is also essential and terms of payment be very clear to both ther parties, with clear understanding of deliverables.

PERCEIVED VALUE: The old saying "you get what you pay for" holds true. A successful event leaves the client feeling that he got more than he paid for. Small touches make all the difference, such as a bowl of fresh fruit that wasn't part of the continental breakfast menu, cookies at break time of a business meeting or a bottle of complimentary champagne given as a surprise during a reception event. Favorable feedback from the guests also raises the client's perceived value of the event.

BUDGETING: Is the foremost control & planning tool. One of the key role of the business manager is to be able to plan and predict and prepare for future. The more accurately one is able to do projections the better the business performance & competitiveness in the market place. Budgets are forward looking tools and challenges managers to dig deep into the business & trends & competition to make accurate projections. Budgets may not always expressed in monetary terms, it may also be targets of serving a particular number of guests, number of staff required, number of rooms to be occupied etc.

KEY ASPECTS OF BUDGETING:

1. Establish challenging goals & objectives for an organization which are clearly expressed in accounting terms.
2. Create & chalk out a plan & provide resources to achieve the same
3. To periodically compare the results with the established budgeted goals
4. Identify the root cause of weak performances if any and take corrective actions
5. Keep continuous improvement the core of the budget in all aspects of business
6. It is approved is applicable for a certain defined period of time
7. It is in short, a plan in financial terms to attain objectives.

PURPOSE OF BUDGETING:

1. To express future performance of a business in accounting terms, that makes it measurable at all times
2. It is all about creating coordinated management goals & policies for an organization.
3. Budgeting provides future estimates of business revenues & expenses & costs. It has details of manpower, technology & resources and its further broken time period wise

BUDGET

It is generally a list of all planned expenses and revenues. It is a plan for saving and spending.

- They are plans for 1 to 10 years for all of the business units.
- Estimates are compared to actual as a means of evaluating performance.
- Budget variances are often used as a means of punishing and rewarding behavior.
- Budgets are updated to reflect outcomes.

OBJECTIVES OF BUDGETARY CONTROL

- To ensure perfect planning for future by setting up various budgets.
- To increase revenue.
- To reduce cost and maximise profits
- To have proper coordination among various departments.
- To maximize capital investments.
- To operate departments with efficiency and economy.
- To anticipate expenditure for future.
- Elimination of waste and increase in profitability.
- Fixation of responsibility.

ADVANTAGES OF BUDGETING

- Maximization of profits.
- Coordination amongst various departments.
- Specific aims.
- Tool for measuring performance
- Determining weakness.
- Corrective actions.
- Cost reduction
- The process of budgeting requires different departments to work together which results in improved communication and co-ordination

- Since budgets are challenging future goals it pushes the management to innovate, look for creative solution or look at different solutions to achieve the goals
- Budget creates a yardstick of performance against which periodic reviews can be done of business performance and any weak areas in performance are highlighted. The highlighted weak areas could be in revenue, cost, or selling or overall optimization of resources

LIMITATIONS OF BUDGETING
- Uncertain future
- Budgeting revision is required
- Budgets may be too easy to achieve
- Non achievable budgets discourage the staff
- Takes a lot of time

APPROACHES TO BUDGETING

1. TOP-DOWN APPROACH: The top management prepares the budget according to the objective of the organization and passes it on to the managers for implementations. The suggestion and inputs may be taken from the managers before the finalization, but consideration to their suggestion is solely on management's discretion.

2. BOTTOM-UP APPROACH: The managers prepare the department wise/business unit wise budget according to the information and past performance data and present the same to the management for their inputs and approval.

The bottom-up approach begins by identifying the different operations and tasks performed by the organization. Each unit of the organization shall disclose the resources and funds required by them in their budgets. The finance department then consolidates the funding requirement of the entire organization, and the HR department shall consolidate the resources needed. The combined budget is then presented to the management for the approval.

TYPES OF BUDGET ON THE BASIS OF TIME:

- **LONG TERM:** A long term budget is usually for a time period of 5-10 years. A long-term budget is also supported by a short-term budget to make it effective.

- **SHORT TERM:** A short term budget is usually for a time period of one year. It is also being easily broken down in time period of monthly & quarterly, as this helps a better control and review of the performance so that any correction in strategy can be done timely to achieve targets.

TYPES OF BUDGET BASED ON FUNCTION:

- **MASTER BUDGET:** The integration of all functional budgets of all departments/units is called a Master Budget. This budget shows the overall profit/loss forecasted for all the functional budgets together in one budget for a specified period of time (generally a financial year) It incorporates sales and cost budgets to achieve overall profit & loss statement.

- **FUNCTIONAL BUDGET:** Functional budget as the name speaks is budget of individual key functions performed in an organization. Example in a Hotel:
- Sales Budget (Rooms)
- Food & Beverage Restaurants
- Banqueting
- Training & development
- Human Resource (Manpower)
- Heat/power Electricity
- Technology
- Repair & Maintenance
- Health Club & Beauty Parlor

TYPES OF BUDGETS BASED ON FLEXIBILITY:

1. **FIXED BUDGET:** Fixed budgets is that budget which remains unchanged with change in the level of activity for example

forecasted fixed expenses or fixed cost which do not change because of change in business. It also works well where the business forecast can be done with high level of accuracy.

2. **FLEXIBLE BUDGET:** The budget that is flexible in nature depending on the change in the level of activity. This budget takes into account the difference of behaviour between the fixed cost and the variable cost. This style of budgeting is realistic, effective and is practical in approach. This method takes into account the varying cost levels at various levels of business activity.

FOUR MAIN TYPES OF BUDGETING METHODS

1. **INCREMENTAL BUDGETING:** This type of budgeting is also called as the traditional method whereby it is prepared by taking the current period's budget as a benchmark, with incremental amounts then being added for the new future period forecasted.

    In Incremental Budgeting, the figures for each expenditure and income start with the previous year's actual numbers and adjusted for inflation, overall market growth, and other factors management deem fit. It's a simple method in which an incremental growth expected in the future time frame is added over the past year's performance.

2. **ZERO BASED BUDGETING (ZBB):** This method of budgeting is implemented without looking at the previous year's data of cost & revenue performance. The advantage of this method is to give a fresh look to all costs and revenues. This method is also used when starting a new project which has no past performance.

3. **ACTIVITY BASED BUDGETING:** This method of budgeting is a top down approach, for example if the sales/revenue target is 100 then it costs out what all activities are required to be done to achieve Rs. 100 and what will be the cost of those activities.

4. **VALUE BASED BUDGETING:** In this method the budget maker reviews budget by asking certain questions: Does a particular

cost that is incurred create value for the customers? What is the cost benefit analysis of a certain cost incurred? In short it seeks justification of costs and reviews cost vs value creation.

PRICING

PURPOSE OF PRICING

A good pricing strategy is one which results in selling of the products to the customers and finds their acceptance to repeat purchase as well.

Some of the factors that affect the pricing of the menu dishes

- Cost of the dish (Raw Material + Over heads)
- Competition set Pricing of similar dishes
- Target profit of the entrepreneur
- Customer's perception & acceptance of the price-value offer

FACTORS AFFECTING MENU PRICING

AMBIENCE: People eat out for a variety of reasons, some of which include fun, companionship; adventure and variety. For the food service operator who provides a good ambience, menu prices can be higher. Excellent product quality with outstanding service goes further over the long run as compared to good restaurant designs, as the ambience may only draw customers.

CUSTOMER TYPE: Some consumers are comparatively less price sensitive than others. All customers however want value for their money. What represents value may vary for different customers. A thorough analysis of who your customers are and what they value most is critical to the success of the food service operator.

LOCAL COMPETITION: The price a competitor charges for his or her product can be helpful in setting a price. It should not however be the only determining factor. If you want to be a successful food service operator then, spend time focusing on your own operations rather than your competitor's.

LOCATION: Location can be a major factor in determining prices. Location can be an asset or a liability. If location is a liability, the menu prices may be lower to attract more customers.

PORTION SIZE: Portion size, which plays a large role in deciding price, is relatively a misunderstood concept. In traditional food service operations, management controls the portion sizes. The best way to determine whether the portion sizes are too large is to watch the dish-wash area and see what comes back from the dining room.

PRODUCT QUALITY & FOOD COST: Food service operators may choose from a variety of quality levels when developing product specifications, planning menus and selling prices. Each food service operator, however, must select the quality level that represents his/her customer's anticipated desires and price the product accordingly. Once the quality is finalized it must be costed as per the portion size which will only lead to a pricing that will help a business sustain and thrive

SERVICE LEVELS: Customers are expected to pay more for the same product when service levels are higher. As the personal level of service increases, prices may also increase. Customers are willing to pay more for increased service levels but make sure that higher prices are also making way for extra profits.

SPECIAL DAYS: This refers to special days or special occasions pricing for example Christmas, New Year's Eve celebration etc.

PRICING STRATEGIES

A good pricing strategy is one which results in selling of the products to the customers and find its acceptance to repeat purchase as well.

TYPES OF PRICING STRATEGIES:

COMPETITION BASED PRICING: This strategy refers to the process whereby the seller decides the pricing of its products & services, based on the competitor's pricing and plans to stay competitive in pricing strategy. This method reviews the prices of the competitive businesses and then finalises own prices around that.

COST PLUS PRICING: This method of pricing comprises of two aspects:

1. Total cost incurred in production of the product or service and
2. An additional amount added to the above cost, which reflects the profit, hence the name cost plus

Adding of the Cost of the production + expected profit amount is Cost Plus Pricing.

CREAMING OR SKIMMING PRICING: This strategy is all about pricing product & services at a premium price. They may be offered at a premium price as a new product and may reduce the price over a period of time. This strategy works on the mind-set of the consumer that if it is high priced than it must be high quality. This method takes advantage of various layers i.e initial premium pricing appeals to the premium segment at the launch of the product and subsequent lower price over a period of time appeals to the middle segment. The price of the product is kept very high to gain high profit, sacrificing the high sales, hence creaming or skimming the market.

DYNAMIC PRICING: A flexible pricing strategy in which, customers pay different prices for the same product based on the market demands

FOLLOW THE LEADER PRICING: The product is priced following the market leader's price.

GOING RATE PRICING: The product is priced as per the current on going rate of the similar products in the market.

IMAGE PRICING: Also known as premium pricing, where by price of one of the product or service is priced artificially high, to create a favourable premium perception amongst the customers.

INTUITION BASED PRICING: No market survey is done and the price of the product is kept by intuition.

LOSS LEADER PRICING: The price of the product is kept less than the actual cost of the product, to gain a lead in the market. The firm sells one product less than the cost price and aim to encourage customers to buy other products from them.

PENETRATION PRICING: The starting product is sold at a very low price, and targets to achieve wider market acceptance within a short period of time. This firm with this policy believes that many customers will switch to their product because of low pricing

PREMIUM PRICING: The product is priced as a premium or superior brand.

PSYCHOLOGICAL PRICING: This pricing strategy is used by firms whereby product is priced above the average pricing of its competition to create a premium image. A pricing strategy designed to create a positive psychological impression on customer's mind.

SEASONAL PRICING: The product is priced according to the high and low demand seasons.

SPECIAL EVENT PRICING: The product is priced specially for some particular event like Christmas, New Year or any other event.

F&B MANAGEMENT TERMINOLOGY:

MARK UP: Markup is the difference between the selling price of a good or service and cost. It is often expressed as a percentage over the cost. A markup is added into the total cost incurred by the producer of a good or service in order to cover the costs of doing business and create a profit. The total cost reflects the total amount of both fixed and variable expenses to produce and distribute a product. Markup can be expressed as a fixed amount or as a percentage of the total cost or selling price.

PERFORMANCE MEASUREMENT: Performance measurement is the way toward gathering, dissecting as well as detailing data with respect to the performance of an individual, group, organization, system or component. Performance measurement is an important tool of strategic analysis. Stakeholders will get a better indication of an organization's strategy from observing what it measures and does than from its declared goals or what it says it does. Performance measurement is applicable to all industry sectors and to all types and sizes of organizations (public, private and not-for-profit).

AVERAGE SPENDING POWER: It refers to the average spend by guests in a restaurant. It is calculated by Total Food & Beverage Sales divided by Number of Covers sold

F&B Sales/Number of Covers sold=Average Spending power

SALES PER WAITER: This is a matrix that is used to measure the productivity of a waiter. It can be calculated by dividing Food & Beverage Sales by number of waiters. This will give the average sales done by each waiter. The higher the amount better the performance of the waiters with regard to revenue generation

SEAT TURNOVER: Seat turnover is the number of times one seat (chair, stool, whatever the customer is sitting on) is used by different individuals ("turns over") in a restaurant during a meal period or time period. Put another way, the total number of seats occupied during a particular period divided by the number of seats available.

The equation for computing seat turnover is the number of visitors served in a chose timespan separated by the number of seats. Assume a café or parlor serves 200 visitors one evening and has a seating limit of 80. The seat turnover works out to 200 divided by 80, or 2.5.

AVERAGE PER COVER: This figure reflects the average spent by guests in the restaurant. It can be calculated as below

Total Food & Beverage revenue of the restaurant/Total Guests Served =Average Per Cover

WAIT TIME: It is important to keep into account of the wait time carefully specially for busy restaurants. Having an accurate estimate for wait time for the guest and restaurant is extremely important. Prolonged wait time for guests may result in flaring of tempers and loss of valuable customers

SALES MIX: In a restaurant this refers to ratio of the menu items that are sold viz a viz the total sales. This matrix is important as each dish has a different profit margins. This can be calculated by total number of units sold of a dish divided by the total units sold of all dishes. Menu Mix is also used by chef to express sales mix.

INCREMENTAL SALES: Incremental sales are buys by clients in addition to what they planned to purchase when they originally entered the store.

For example, when a client walks into a hotel and plans to stay in a deluxe room by the front office representative is able to upsell a Club room at and additional amount this is incremental sales

PERFORMANCE MANAGEMENT FORMULA'S

1. Revenue - Expense = Profit
2. Profit=Sales-Cost of Sales-Cost of labour-Cost of Overhead expenses
3. CoGS(Cost of Goods sold)=Opening inventory+ Purchases-Closing inventory
4. Gross Profit= Total Revenue-CoGS
5. Inventory Turnover ratio=(CoGS/Opening inventory+ Closing Inventory/2)
6. Revenue =Number of Units sold X Price per Unit
7. Food Cost% =Food Costs (Food Cost of Sales)/Total food sales X 100
8. Beverage Cost %=Cost of beverage sold/total beverage sale X 100
9. Labout Cost %= Cost of Labour/Total Revenue X 100
10. Average Per Cover Food = Total Food Sales/Total Number of Covers served
11. Average Per Cover Beverage: = Total Beverage Sale/Total Number of Covers served
12. Average Per Cover Food &b beverage= Total food & beverage revenue/total number of covers served
13. F&B profit %= Total F&B Profit/Total F&B Revenue
14. Revenue Contribution of Individual Outlet= Revenue of the specific Outlet/Total F&B revenue
15. Seat Turn over= Total Covers Served/Number of seats in the restaurant
16. Popularity Index=Total Number of an item sold/Total number of all items sold
17. Employee Turnover Rate =Employee departed/Number of employees X 100
18. Customer Retention Rate=Total Customers-Total New Customers/Total Customers X 100

FINANCIAL MANAGEMENT

Financial management is about planning, controlling and careful use of the funds that ensure efficient operation of a business/organization.

KEY FUNCTIONS OF FINANCIAL MANAGEMENT

- Planning, Organizing & controlling of all financial activities of the firm (Incoming revenue & outgoing expenses)
- It ensures wise allocation of financial resources for smooth operations
- Aims to reduce the overall costs by applying control & audit measures

FINANCIAL MANAGEMENT IN THE HOSPITALITY INDUSTRY

Financial management lays the very foundation of a successful business. Likewise, the most successful hotels rely on fundamental financial management principles to enable them to manage their property profitably.

Best practices of financial management in the hospitality industry include:

- Creating an annual budget;
- Building a detailed financial tracking model and
- Having on-going audits.

FINANCE TERMINOLOGY

COST: It is the monitory expenditure which a firm has to incur in return of sales and purchases. It refers to the amount incurred by any organisation to purchase or hire the factors for production either for products or services.

INFLATION: This is about the decline of the purchasing power of the currency over a period of time. This is about sustained upward trend of the overall prices of products and service.

DEFLATION: This is when there is a general overall decline in the prices of products and services and is opposite of Inflation. Deflation happens when the inflation is below 0%

DUE DILIGENCE: Due diligence is the process of examining all the material facts of a contract or a deal before a legal contract is signed by both the parties. Put differently, it could also mean verifying the accuracy of a statement.

CURRENT LIABILITIES: When a company purchases goods on credit which needs to be paid back in a short period of time, it is known as Accounts Payable. It is treated as a liability and comes under the head 'current liabilities'. Accounts Payable is a short-term debt payment which needs to be paid to avoid default.

AUDIT: Audit is the examination or inspection of various books of accounts by an auditor followed by physical checking of inventory to make sure that all departments are following documented system of recording transactions. It is done to ascertain the accuracy of financial statements provided by the organization.

BANKRUPTCY: In this situation an organization is unable to honor its financial obligations or make payment to its creditors, & files for bankruptcy. This is a legal process which is initiated against the companies who are unable to pay their financial debts.

CAPITAL BUDGET: Capital budget consists of expenditure of assets like building, land, machinery, equipment etc. It is the process of allocation of resources for major capital investment/expenditure.

CONTINGENCY FUND: Contingency Fund is created as an imprest account to meet some urgent or unforeseen expenditure of the government.

BUDGETARY DEFICIT: Budgetary deficit is the difference between all receipts and expenses in both revenue and capital account of the government.

CUSTOMS DUTY: Customs duty refers to the taxes imposed on products when they are transported over international borders between countries.

MICRO-ECONOMICS: Microeconomics is the study of individuals, households and firms' behaviour in decision making and allocation of resources. It generally applies to markets of goods and services and deals with individual and economic issues.

MACRO-ECONOMICS: It is the study of behaviour and performance of the economy as a whole. It focuses on national output, unemployment and inflation.

COST BENEFIT ANALYSIS: A process by which you weigh expected costs against expected benefits to determine the best (or most profitable) course of action.

CASH FLOW: Every business needs cash to operate. The term cash flow, refers to the amount of operating cash that "flows" through the business and affects the business's liquidity. Smaller businesses must maintain even tighter control over the cash flow which is essential for the smooth and sustainable business.

NET PROFIT: Net profit denotes the amount of earnings left with the firm, after deducting all expenses, interest and taxes. It is a key, indicator of company's ability to convert sales unto profit.

EBITDA: EBITDA stands for Earnings Before Interest Taxes depreciation & Amortization. It acts as a tool to measure a company's financial performance. It reflects companys financial earnings before financial deductions but does not indicate company's cash flow.

AMORTIZATION: Amortization is an accounting technique which is practiced to spread an intangible assets value over a period of its useful life.

CAPITAL INVESTMENT: Capital investment refers to money used by a business to purchase fixed assets, such as land, machinery, or buildings.

RETURN ON INVESTMENT: ROI=Net Profit/Capital Employed × 100 Return on Investment (ROI) is a performance measure used to evaluate the efficiency of an investment. ROI measure the amount of return on a particular investment, relative to the investment's cost.

NET OPERATING PROFIT: NOP is the profit a company is left with after subtracting for cost of goods sold, operating expenses, interest and taxes. It is calculated on the profit and loss statement.

DEPRECIATION: The value of any asset can be said to depreciate when it loses some of that value over a period of time. Depreciation occurs due to wear and tear.

BREAK EVEN ANALYSIS: In economics and business, specifically cost accounting, the break-even point (BEP) is the point at which cost or expenses and revenue are equal: there is no net loss or gain, and one has "broken-even". It is non-profit nor loss situation.

OPPORTUNITY COST: It refers to the cost of the next best alternative action that is sacrificed in order to pursue the chosen action.

CapEx: Capital Expenditure-capital expenditure is all the expenses that a firm makes to acquire, maintain or improves its fixed assets like land, building, equipment, vehicle etc.

ASSETS: Assets are all items of value that an firm owns for example land, plant , machinery, cash, office equipment & intellectual property.

LIABILITY: Liabilities is what a firm owes to other parties , in short - liabilities take money out and assets put money in your pocket.

DIVIDEND: A dividend is the distribution of some of a company's earnings to a class of its shareholders, as determined by the company's board of directors.

NIGHT AUDIT: The auditing process for the day is generally conducted at the end of the day during the following night, hence the name 'Night Audit'. It can be performed by the conventional method of using papers, receipts, vouchers, coupons, and files. But performing audit using modern PMS systems is easy, fast, and efficient.

BANK RECONCILIATION: Bank reconciliation is a process performed by a company to ensure that its records & cash book are correct. This is done by comparing the company's recorded amounts with the amounts shown on the bank statement. Any differences must be justified. When there are no unexplained differences, accountant's state that the bank statement has been reconciled

PROPERTY MANAGEMENT SYSTEM: A property management system (PMS) is software that facilitates a hotel's reservation management and administrative tasks. The most important functions include front-desk operations, reservations, channel management, housekeeping, rate and occupancy management, and payment processing.

GROSS REVENUE: Is the total sales generated by the hotel by selling various services & products. This is no way reflects the profitability of the hotel. It simply shows the ability of the hotel to makes sales through different products & services across the hotel.

GROSS PROFIT: In any given time is the gross revenue minus all expenses incurred in producing the goods.

Gross Profit=Revenue-Cost of goods sold

DEPRECIATION: Is the decline in the value of an asset over a period of time for example plant, machinery etc. because of wear & tear.

ADR=Average Daily Rate Is the average of all rooms types and rates. It is achieved/calculated by dividing the room revenue earned by the number of rooms sold.

ADR=Rooms Revenue/Number of rooms Sold

RevPAR-Revenue Per Available Room RevPAR=Average daily Rate x Occupancy percentage

This metrics shows the revenue earned from the available per room irrespective whether it is occupied or not. This is considered one of the key performance metrics by hoteliers of room division performance. It reflects the ability of a hotel to fill its hotel room at an average price. It shows if the RevPAR of a hotel increases it shows average room rate or occupancy rate is increasing. It helps in better pricing strategies to sell better.

However, it does not reflect the profitability of the hotel in any way.

RevPAR=Rooms Revenue/Number of Rooms Available

COGS: COST OF GOODS SOLD: At any given time, cost of goods sold are, all the direct expenses incurred in producing goods for sale

GROSS MARGIN: Gross margin is the difference between revenue & cost of goods sold (COGS) divided by revenue.

NET SALES = Gross sales – (Customer Discounts, Returns, Allowances)

The sum of an organization's gross revenue minus its returns, allowances, and discounts is known as Net Sales.

GROSS PROFIT= Net sales – Cost of goods sold

Gross profit refers to an organization's profits earned minus the prices of manufacturing and distributing its products

OPERATING PROFIT = Gross Profit – Total operating expenses + Operating incomes

Operating profit is an accounting metric which measures the profits of a company generated from its core business functions. The profitability of a business can have measured with the help of Operating profit.

NET INCOME: Gross Income – Expenses = Net Income

Revenue – Cost of Goods Sold – expenses = Net Income

ACCOUNTS PAYABLE: It is money owed by a business to its suppliers shown as a current liability a company's record.

ACCOUNTS RECEIVABLE is a legally enforceable claim for payment held by a business for goods supplied and/or services rendered that customers/clients have ordered but not paid for.

JOURNAL: A journal is a written document in which monetary transactions are entered the first time they are processed in a chronological order.

LEDGER: The ledger is a summarized version of the monetary amounts penned down in journals which includes the individual transactions by their date.

TRIAL BALANCE: A trial balance includes a list of all the overall ledger accounts (both revenue and capital) contained within the ledger of a business. It shows debit & credit balances

PETTY CASH: Petty cash is an amount of discretionary funds in the form of cash used for small payments. Petty cash is the little amounts of payment done during the daily course of operations.

BOOK-KEEPING: Book-keeping is a procedure which involves the recording of transactions related to the business so as to produce an accounting record.

BOTTOM LINE: Bottom line refers to the last line in a company's balance sheet which is the net profit or net-earnings. The phrase bottom line is often used in conversation to refer to net profit, all those actions & strategies that help increase profits means that make bottom line better.

TOP LINE: Top line refers to the company's gross revenue or total sale

GOPPAR-GROSS OPERATING PROFIT PER AVAILABLE ROOM:

Gross Revenue-Gross Expenditure/number of available rooms in the hotel

This metric is useful for hotel owners as this gives a bigger picture to them in the sense that how well their asset as a hotel is performing.

It is one of the key performance indicators.

Number of rooms	100
Days in a year	365
Total number of rooms available per year	**36500**
Revenues per department	
Rooms	3000000
Food and beverages	1000000
Other departments	300000
Total Revenue	**4300000**
Expenses	
Rooms	550000
Food and beverages	500000
Other departments	150000
Undistributed	800000
Total Expenses	**2000000**
Gross Operating Profit (GOP)	**2300000**
Gross Operating Profit Per Available Room (GOPPAR)	**63.01**

TYPES OF COSTS

TOTAL COST: Includes all expenses whether paid or not for production or selling a unit or providing services to customer.

MARGINAL COST: The amount by which total cost varies with the volume of production.

STANDARD COST: Also called budgeted cost and is used as a benchmark for the manager.

CONVERSION COST: This includes costs incurred (like direct wages and production overhead) to transform raw material into finished products.

DIRECT COST: Cost which can be allocated to a product is termed as direct cost, includes raw material, direct labor cost and other direct cost.

FIXED COST: This cost is also called capacity cost or period cost. The cost which remains constant with increase or decrease in the volume of production. E.g.- rent, interest, insurance

CONTROLLABLE COST: costs which can be controlled by the department. E.g.- material cost, direct wages, direct expenses.

UNCONTROLLABLE COST: Costs which cannot be controlled by the department. E.g.- rent, interest

PRODUCTION COST: The cost incured in production of food, goods or services is termed as production cost. This includes supplying material, lobor, services, finishes, packaging and storing of product.

ADMINISTRATION COST: The cost incurred for making policy, direction and controlling are termed as administration costs.

SELLING COST: Cost incurred in marketing and selling

DISTRIBUTION COST: The cost include in distribution of products, which includes packing of products available for dispatch and ends with making reconditional returned empty packages.

ORDERINGS COST: This includes the entire cost of acquiring raw material, not only the cost of raw material but also includes the requisition, purchase, ordering, transporting, receiving, inspection and storing etc.

CARRYING COST: The which incurred for holding a given level of stock termed as carrying cost, which includes the investment cost, storage cost, insurance, taxes, storage cost, insurance, taxes, cost of deterioration and obsolescence.

FOOD COST: Total cost incurred to prepare the final product which include cost of raw material, storing cost, processing cost, preparation cost and labor cost.

Formula = (beginning inventory+purchase-ending inventory)/food sales

BEVERAGE COST: Total cost incurred to prepare the final product which include the cost of raw materials (cocktails, mocktails), storing cost, processing cost, preparation cost and labor cost.

Formula = (beginning inventory+purchase-endinginventory)/beverage sales

DIRECT MATERIAL COST: In case of food industry food cost is the direct material cost, includes all the food articles either used in raw. Semi cooked or cooked from in order to finish the dish and sell it.

DIRECT EXPENSES: The direct expenses other than direct material cost and direct wages which can be identified with all allocated to the cost center.

DIRECT WAGES: The direct wages/salaries are the wages which can be allocated to the cost center or the cost unit, sometime payment of direct wages and indirect wages falls within the definition of direct wages, includes – laborers engaged in altering the condition-inspectors, analysts etc. specifivally required for the production of the product-wages paid to foremen, charge hand etc.

PRODUCTION OVERHEAD: This includes all indirect material cost, indirect wages, all indirect expenses incurred for the production of goods in a unit or business house.

ADMINISTRATIVE OVERHEAD: This includes all indirect material cost, indirect wages, and indirect expenses incurred in the direct control and administrative of a production house, includes- printing, stationery, salaries paid to administrative employes, etc.

SELLING OVERHEAD: This includes all indirect material cost, indirect wages and indirect expenses incurred in the promotion of sales and retention of customers, includes – printing, stationary, mailing literatures, catalogues, salary oaid to the employees, etc. also includes bad debts and collection charges, cash discount allowed, after sales srvices.

DISTRIBUTION OVERHEAD: This includes all indirect material cost, indirect wages, indirect expenses with making the packed product available for dispatch and ends with making the re-conditioned reture empty packages available for reuse ex-packaging cases, delivery vehicle etc.

TYPES OF COST ON THE BASIS OF NATURE OF COSTS-

FIXED COST: These costs do not vary with the change in volume of production.

VARIABLE COST: It is the cost that vary with the change in volume of production.

SEMI-VARIABLE COST: This is also called as semi fixed cost or also as mixed cost in short means that a base cost will for sure incur however irrespective fo the volume and along with an addition cost that will vary with the fluctuating volumes.

MATERIAL COST: It refers to the cost of material used for production of product or services.

LABOUR COST: Labour cost is the cost of labour which means the sum of all wages paid to the employees as well as the amount paid towards employee benefits and payroll taxes etc.

OVERHEAD COST: Overhead costs are those costs incurred during the operations of a business that cannot be traced or contributed to any particular cost unit! Overheads can be fixed, variable & semi variable.

TYPES OF COST-ON THE BASIS OF RELEVANCE OF DECISION MAKING:

OPPORTUNITY COST: It refers to the cost of the next best alternative action that is forgone in order to pursue the chosen action.

SUNK COST: Sunk cost are those cost that have incurred and do not have any potential of recovery, for example your rent or any marketing campaign etc.

REPLACEMENT COST: It is the cost of replacement of an asset, plant, machinery, equipment etc.

IMPUTED COST: Also called as implied cost which are considered just for the purpose of decision making and do not involve any actual cash outflow.

REAL COST: It refers to the cost of all efforts and sacrifices made by the owners of factors of production in production of a commodity.

SOCIAL COST: It refers to the cost of hardships and sacrifices that a society has to bear due to operation of business activities.

CONVERSION COST: It refers to the cost involved in transforming raw materials into finished products. These types of cost do not include the actual cost of raw material. It includes the cost of direct and indirect labour, overheads and expenses.

TYPES OF MARKETS

PERFECT COMPETITION (WITH INFINITE BUYERS AND SELLERS): There are numerous buyers and sellers. With so many players in the market, it is kind of impossible for any one participant to alter the prevailing price. If at all they do so, the buyers and sellers have infinite alternatives to pursue.

MONOPOLY (WITH ONE PRODUCER): Here there is a single producer of a particular good or service, and generally no reasonable substitute.

OLIGOPOLY (WITH A HANDFUL OF PRODUCERS): An oligopoly is similar to monopoly. But here rather than having only one producer of a good or service, there are a handful of producers.

MONOPOLISTIC COMPETITION (WITH NUMEROUS COMPETITORS): This is a type of market system which combines elements of a monopoly and elements of perfect competition. There are numerous competitors in the market but each competitor is differentiated from the other. An example- market for music. While there are many artists, each artist is different from another.

MONOPSONY (WITH ONE BUYER): Market systems may also be differentiated according to the number of buyers. A perfectly competitive market theoretically has numerous buyers and sellers where as a monopsony has only one buyer for a particular good or service, giving that buyer significant power in determining the price of the products produced.

KEY METRICS FOR SUCCESSFUL HOTEL OPERATIONS

- Energy Management
- Quality in product, process
- Customer Centric work culture
- Water Consumption
- Employee Performance as Per The KPI (Key Performance Indicators)
- Customer Loyalty Programme

- Customer Experience Measurement
- Online Ratings by Customers
- Marketing ROI
- Measure, Manage, Optimize, Repeat
- Principles of Work Safety & Sanitation. Waste disposal
- Application of Menu Engineering
- Application of Principles of Purchase
- Product Quality Consistency
- Food Loss
- Control Over Pilferage & Wastages
- Food Cost as per Budgeted Targets

MATERIAL MANAGEMENT

Material Management is the process of planning, selecting, negotiating, purchasing, procuring, receiving, inventory management, storing and issuing of requirements and co-ordinating with various user departments for ensuring smooth procurements of requirements.

A well-managed material management/supply chain department is the difference between a successful and a struggling hotel brand. A professionally managed supply chain department provide a big competitive edge to any hotel.

Its function includes several important aspects connected with material, such as, purchasing, storage, inventory control, material handling, standardization etc.

AIM OF MATERIAL MANAGEMENT: Is to procure the required material that is:

- Right Quality
- Right Quantity
- At the Right time
- At the Right place
- Procurement at the Right cost

PURPOSE OF MATERIAL MANAGEMENT

- To satisfy the demand during period of replenishment & ensure smooth operation/production
- To carry reserve stock to avoid stock out
- To stabilize fluctuations in consumption

- To establish standardized quality systems & procedure of ordering to vendors & receiving & storage

NEED OF MATERIAL MANAGEMENT

- Around 50% of the revenue is usually consumed or is committed in procurement
- To keep smooth flow of procurement leading to smooth production and services
- To identify the most suitable vendor/supplier for the requirements
- To negotiate purchase & drafting of contracts/purchase orders/ tenders etc.
- To co-ordinate between various departments and ensuring their requirements are timely procured as per prescribed quality standards

OBECTIVE OF MATERIAL MANAGEMENT

- Lower procurement & storage cost
- Maintain Continuity of supply
- Maintain Consistency in quality
- Good supplier relations
- Development of personnel

MATERIAL PLANNING & CONTROL: Materials planning and control is done based on the sales forecast and production plans. It involves estimating the future business and raw material requirements, based on which the inventory & par stock levels and ordering levels are maintained.

DPEARTMENTS UDER MATERIAL MANAGEMENT

RECEIVING: The primary role of receiving department is to ensure that all the goods ordered by the purchase department are received as per the Purchase orders & as per the specified quality and quantity and also as per the contracted rate. The location of the receiving department should be at a location which is easily accessible and has easy downloading facility for the trucks/supplier's vehicles. There should be ramp so that trollies can be used to carry the material from the trucks to receiving with ease. There could also be a provision of a lift/elevator.

The layout should be such that it can be easily cleaned as frequent delivery of variety of items including meat & perishables can make it dirty often.

Receiving should check that all packaged items have intact packaging

All countable items should be counted or weighed as per the unit applicable

All items should be received as per the prescribed specification

As and when required the user departments help me be taken to ensure quality of the products.

STORES: The key role of the stores department is to receive, store and issue

supplies for the operations. Stores work closely with purchase & receiving department on a daily basis.

FUNCTION OF STORES DEPARTMENT:

- To receive and store supplies as ordered by the purchase department as per the prescribed storage guidelines for that product.
- To verify the correctness of the quantity, quality, packaging size, specifications etc.
- Are as mentioned in the purchase order.
- To maintain updated records of the supplies in the inventory system
- To ensure all received products/supplies are stored as per the guidelines to ensure safety & care of the goods avoiding wastage, breakage or pilferages
- To issue material to all departments against the authorized & approved requisitions only

PURCHASE: Purchasing is the process of procurement of goods, supplies & equipment to ensure smooth flow of hotel operation and quality delivery of services to its esteemed guests. Purchase department is responsible, for meeting hotels requirements as per required quality, quantity in a timely manner at competitive market price. Purchasing includes selection of sources of supply finalization in terms of purchase, placement of purchase orders, follow-up, maintenance of smooth relations with suppliers, approval of payments to suppliers, evaluating and rating suppliers.

Some of the key functions of Purchase Department are:

- Negotiate prices of requirements.
- Compare with 3 vendors before finalizing contracts.
- Ensure quality products & service by vendors and apply standard purchase specifications.
- Establish contracts for the regular requirements, to ensure improved bargaining capacity to achieve year around good pricing and quality for supplies.
- Ensure timely deliveries of requirements as per specified qualities.
- To share updated information with user departments about new/ innovative products and substitutes of requirements.
- Implement strong and effective purchasing policies as per the guidelines of the management.
- Maintain strong co-ordination with the user departments and work closely with them in ensuring timely delivery of requirements as per specifications provided.

TYPES OF PURCHASE METHODS

STANDARD PURCHASE CONTRACT: This method of purchasing is all about negotiating annual prices for regular requirements. Quotations are invited from the form suppliers for regular/recurring raw material requirements and negotiated for an annual price and contracts are awarded to suppliers with agreed terms and conditions.

ONE TIME PUCHASE ORDER: This method is for requirements which are mentioned in the purchase order, once that many quantities/units are supplied the purchase order is completed and no more quantities are supplied. For example, buying 50 units of TV. Once 50 units are supplied the Purchase order is completed.

CASH PURCHASING: Cash purchase is means to purchase requirements from the market against cash. This method is effective and used during emergency situations & for items which are required in only small quantities and are of smaller value.

TYPES OF PURCHASE ON THE BASIS OF AUTHORITY

1. **CENTRALIZED PURCHASING:** Centralized purchase method is a purchase process that consolidates the requirements of the entire company or multiple businesses or units of the same company. This method gives additional purchasing power to the purchase manager as the quantity requirements are consolidated that helps apply economies of scale and per unit purchase pricing of the units gets cheaper.

2. **DE-CENTRALIZED PURCHASING:** This method is just the opposite of the centralized purchase method. This method gives authority to purchase individually to different business units under the same organization.

KEY STEPS IN PURCHASE CYCLE:

1. Identify need for an item/service to be purchased
2. Draft detailed specification for the same
3. Identify-compare and select vendor/supplier
4. Place order for goods & services as per specification
5. Receive goods & services as per specification
6. Storing goods & raw material as per there designated store
7. Issuing goods & raw material as per the requisitions duly approved

CHARACTERISTICS OF A GOOD SUPPLIER:

The products that are used in a hotel reflect the quality of the hotel hence making suppliers a partner in maintaining quality in a hotel.

Considerations while finalizing qualities of a good vendor:

- Select those vendors who understand brand standards & quality and are competent to understand and supply as per specification provided
- Select Vendors who have strong credibility in the market place & are trusted
- Select vendors who are punctual and can handle any emergency demands
- Select vendors who are ethical, responsible & are experts in their product line, and can provide guidance how to best use or store or may be train the hotel team
- Ease of communication is extremely important while executing regular orders and supplies.

STORES MANAGEMENT: Stores management involves physical control of materials, storage of raw material as per specification, minimization of obsolescence and damage through timely disposal and efficient handling, maintenance of stores records, proper location and stocking. A store is also responsible for the physical verification of stocks and reconciling them with book figures.

INVENTORY CONTROL: Inventory generally refers to the materials in stock. It is also called the idle resource of an enterprise. Inventories represent those items, which are either stocked for sale or they are in the process of manufacturing or they are in the form of materials, which are yet to be utilized.

Inventory control is a planned approach of determining what to order, when to order and how much to order and how much to stock so that costs associated with buying and storing are optimal without interrupting production and sales.

Inventory control basically deals with two problems:

i.   When should an order be placed? (Order level),

ii. How much should be ordered? (Order quantity).

KEY TERMS & CONCEPTS OF MATERIAL MANAGAMENT

PAR STOCK LEVELS: To ensure smooth flow of functions across all departments of a hotel is extremely crucial. Not available items in stores may have an adverse impact on guest experience. Hence maintaining par stocks in stores is an essential step in maintaining overall quality in Hospitality. Par Stock is that minimum amount of supplies, that is required to be kept in stock at all times to meet everyday demands of various departments to ensure smooth operations without any interruption.

STOCK VARIANCE: It is the measure of volatility as it measures how much the stock tends to deviate from its mean. If variance is high, the stock widely fluctuates and vice versa.

BUFFER STOCK: Also, sometimes called as the safety stock. It is that extra level of stock that is maintained in the inventory to mitigate the risk of running out of stock. The reason behind is to overcome the uncertainties in the supplies and to ensure uninterrupted smooth flow of services and availabilities of raw materials

CASH PURCHASE: Cash purchase occurs when something is required urgently or is required rarely or in small quantities. This method of purchase occurs when immediate cash payment is made against the delivery/purchase of goods or services. This method is not encouraged much but is essential in certain circumstances for example to compensate for short supplies.

BLIND TASTING: Blind tasting is that method which involves tasting something without knowing about its brand or identity. Blind tasting is conducted for various items like wine, food etc. This method is used to neutralize any inclination towards a brand and ensure neutral tasting and assessment of products

JUST IN TIME: Just in Time is a philosophy rather than a technique. By eliminating all waste and seeking continuous improvement, it aims at creating manufacturing system that is response to the market needs.

JIT provides an efficient production in an organization and delivery of only the necessary parts in the right quantity, at the right time and place while using the minimum facilities"

STANDING PURCHASE ORDER: Standing purchase orders are contractual agreement between the hotel & the supplier for routine & regularly required goods and services. For example, supplies of milk, cream, fruits and vegetables, cleaning chemicals, pens, pencils, stationary etc. This method helps save time in negotiations as the rates are well negotiated for a year, its helps maintain consistent quality and saves time

IMPORTANCE OF STANDARD PURCHASE SPECIFICATONS: It is essential that most of the supplies have clear & precise specification which is crucial in maintaining consistent standards across all departments & customer touch points. Purchase specification must be simple to understand without use of words that can be misinterpreted. However, specification may be changed or amended whenever the management approves to change the quality.

- It ensures that the user department provides clear and crisp details of the product that are required
- It helps the vendor to know the quality they are quoting for and avoids any confusion or potential future conflict between the buyer & the supplier
- It reduces the time while ordering frequently purchased items
- It helps in obtaining competitive pricing from the market for the same quality as per specification
- It also provides clear quality etc. guidelines to the receiving department at the time of receiving, hence eliminating any doubt between the supplier & the receiving in-charge
- Clear purchase specification help maintain consistent quality by purchasing the same products
- It also helps in maintaining standard food cost and hence helps in pricing as well.

REQUIREMENTS OF EFFECTIVE SPECIFICATIONS-

- Name of the product/service supported a brief description
- Brief note about the quality
- Its measurement unit should be specified for example it is required in numbers, kg, liter, size etc. configurations
- In what condition the product should be received- frozen- fresh- canned etc

BEST PRACTICES WHILE RECEIVING

- Count or measure goods as per the applicable unit Could Be Numbers, Liter, Kg etc.
- Check quality of the product as per the standard specification provided with the purchase order
- Verify quantity and tally it with the purchase order and check for any under supply of over-supply.
- Check for any fraud etc. for example addition of water injected in chicken leading to extra weight in chickens or ice pockets in chicken which tend to over weigh the chicken
- Ensure that all supplies are made during receiving hours and not later than its prescribed timings unless there is an emergency. Increased practice of deliveries after the closure of receiving hours leads to more frauds and mal practices.
- All goods must be verified for quality & quantity before they are sent to stores and never directly to stores.
- If goods are not supported without an invoice, the receiving in-charge must create a memorandum invoice for the same.

KEY CONCEPTS IN MATERIAL MANAGEMENT

FORCES MAJEUR: This term is essential to be understood in Purchase department. This clause is included in purchase contracts, which removes liability from fulfilling the contract in case of force majeure. During force majeure a vendor cannot be held accountable to perform or provide uninterrupted services or deliveries as he would have during normal times. Forces Majeure is a "French word" which means "greater force", which refers to something which is an act of god, an event like a tsunami, tornedo, volcanic eruption, hurricane for which no party can be held accountable. Forces majeure also refers to act of man, which are unforeseen circumstances, unavoidable circumstances like riots or war.

SHORT SUPPLY: When a vendor delivers less quantity than what has been ordered by the Purchase department it is termed as short supply. A short supply report is made and immediately shared with the user department head. If the user department feels that the quantity that has been short supplied is essential for the smooth flow of the operation, they may request the purchase department to procure the short-supplied quantity immediately either from another vendor or make urgent cash purchase from the market. In case the product quantity short supplied is purchased at a higher price from the market, the differential amount is debited to the supplier who has sent short supply along with the cost of conveyance.

For example if 50 kg of a vegetable is short supplied, and the contract price for that for Rs.50/kg, and if we purchased 50 kg from the market t Rs 70/kg, the difference of Rs. 20/kg would be debited as: Differential rate per kg = Rs. 20

Quantity cash purchased=50 Kg

Amount debited Rs. 20 X 50= Rs. 1000 (plus additional conveyance charges if incurred

NOT SUPPLIED: This phrase refers to the items which has been ordered and are expected to be delivered but the supplier fails to deliver. Not supplied items need to be informed immediately to the user department to take either of the action- 1 wait for delivers tomorrow or make urgent procurement if they are emergency requirements

ABC ANALYSIS: The concept of ABC analysis highlights that all items in the inventory are not of same value, some are costlier over other products. As per ABC analysis products in an inventory could be categorized into three categories based on their value (A, B & C based on their value/importance) "A" being highest value, B– Lesser value than A, and C Category has lesser value than B category items. This categorization helps in different methods of control & management. This categorization helps management more on the high value items i.e. A category items rather than investing too much time on low value many items. This method helps exercise more control on higher value items and less attention on low value many trivial items.

VED ANALYSIS: VED Analysis stands for Vital, Essential & Desirable which helps differentiate items on the basis of their importance & necessity required in production or any other activity. **Vital items** are those items which if out of stock would bring the production to a halt or are those items whose stock out would cost a lot to the organization

Essential Items are those items, these items are just next to vital in importance level. Management should ensure the availability of these items as well but the non-availability of these items may cause temporary loss or it may also be possible to repair the stock out part

Desirable items are those items which are least important among these three, and any unavailability of these items may result in minor stoppage of work but easy replenishment of these items is possible within a short duration of time

HML: High-Medium & Low based on importance of the price per unit

SDE: Scare–Difficult-Easy on the basis of ease of procurement or ease of availability

FSN: Fast Moving-Slow Moving & Non-Moving, on the basis of the movement from the stores.

DAILY RECEIVING REPORT: This is a daily report prepared & signed by the receiving manager. This report provides details of all the supplies received by the receiving department i.e. Name of the supplier, items received & quantity received. The report is also accompanied with the invoice/challan provided by the supplier along with the supplies.

LEAD TIME: With regard to purchase department- lead time is the time taken to process an order i.e. the total time taken, from the time an order is placed with a vendor till the time it is delivered and received at the hotel. It is the time between the initiation of the order and its execution completion. It's the total time taken, between the release of an order of production of an item till the time of its completion and converted into a finished product.

CARRYING COST: Is the sum total of all the costs, that a business pays, to hold an inventory in stock. Many companies miss to calculate this cost which could be substantial capital locked up. This also helps review any overstocking in inventory.

Some of the costs incurred are actual cost of inventory items,

- Interest accrued
- warehouse rental,
- opportunity cost,
- employee costs,
- storage cost/fees,
- insurances,
- impact of quality,
- shrinkage of perishable raw material,
- deterioration of quality

REORDER LEVEL: Reorder level or reorder point is the inventory level at which a company would place a new order. Reorder level depends on a company's work order lead time and its demand during the time and whether the company maintain a company a safety stock.

EOQ-Economic Order Quantity: Economic order quantity is that optimum quantity ordered for purchasing at a given point, so as to achieve minimized carrying cost & ordering cost of the products without disrupting the smooth flow of operations.

The 'order quantity' means the quantity produced or procured during one production cycle. Economic order quantity is calculated by balancing the two costs. Economic Order Quantity (EOQ) is that size of order which minimizes total costs of carrying and cost of ordering. i.e., Minimum Total Cost occurs when Inventory Carrying Cost = Ordering Cost.

BEST BEFORE: Best before date means till that date the food will be in its best quality, however after the best before date it may lose its nutrients, freshness and taste to some extent but may still be fit and safe to consumer.

EXPIRY DATE: Expiry date simply tells the consumer about the last day a product is safe and fit to be consumed. It clearly means that after the expiry date the product is unhealthy for eating and if consumed may result in health problem and even food poisoning. Food items after expiry date should be destroyed and discarded and never consumed

OVER SUPPLY: This refers to a situation in which a vendor sends more supplies than what has been ordered for. Receiving department in ideal situation should only be accepting the quantity which has been ordered for by the purchase department. However sometimes for frequently ordered items the user department may approve to accept small oversupplies keeping in view the demand ahead in recent future subject to the storing capacity of the establishment.

DEBIT NOTE: This raising of note to debit the differential amount to the supplier because of its short supply resulting in cash purchase is called debit Note

For example, if 50 kg of a vegetable is short supplied, and the contract price for that for Rs. 50/kg, and if we purchased 50 kg from the market @ Rs. 70/kg, the difference of Rs. 20/kg would be debited as below

Differential rate per kg= Rs. 20

Quantity cash purchased=50 Kg

Amount debited Rs.20 X 50= Rs. 1000 (plus additional conveyance charges if incurred).

FIFO-FIRST IN FIRST OUT: First in first out is a strategy which is used mostly for perishables items or items which have a shelf life. The essence of this method is that the items purchased first to be used first to ensure items in stores don't get spoiled because of expiry date.

LIFO: LAST IN FIRST OUT: Last in, first out (LIFO) is a method used to account for inventory that records the most recently produced items as sold first. Under LIFO, the cost of the most recent products purchased (or produced) are the first to be expensed as cost of goods sold (COGS), which means the lower cost of older products will be reported as inventory.

WASTAGE: Wastage is when some product or resource of the hotel has been wasted or destroyed because of carelessness but it may not necessarily be intentional.

1. For example, a trainee in kitchen may not be able to extract the best yield in potato peeling because of lack of training or practice, but ends up wasting potatoes in thick peels.

2. Wastage of perishable items stored in cold store because of the cold storage machine breakdown is also wastage.

3. Serving bigger portions of dishes then what is prescribed as per the standard portion size is also wastage

PILFERAGE: Pilferage is an intentional action by someone which results in loss of hotels products or its resources. For example, a housekeeping employee pocketing and carrying home guest amenities.

BREAK-EVEN POINT: No profit and Loss situation. Break even quantity = Fixed costs/(Sales price per unit – Variable cost per unit).

Entrepreneurship & Leadership

ENTREPRENEURSHIP

ENTREPRENEURSHIP: Entrepreneurship is the ability and readiness to develop, organize and run a business enterprise, along with any of its uncertainties in order to make a profit.

ENTREPRENEUR The entrepreneur is defined as someone who has the ability and desire to establish, administer and succeed in a startup venture along with risk entitled to it, to make profits. In a nutshell, anyone who has the will and determination to start a new company and deals with all the risks that go with it can become an Entrepreneur.

TYPES OF ENTERPRISES: Sole Proprietorship, Partnership Firm, Company, Limited Liability Partnership, One-person Company, Small Companies etc.

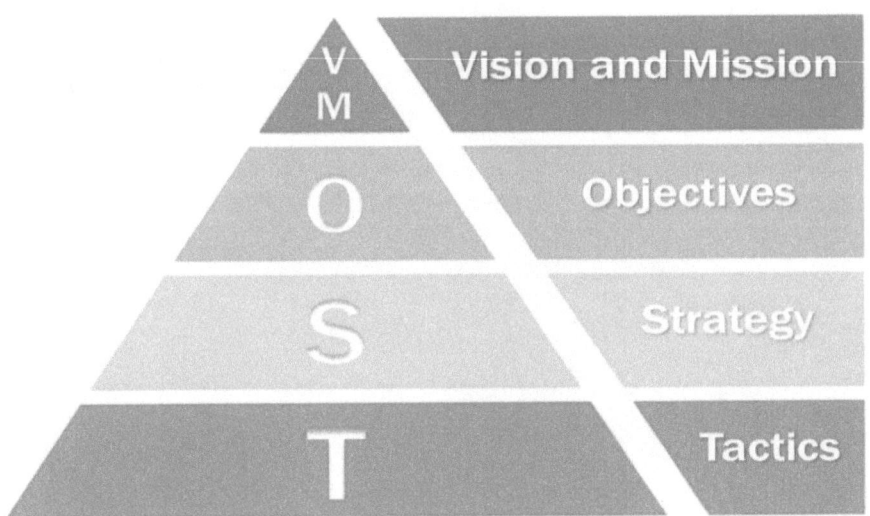

VISION: It is about What we want to become over a period of time? It's a description of the business that one aspires to build that inspires and motivates.

MISSION: Is the reason for existence of the business. Mission drives the values and the business. Mission focuses, guides and directs a business in a particular direction. It answers- what we do? Who we do it for? And How we do it?

OBJECTIVE: These are one step below mission, this can be explained as a collection of individual goals to accomplish a mission. Objectives are specific targets.

STRATEGY: This answer's what all is required to be done to achieve objectives? This refers to the overall approach of getting things done.

TACTIC: The specific steps or activities undertaken to accomplish a strategy. Tactics support the strategy. This refers to what activities will be taken to enact the strategy.

WHO IS AN ENTREPRENEUR?

An entrepreneur is an individual who creates a new business, bearing most of the risks and enjoying most of the rewards. The entrepreneur is commonly seen as an innovator, a source of new ideas, goods, services, and business/or procedures.

Entrepreneurs play a key role in any economy, using the skills and initiative necessary to anticipate needs and bring good new ideas to market. Entrepreneurs who prove to be successful in taking on the risks of a start-up are rewarded with profits, fame, and continued growth opportunities. Those who fail, suffer losses and become less prevalent in the markets.

QUALITIES OF SUCCESFUL ENTREPRENEURS

ACTION ORIENTED: They have a clear understanding that only having an idea or only knowledge will not be enough unless it is executed well hence they give lot of importance to action. They believe in taking consistent action for a considerable period of time to see results and don't give up easily when they don't see results initially.

ADAPTABILITY: An entrepreneur must be able to adapt to the changing market conditions and competition & consumer demands. They also have to be adaptable to new challenges within the firm as well as ever changing market conditions. Adaptability is about being effective in the face of changing & challenging conditions around you.

ALLIED EFFORT: An entrepreneur should be open to suggestions and agree with his/her fellow teammates giving them the importance that they need.

DECISIVE: Being decisive is an essential trait, which means being firm about one's decision and having belief in that. This leads to action, staying indecisive can be a major obstacle as it leads to inaction and loss of motivation. Staying indecisive for very long can rob one of opportunities and may hamper one's self confidence and may lead to over analysis.

FOCUSED: It is the ability to stay focused on the objective as the path of an entrepreneur is full of set-backs and challenges. This skill is all about the end in mind, having a bird's eye view on the final objective and making effort with the goal in mind.

GROWTH MINDSET: People with growth mindset thrive on challenges and risks. They see failure as an opportunity to learn and grow and hence take risks. They do not interpret failure as a reflection of being not intelligent. Growth mindset people believe that even if I have failed once does not mean I cannot learn that skill over a period of time and challenges the fixed mindset or fixed belief that hinders them from growth and progress. They believe in maximizing their potential, they believe in overcoming challenges, and they are inspired by the success of others.

PASSIONATE: It is passion of an entrepreneurs that keep them going when they are going through the hardships or challenging times in a business. Passion is high when we love what we are doing and that makes us put in extra efforts without losing enthusiasm which gives outstanding results

PERSISTENCE: Entrepreneurs don't give up easily, in face of defeat rather they see failure as opportunity to growth and come back stronger. They are determined to see their endeavour succeed. They don't believe that it cannot succeed so they fuel their efforts and take action rather than accepting defeat and giving up

PRAGMATIC: This approach means that, they look at various ways to achieve their objective, they don't maintain a dogmatic view of situation of problems which is about sticking to limited ways of solving a problem. They approach situation in an innovative and flexible way to figure out different ways to solve a problem or to overcome an obstacle.

PRODUCT & SERVICE KNOWLEDGE: They work tirelessly to gain knowledge about the product and services and the customers they will be serving. They maintain a keen ability to learn more and more about the business they are in, to keep it sustainable and competitive in the market place.

RESOURCEFUL: Successful entrepreneurs are resourceful, it is the ability to solve problems and generate resources as and when required to overcome obstacles. It is the ability to think creatively in difficult solutions and come out with resources or create resources even in challenging situations.

RISK TAKING ABILITY: Risk is essential when an entrepreneur sets out on a journey to establish a company. There is no surety that a new idea of a business will survive and will not fail. No research or knowledge is enough to ensure 100% success of any venture, so eliminating risk or failure is not possible. But gaining knowledge about the business and by passion one can overcome the risk and come out successful.

SELF CONFIDENT: They have a high sense of self-worth and doubt themselves if they can achieve the goal. They believe in growth mind-set and keep learning new skills and knowledge to ensure their continuous growth

SELF DISCIPLINE: By becoming self-disciplined they are able to eliminate all the hindrances which could be poor productivity, too many interruptions, clutter at work etc. to ensure they stay highly productive and make good progress towards their goals.

ENTREPRENEURS HAVE GROWTH MIND-SET.

WHAT IS THE DIFFERENCE BETWEEN FIXED MINDSET & GROWTH MINDSET?

FIXED MIND-SET: People with fixed mindset believe talent alone is required to succeed, these people do not work hard to develop new skills or knowledge set and make no effort towards developing their skill set. They feel they were born with a certain skills and talents and that alone is enough to succeed. In a way they are static and people with fixed mindset do not take chances and risks and avoid failure at all costs and stretch themselves to be more what they want to become. They somewhat feel that they cannot change the way they are, they continue to believe that they are born with a certain level of intelligence which cannot be changed and they continue to behave according to that. Fixed mindset prevents growth and skill development as they continue to firmly believe that their qualities are fixed traits and cannot be changed. Such people always want to appear intelligent

GROWTH MINDSET: People with growth mindset thrive on challenges and risks. They see failure as an opportunity to learn and grow and hence take risks. They do not interpret failure as a reflection of being not intelligent. Growth mindset people believe that even if I have failed once does not mean I cannot learn that skill over a period of time and challenges the fixed mindset or fixed belief that hinders them from growth and progress. They believe in maximizing their potential, they believe in overcoming challenges, and they are inspired by the success of others. Four dimensions of a successful enterprise: strategy, operations, marketing and finances

TYPES OF ENTREPRENEURSHIP

SMALL BUSINESS ENTREPRENEURSHIP: Entrepreneurs in this category have small business and make profit that supports their business and family. E.g. groceries store, hair dresser, stationary store, book store, small size café etc. They usually hire manpower from close vicinity and have invested their own money and are not seeking investments for venture capitalists.

LARGE BUSINESS ENTREPRENEURHSIP: Small business owners sometime turn big when there is an innovation or opportunity, or simply when the company grows rapidly. Entrepreneurs in this category are part of a large businesses. Such organizations often create products and services as per the demand in the marketplace.

SCALABLE STARTUPS ENTREPRENEURSHIP: These entrepreneurs are those who have a concept/idea which can scale up very fast and they believe that their concept will revolutionize the way things are being done in a particular sector. Many of such businesses are innovations and technology based. They often are on a look out for venture capitalists or angel investors

INTRAPRENEUR: An intrapreneur is someone who works inside a large corporation/business firm, he is someone who manages large projects and is often taking key decisions that have impact on a business outcome. The key difference between and intrapreneur and entrepreneur is that intrapreneur finances are not at stake and he gets his salary even if the business fails. An intrapreneur uses all his entrepreneur skills without incurring any risks.

SOCIAL ENTRERENEURSHIP: Such businesses are deigned balancing the profit and social contribution together as success parameter. This category aims to work responsibly and look at fair profit and aim to make a positive difference in the society.

INNOVATIOVE ENTREPRENEURSHIP: Innovative entrepreneurs are buys innovating and coming out with new ideas and business concepts that disrupts the market place. They want to make a positive change in the way people live their lives. They aim to stand out in the market place by creating unique products and services. Steve Job of apple for example

HUSTLER ENTREPRENEURSHIP: Entrepreneurs who are willing to put in a lot of hard work to see through their enterprise succeed. They often start with small business but by their sheer hard work grow their business.

IMITATOR ENTREPRENEURSHIP: Such entrepreneurs look at a particular business model, product or service and create their business based on the same concept but try and make that better than what currently exists. They have a lot of self-confidence and they focus on learning from other people's mistakes.

RESEARCHER ENTREPRENEURSHIP: Researches take a lot of time before they start their business. They aim at having an in-depth knowledge of business so that they can cut down the chances of losses or failure of the business endeavour.

BUYER ENTREPRENEURSHIP: These entrepreneurs invest/buy businesses that they like in the market place, they have financial strength and prefer to invest/buy existing businesses in the market. They buy existing business make the changes in them and work towards increasing its profits.

IMPORTANCE OF RISK IN BUSINESS:

- If a business takes a risk and fails, its people learn from that failure. Risk management is important in an organization because without it, a firm cannot define its objectives for the future.

- The ability to manage risk will help companies act more confidently on future business decisions.

- Their knowledge of the risks they are facing will give them various options on how to deal with potential problems.

- The real risk in business – and there are always risks – is not knowing which risks are worth taking.

- The importance of risk management in an organization is quantified by how well it deals with the many factors that exist within and externally of the business.

- The importance of risk management in an organization is what creates a positive working culture, maintains compliance across the organization, upholds strong corporate values, sets the tone for handling high profile crises and remains competitive and present in the public consciousness.

- Risk Appetite: According to ISO 31000, a risk appetite definition is "the amount and type of risk that an organization is prepared to pursue, retain or take." The challenge with developing a risk appetite definition is how to implement and enforce it, making it relevant to business units on a day-to-day and case by case basis.

- A risk appetite statement is a higher-level statement that broadly considers the levels of risk that management deems acceptable.

WHAT IS A BUSINESS PLAN?

A business plan is a written description of your business's future, a document that tells what you plan to do and how you plan to do it. If you jot down a paragraph on the back of an envelope describing your business strategy, you've written a plan, or at least the germ of one.

IMPORTANCE OF A BUSINESS PLAN

- To clearly define the objectives of the business
- To clearly define the product and services being offered
- To have improved understanding of the target customers
- To clearly define the revenue model
- For better understanding of the market & competition
- To assess feasibility of the business thereby reducing the risk of failure
- To determine the financial requirements
- To attract investors by explaining to them a detailed business plan
- To research the market trends and needs and expectations
- To attract partners
- To create a marketing plan for the product and services
- To plan positioning of the product and the services
- To understand clearly the opportunities to can be tapped

IS A BUSINESS PLAN OVERRATED?

No, business plans are NOT overrated because long-term success requires planning. However, writing up a business plan isn't necessary to succeed. What matters is that you have a game plan and that your team knows what that is and what to do!

COMPONENTS OF A GOOD BUSINESS PLAN:

EXECUTIVE SUMMARY: This serves as an overview of the main aspects of your company and business plan that you will discuss in greater length in the rest of your plan.

BUSINESS DESCRIPTION: This is where you explain why you're in business and what you're selling. If you sell products, describe your manufacturing process, availability of materials, how you handle inventory and fulfillment, and other operational details.

MARKET RESEARCH & STRATEGY: These describe your marketing strategy, including sales forecasts, deadlines and milestones, advertising, public relations and how you stack up against your competition.

MANAGEMENT & PERSONNEL: Provide bios of your company executives and managers and explain how their expertise will help you meet business goals. Investors need to evaluate risk, and often, a management team with lots of experience may lower perceived risk.

COMPANY SYNOPSIS: The Company Synopsis section is where you provide readers with a more in-depth look at your company and what you have to offer.

CUSTOMER DEFINITION: This here is *knowing your audience*. Once you have a good idea of your customer personas and demographics, you'll want to explain how you're designing your products/services, branding, customer service, etc. to appeal to your target audience and meet their needs.

CUSTOMER ACQUISITION: Now that we know who your customers are, the next question is — how do you plan on getting them? This essentially refers to your marketing plan where you'll go into detail about how you intend on raising awareness for your brand to expand your customer base

FUNDING: This is your opportunity to tell investors:

- What your funding goals are
- How they can help you achieve those goals
- What they have to gain from getting involved in your company

FINANCIAL DOCUMENTS: This is where you provide the numbers that back up everything you described in your organizational and marketing sections. Include conservative projections of your profit and loss statements, balance sheet, and your cash flow statements for the next three years.

SCALABLE BUSINESS

A scalable business model is a business that sees increasing returns as it invests more in capital, labour and services. This generally means that unit costs decline as your business expands.

Steps to determine that the business in largely scalable

- Understand Your "Fixed Cost to Build
- Determine Your On-going Operating Costs
- Determine Your End State Economics
- Determine What It Will Take to Get There

IMPORTANCE OF COMPETITIVENESS IN ENTREPRENEURSHIP

BRINGS ABOUT INNOVATION: Competition makes people innovative. Innovation is crucial to the progress of any business. It brings about new ideas and sees them getting effectively tested in a relatively short amount of time

OPTIMUM DECISION MAKING: This is essential for the business to thrive in the market. It involves analyzing the competitors, market needs, trends etc. and using the generated reports to make optimal decisions that work for both the business and service/product consumers.

COMPETITION IDENTIFIES STREGTHS & WEAKNESSES: Although a painful pruning process, competition helps businesses to identify strengths and weaknesses opportunities for growth in their model.

MOTIVATES MARKET RESEARCH: In the world of business, there will be instances in which a customer leaves you for a competitor, or leaves a competitor for you. When either of these instances occurs, learn about what specifically caused the customer to change businesses. Gathering this information enables you to better understand your target audience.

COMPETITIVE ADVANTAGE: Competitive advantage refers to factors that allow a company to produce goods or services better or more cheaply than its rivals. These factors allow the productive entity to generate more sales or superior margins compared to its market rivals.

WAYS TO GAIN COMPETITIVE ADVANTAGE IN BUSINESS

- Create a Corporate Culture that Attracts the Best Talent
- Define Niches that are Under-serviced
- Clarify Your Strengths

- Establish Your Unique Value Proposition
- Cost focus
- Cost leadership
- Innovation. Etc.

SUSTAINABLE COMPETITIVENESS: Sustainable competitiveness as the set of institutions, policies, and factors that make a nation productive over the longer term while ensuring social and environmental sustainability. Sustainable competitive advantages are company assets, attributes, or abilities that are difficult to duplicate or exceed; and provide a superior or favorable long term position over competitors. Examples of Sustainable Competitive Advantages:

- Low Cost Provider/Low pricing
- Market or Pricing Power
- Powerful Brands
- Product Differentiation
- Strong Balance Sheet/Cash
- Adapting Product Line

MID-CAREER DILEMMA

- It happens around age 40. It is not a midlife crisis but just a state of dilemma or confusion about their life and their careers.
- The genesis of a mid-career dilemma is in what I call "the experience trap."
- Experience is a double-edged sword. When you don't have it, you want it. When you have it, you don't have enough of it. You want more of it so you go get it. This goes on for years.
- Then, one day, all of a sudden, you have too much of it for a job. You are sort of "over experienced," if we can say it that way. Then you are stuck – you don't have enough experience for the next job and you are "over qualified" for the job that your younger peers are engaged in. That's the onset of the dilemma.

KEY CONCEPTS FOR ENTREPRENEURSHIP

WHAT IS VALUE PROPOSITION? A value proposition refers to the value a company promises to deliver to customers should they choose to buy their product. A value proposition is part of a company's overall marketing strategy. The value proposition provides a declaration of intent or a statement that introduces a company's brand to consumers by telling them what the company stands for, how it operates, and why it deserves their business.

WHAT IS SOCIAL ENTREPRENEURSHIP: It is a combination of social and commerce issues. They are not only concerned with profits. Success is defined by how they improve the world. Their focus is mostly placed on the social or environmental changes made while earning profits.

STRATEGY & DEVELOPMENT: Who does your business serve? What are its core competencies and how will you leverage them? What are your business's goals for the year? What is your business's vision and mission, questions like these, all fall within the dimension of a business strategy. It serves as the foundation and hub for all of the other dimensions, and having a weak strategy core often causes many businesses to put the cart before the horse.

OPERATIONS: The dimension of operations is the realm of execution and productivity. In short, it covers getting stuff done. Many businesses have a decent sense of strategy and struggle with operations.

What separates a lot of good businesses from great ones is their execution. Businesses that get the right stuff done grow faster and more consistently than businesses that struggle with execution.

MARKETING: There's a reason that so many of the gurus in business are marketers or salespeople: good marketing equals more money. We all know that cash-flow is the pulse of any business, and marketing is what gets you cash-flow. Though we often talk about increased revenue when we speak of marketing, it's also just as true that effective marketing ensures that a business's resources are leveraged in the best way possible, thus making it a great way to keep money in your business as well as to make more.

FINANCES: Many people are continually scared because they have no idea what they made last month and this month, nor do they have any idea what's coming in in the future. A challenge with this particular dimension is understanding what level of granularity you need for effective decision-making. Most people don't need to have a daily sales report, but a monthly sales report may not give you enough time to react or plan.

It's absolutely true that you can get lost in the financial data and questions in your business. What's also true is that you're absolutely lost without them.

SCALABLE ENTERPRISE: Enterprise's infrastructure and services able to scale with demands. Scalability is the ability of a system to grow to meet a company's business needs. It is the ease with which the supply of a product, service or process can be expanded to meet changing levels of demand. In today's high-technology marketplace, economists are increasingly talking about the importance of instant scalability.

A company with good scalability is one that is able to maintain or improve its profit margins while its volume of sales increases.

COST ADVANTAGE: this advantage comes into play when the organisations compete on the basis of cost and are eager to understand the sources of their cost advantage or disadvantage and about the factors that are driving these costs.

DIFFERENTIATION ADVANTAGE: this plays a role in the firms that strive to create superior products or services using a differentiation advantage approach.

LEADERSHIP

FROM THE BOOK LEADERSHIP PLUS- AUTHOR NEERAJ CHANDHOK

PSEUDO LEADERSHIP   TRUE LEADERSHIP

LEADERS BELIEVE IN NOT ONLY KNOWING BUT DOING: They understand the difference between movement and progress. Some of us feel that moving around a lot being busy and running around all day we have accomplished a lot. However, it is not about running around and being busy, it is about what are we busy doing and what is the purpose and direction of our hard-work that defines our progress. leaders take big actions and never fall in the trap of procrastination or wanting to know everything ending up over analysing which is a trap, called paralysis of analysis.

LEADERS LEVERAGE TEAM COLLECTIVE STRENGTH

You can do what I cannot do; I can do what you cannot do; Together we can do great things - Mother Teresa.

There is a famous Chinese quote which says that "the wise adapt themselves to the circumstances as water adapt to the pitcher."

Some of the adaptations required for leaders are:

- Open to accept new ideas and suggestions
- Evolve as per new situations and technologies
- To stay abreast with constantly changing business and work place environment
- Leaders don't let emotions cloud their vision

"I've learned that people will forget what you said, people will forget what you did, but people will never forget how you made them feel." – Maya Angelou

Leadership is not a title or a designation it is rather a responsibility and a behaviour. Mostly leadership is confused with someone who is heading a company. In fact, for leadership there is no requirement of a designation. Designation only means a position achieved in hierarchy of an organization. Leadership is not about having more power, authority, a plush office or a flashy designation; it is about responsibility, a behaviour. It is about a collective goal; it is about influence. Leadership is not about me; it is about we or us leveraging through people. It is about creating a shared identity. Leadership is all about influence and relationship and not about controlling. Once the goals are accomplished, the team feels they have done it. Leaders tirelessly work to safeguard their team and push them to achieve more & to do things beyond the ordinary. They inspire by being an example, work with team, share credit, take responsibility of consequences, face criticism, face fear, overcome failure, show resilience, courage and grit to emerge as a leader. One becomes a leader when one is able to influence a group of people to take action towards a shared vision or a goal. Leadership is about influence which is achieved by building trust and deep-rooted relationships.

ESSENCE OF LEADERSHIP- LEAD LIKE A SHERPA

Just as a CEO is hired by an organization to lead the company to the best of heights similarly Sherpa's job is to lead the members of the expedition to the top of the mountain. Sherpa's are used to facing obstacles, dangerous snow covered unforeseen hindrances which they face with courage like a CEO who navigates business through a maze of choices and complex problems. The CEO tries to overcome the problem of complexities based on his expert judgement and experience, collaborates and leverages the competencies and strength of his team. The leader inspires and keeps the team motivated and energized towards achieving a common goal.

The behaviour of Sherpa's truly represents the essence of a Leadership:

- To guide & inspire the team to the destination.
- To create a detailed plan and prepare for the expedition
- To face the challenges head on and chalk/carve a path for the team
- They are part of the team and work along with the team at all times, which develops respect, trust and strong relationships.
- Give them expert guidance, inspiration and push them to stretch and give their best

- Face difficult and life-threatening circumstances, with grace, courage and grit which inspires confidence of the team. They guide mountain expeditions in the face of huge challenges to stay ahead and take care of the entire expedition in all aspects, yet, when the mountaineers reach the summit they feel they have achieved it. This is the power of leadership and the Sherpa's celebrate the victory with them.

TYPES OF LEADERSHIPS:

AUTOCRATIC: The leadership in this style has total authority and impose their will on employees.

PARTICIPATIVE/DECOMCRATIC: This is also called a democratic style, this styles values the inputs of the team members but the responsibility of the final decision is with the leader Makes employees feel valued as they participate in decision making.

SERVANT: Servant leaders focus on the needs of the team members before their own and they extend all the help, guidance and support to the teams to perform better. This creates a unselfish mindset, fosters teamwork and create a culture of trust.

LAIZZEZ FAIRE: This style is about hands-off approach which means the employee are skilled in nature and are motivated to their task and the leaders keep a hands off approach and leaves the team the work on their own mostly.

BUREAUCRATIC: This refers to organizational leadership which is highly formalized through policies, procedures, hierarchy etc here rules and clearly defined guidelines are set and one follows the chain of command.

TRANSFORMATIONAL: This style of leadership inspires and motivates the employees to produce high level of productivity and can be instrumental in bringing huge change in organizational performance.

TRANSACTIONAL: This style refers to certain rewards/recognition which is based on achievement or accomplishment of certain task/goal. Often used in achieving sales targets and giving commissions or incentives on achieving the targets.

Soft Skills

SOFT SKILLS-KEY TO SUCCESS IN HOSPITALITY

SOFT SKILLS: Soft skills are character traits and interpersonal skills that characterize a person's relationships with other people. In the workplace, soft skills are considered to be a complement to hard skills, which refer to a person's knowledge and occupational skills. Some of the soft skills are etiquettes, communication, teamwork, listening etc.

HARD SKILLS: Skills like maths, science, accounting, computer programming that are teachable and measurable are called hard skills. Hard skills can be learned and acquired by practice & through education. Hard skills focus on skills and practical skills. Hard skills can be learned through books or through on the job training. Hard skills aim at increased skill that assists in employability.

HARD SKILLS VS SOFT SKILLS

Hard skills can be measured however soft skills are often intangible and hard to quantify. Hard skills are clearly reflected in the resume, cv or by job related assignments. To assess soft skills, one may ask situational questions and by assessing a candidate's reactions during the interview which gives an insight into the overall personality of a candidate.

IMPORTANCE OF SOFT SKILLS IN CAREER: Soft skills refer to how one carries and behaves in the professional field. It refers to collaboration, team work, not getting stressed under pressure, communicating effectively, cheerful, energy, initiative to name a few traits. Soft skills are those traits & skills that help's an individual to work harmoniously & effectively with other people. It is that inter personal skill that defines one's relationship with others. The technical skills for example, a degree in a particular stream is crucial in getting a foot in the door i.e makes one qualify for an interview but to clear the interview & to perform successfully in teams & work space one would requires strong inter personal skills. Soft skills help one become more productive and relevant in marketplace.

The challenge with the soft skills is that the employer and organization take it for granted that all those recruited or hired in the company know very well what kind of behaviour is expected from them while they are at the work place. Also, another challenge is that there is very little training that is provided in soft skills. No matter what job or position one is at, soft skills can be a major differentiator and game changer and gives one an edge over the competition.

IMPORTANCE OF SOFT SKILLS:

- Customer Interaction & customer satisfaction requires expert soft skills
- To know hard skills without soft skills will not result in successful outputs. Hard Skills + Soft skill is the winning strategy.
- Work places are inter personal places which requires continuous communication, active listening, collaborating for projects, debating over ideas, solving problems together, maintaining good relationship is key to a great work environment.
- Hard Skills are easy to lean than soft skills, soft skills development is about committing to change oneself and takes conscious & continuous effort on part of an individual

KEY SOFT SKILLS:

EQ-EMOTIONAL INTELLIGENCE: Emotional intelligence plays a big role in defining happiness & success in one's life. EQ is about being well aware of one's emotions and also the ability to be aware of the emotions and needs of the others. It is about controlling and understanding own emotions. We often come across extremely talented and intelligent people who struggle to work in team amicably or to succeed. Emotional Quotient or Emotional intelligence helps one overcome life's obstacles and challenges & defuse conflicts. Emotional intelligence is reflected in one's mental, physical health & in relationships. It is a key determinant in achieving life goals, career targets & building strong relationships. EQ is a better indicator of a good team player, leader & self-motivated performer.

WHAT IS EMOTIONAL INTELLIGENCE:

Emotional intelligence can be broken down into four main categories-

SELF AWARENESS: Knowing about self-weaknesses & strengths. It is also about how one is affected by self-emotions.

SELF MANAGEMENT: Is about controlling one's emotions in a positive way, it is about controlling emotional outbursts, accept changes & adapt & taking initiative.

RELATIONSHIP MANAGEMENT: It is the ability to maintain and foster good and healthy relationship, influence, manage conflicts and be able to work effectively in a team.

SOCIAL AWARENESS: Is having empathy for others, be able to feel the emotions and needs of the others and be comfortable socially.

IQ- INTELLIGENCE QUOTIENT: Refers to one's reasoning ability.

IQ is the measurement of one's intelligence achieved through intelligence test and is expressed in numbers. The average IQ is 100, if you score above 100 you are considered smarter than the average and score below 100 means less than the average.

WHAT IS THE DIFFERENCE BETWEEN IQ & IQ?

IQ=Intelligence Quotient- is about analytical, comprehension,

EQ=Emotional Quotient (also known as Emotional Intelligence)

IQ is about ability to feel, think

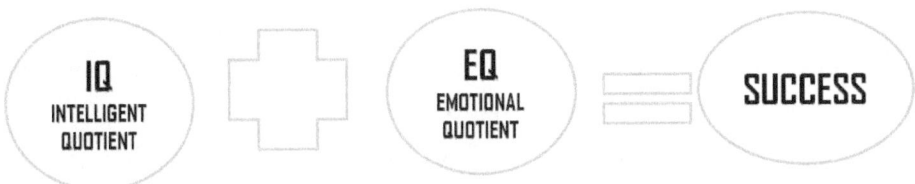

TEAM WORK: Teams are formed when individuals with a common taste, preference, liking, and attitude come and work together for a common

goal. Teams play a very important role in organizations as well as our personal lives.

"Coming together is a beginning. Keeping together is progress. Working together is Success-Henry Ford"

Targets must be met and revenues have to be generated. Tasks must not be kept pending for a long time and ought to be completed within the desired timeframe. A single brain can't always come with solutions or take decisions alone. He needs someone with whom he can discuss his ideas. In a team, every team member has an equal contribution and each team member suggests a solution best suited to the problem. All the alternatives can be explored to come out with the best possible solution. Thoughts can be discussed among the team members and the pros and cons can be evaluated

PROBLEM SOLVING: Problem solving is the act of defining a problem; determining the cause of the problem; identifying, prioritizing, and selecting alternatives for a solution; and implementing a solution. Clearly defining a problem is half the problem solved.

"CAN DO ATTITUDE": Can Do attitude at work can be a highly differentiating approach, which means that one has confidence & is resourceful & is willing to put in an extra effort on a challenging assignment. This also means that one will not waste time complaining & will not give up. An individual with can do attitude looks at situations and problems positively and as challenges and is solution driven rather than complain driven. Such an individual when faced with an uncomfortable situation or obstacle tries to overcome them, rather than giving up to them

When we say someone has a can-do approach it means that one's is self-confident and is ready to accept new challenges, tasks & problems without complaining & won't give up easily

ACTIVE LISTENING: Active listening is about paying complete attention to what is being said, that means giving undivided attention. It means giving all your attention to the speaker. It is about listening with all five senses. Some of the signs that one is actively listening is by maintaining eye contact, nodding head and saying yes or may be smiling. Since major part of communication is boy language and tone and of course the spoken words, active listening is listening and understanding the communications in all these aspects

ADAPTABILITY: Adaptability skills is a person's ability to adjust to changes in their environment quickly & easily. It is about being comfortable with changes around oneself. Being adaptable in one's career would imply that one can adapt easily to changing expectations, market trends, expectations & even locational change. Being adaptable in your career, can mean you are able to respond quickly to changing ideas, responsibilities, expectations, trends, strategies and other processes at work. Being adaptable also means possessing soft skills like interpersonal, communication, creative thinking and problem-solving skills.

ATTENTION TO DETAIL: Attention to detail is a very soft skill and is also a very sought-after skill by the employers. It is related to the attentiveness & accuracy with which an allocated task is done. It refers to capability of being attentive to all small & big details of the job and concentrate completely of the task one is assigned.

RESILIENCE: Resilience is the ability of being able to adapt well and bounce back quickly from setbacks in life. It refers to bouncing back from a failure, disappointment or from an unexpected loss. Another word often used for resilience is grit. Grit is the ability to face a difficult or a set back with courage for a sustained period of time and trying one's best to change the situation

EMPATHY: Empathy is an essential skill for service provider, it is the ability of one to put self into the shoes of the customer and feel as he feels. This enables and gives a big edge to the service provider as he is able to have a better improved perspective and starts thinking like the customer which helps the server serve better. Customer feel valued and satisfied when served with empathy.

Empathy is often confused with sympathy or compassion or pity, so it is essential that we understand all of them.

Pity- I feel sorry for your suffering

(Feeling of discomfort because of someone's sufferings

Sympathy-I care about your suffering

(Thoughts)

Empathy-I can feel your suffering like you feel

(Thoughts & Feelings)

Compassion-I want to comfort & relieve you in your sufferings

(Thought –Feeling & Action)

Pity Sympathy Empathy Compassion

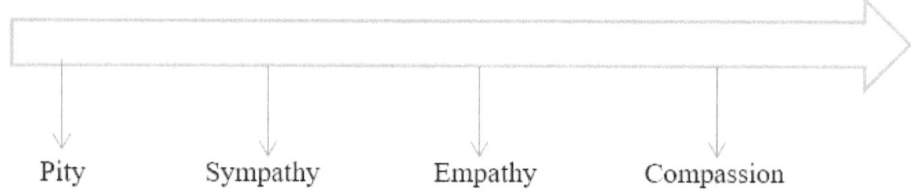

| Pity | Sympathy | Empathy | Compassion |

What is the difference between Empathy & Sympathy?

- Empathy is a term we use for the ability to understand other people's feelings as if we were having them ourselves.
- Sympathy refers to the ability to take part in someone else's feelings, mostly by feeling sorrowful about their misfortune.

Empathy is much stronger feeling than sympathy.

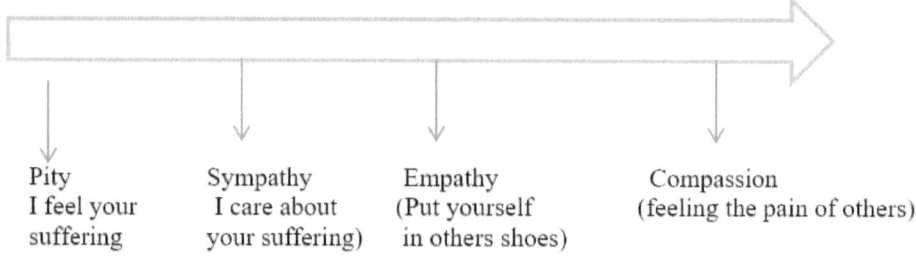

| Pity | Sympathy | Empathy | Compassion |
| I feel your suffering | I care about your suffering) | (Put yourself in others shoes) | (feeling the pain of others) |

CUSTOMER SERVING SKILLS

Customer service is an essential part of delivering customer satisfaction. It has to be timely, competent, customized and with empathy. Excellent customer service is always planned and never by accident. Good customer service is all about getting it right in the first time.

Some of the key customer service skills are:

- Empathy
- Adaptability
- Excellent communication skills
- Excellent listening skills
- Being confident and persuasive
- Problem solving

TAKING CRITICISM: Criticism takes into account of a person's actions at work and highlight the fault, drawbacks so that they can be improved upon. Taking criticism is not just about accepting what people say. It is also the ability to ignore distractive comments and critics whiles pressing on to achieve an objective. Taking criticism with the aim to improve and not taking it personally is a rare skill. Taking criticism positively and still staying motivated leads to continuous development and improvement. Often criticism is not pleasant, if it's unfair and with an objective to put down than it may lead to frustration. Criticism should be fair and corrective in nature and not only fault finding in nature.

STRESS AND TIME MANAGEMENT: Time management helps you to reduce long-term stress by giving you direction when you have too much work to do. It puts you in control of where you are going and helps you to increase your productivity.

Time management methods involve finding ways to work more efficiently, so as to maximize one's use of time. A variety of techniques and tools for list-making, task analysis scheduling, and task prioritization are typically used for this purpose.

The basic time management process involves the following steps:

- Developing a thorough understanding of all the various steps that must be performed to get a particular task completed
- Writing these steps down in the order they must be performed
- Identifying dependencies among steps that may cause bottlenecks to occur
- Scheduling the steps (using memory tools, including day planners, memo boards, sticky notes, shared calendars, project management software and personal information managers to assist in their timely performance)
- Tracking execution of the steps as they occur
- Using what is learned from experience executing the steps to improve the efficiency with which various steps may be performed.

MULTI TASKING:

- Performing two or more tasks simultaneously
- Switching back and forth from one thing to another
- Performing a number of tasks in rapid succession

NETWORKING SKILLS: Networking skills are the competencies you need to have to maintain professional or social contacts. Networking is a critical skill in sales, business development and a number of other industries. Networking skills are necessary to make and develop relationships with new contacts and promote something of value.

NETWORKING SKILLS:

- Communication
- Active listening
- Social skills
- Public speaking skills
- Nonverbal communication
- Interpersonal skills
- Empathy
- Positivity

- Humour
- Focus

COMMUNICATION: Communication can broadly be defined as exchange of ideas, messages and information between two or more persons, through a medium, in a manner that the sender and the receiver understand the message in the common sense, that is, they develop common understanding of the message.

The word communication is derived from the Latin word 'communicare', which means to share, impart, participate, exchange, transmit or to make common. It emphasises on sharing common information, ideas and messages. It is not merely issuing orders and instructions.

BARRIERS TO COMMUNICATION:

- Physical
- Emotional
- Linguistic
- Perceptional
- Cultural
- Psychological
- Technological
- Organizational Structure
- Attitude

TYPES OF COMMUNICATION

VERBAL COMMUNICATION: To be able to speak clearly and choose the appropriate words to express.

NON-VERBAL COMMUNICATION: Refers to the body language and facial expression during communication.

LISTENING: Listening is the ability to accurately receive and interpret messages in the communication process. Listening is key to all effective communication. Without the ability to listen effectively, messages are easily misunderstood.

Written communication-is the ability to write letters, text messages, correspond in writing or share reports,

ACTIVE LISTENING: Is also an extremely important communication skill as it helps one to listen patiently and understand the communication in the spirit it is made.

VISUAL COMMUNICATION: Refers to the ability to communicate effectively by way of pictures, symbols or use of any other visual aid effectively.

IMPORTANCE OF ACTIVE LISTENING

1. Pay undivided attention to the words of the speaker and try and picture the communication
2. Listen attentively without interrupting the speaker (take notes if required to ensure all points are understood)
3. Pay special attention to the no verbal and tone of the speaker for example s the tone irritated, cheerful or enthusiastic or may be full of boredom or frustration. Look for non-verbal cues & gestures. This can be helpful even during the telephonic calls when you are not able to see the customer or the speaker.
4. Try not to pre judge the conversation and start any conversation with an open mind
5. Do not try to dominate the speaker with your own version of the discussion, ask questions with an objective to understand better
6. Try to summarize the understanding of the conversation at the end of the communication to ensure

ORGANIZATIONAL SKILLS

Organizational skills are planning, scheduling and arranging your thoughts & tasks & allocate time to them so as to be able to complete them timely and effectively without getting over stressed and overwhelmed. Good organizational skills benefit. Displaying string organizational skills showcases that you have ability to focus, think strategically and accomplish goals effectively within timelines.

BENEFITS OF BEING ORGNANIZED:
1. To completes tasks within deadline
2. To show consistent performance
3. It builds self-confidence & confidence of the organization in you
4. One can multi task

SIMPLE TECHNIQUES TO ORGANIZE BETTER:
1. Clear the clutter at work place and have a clear to do check list with priority
2. Keep a notebook handy to avoid missing out noting down any crucial information
3. Use –Touch it only once – rule at work which means any paper, tool or file. It means dealing with a tool, e mail one time and complete the task with regard to that.
4. Assign a respective space to all tools, documents, files etc. so that one does not spend additional time looking for things
5. Also have clarity about a not to do things which are simply not adding any productivity to the overall output (disruptions, social media, gossips etc.)
6. Take initiative and not keep waiting for an external inspiration to get going about a challenging task.
7. Develop a routine and stay disciplined around that. That refers to committing and scheduling time to certain tasks, to stay on top of your work performance (this will help piling up of some unnecessary work which should have been done every day).

LEADERSHIP SKILLS: Leadership skills are skills you use when organising other people to reach a shared goal. Whether you're in a management position or leading a project, leadership skills require you to motivate others to complete a series of tasks often according to a schedule. Leadership is not just one skill but rather a combination of several different skills working together. Some examples of skills that make a strong leader include:

- Patience
- Empathy
- Decisiveness
- Active listening
- Reliability
- Dependability
- Creativity
- Positivity
- Effective feedback
- Timely communication
- Team building
- Flexibility
- Risk-taking
- Ability to teach and mentor

COLLABORATION: In today's competitive world the problem and challenges are so complex that no single person has solution to all of them which calls for collaboration.

BENEFITS OF COLLABORATION:

1. It helps organizations solve complex problems
2. It makes organization more efficient, productive & competitive
3. It encourages improved communication & relationship between the employees.
4. Collaboration of different talents and experts leads to improved overall learning of the employees.
5. Collaboration leads to improved and positive work culture leading to happier and positive work force
6. With increase in the overall satisfaction of employees results in increase in the employee retention rate
7. Effective collaborating teams have a competitive advantage in the market place, & also lead to reduced cost of operations.

ADAPTABILITY: It is a soft skill. It refers to being able to rapidly learn new skills and behaviors in response to changing circumstances and surroundings. Employers usually look for adaptability when hiring new staff.

Someone who is adaptable is also flexible. They usually work well on their own as well as with team members.

WORK UNDER PRESSURE: The ability to work under pressure involves dealing with situations which are usually out of your control. One can stay calm, plan effectively and manage time in order to reduce the pressure and solve the issue correctly.

Human Resource Management

HUMAN RESOURCE MANAGEMENT

Human Resource Management is a key department in hospitality as this industry is completely people driven. HRM is about managing the most valuable component of Hospitality that is humans. Managing this department effectively results in bringing competitive advantage to a Hotel. Any organization requires three major areas to function effectively to survive and Thrive-Finances, machines & humans. And humans operate finances & machines and organizations are known to turn around by changing the leadership, or teams or by better training team for improved performances proving Human resource management to be most valuable asset management.

KEY FIVE FUNCTIONS OF HUMAN RESOURCE MANAGEMENT

Recruitment & selection

Employee motivation

Employee evaluation

Industrial Relations

Employee Training & development

KEY OBJECTIVES OF HUMAN RESOURCE DEPARTMENT:

- HRM is responsible for procurement, development, maintenance of human resource
- One of its key objectives is to achieve individual, organizational and social objectives

- Human Resource Management also includes the study of management, psychology, communication, economics and sociology.
- HRM is about teamwork and team spirit and organizational culture
- It is an ongoing purpose

KEY TERMS AND CONCEPTS IN HUMAN RESOURCE MANAGEMENT

EXIT INTERVIEWS: Exit interview are those interviews which are done with the employees who are leaving an organization. These are conducted with the purpose of finding out the reasons for a company's employee turnover, to identify training and development needs, how employees feel about the compensation and benefits, how employees feel about company culture and work environment, growth opportunities, workload and work relationship. This information is beneficial for finding the areas of improvement and working upon them.

PERFORMANCE APPRAISALS: It is a process of identifying and measuring the human performance, it's about developing performance dimensions and ratings scales. Performance appraisals form the basis for increments, promotions, salary increases, layoffs, terminations etc.

CAREER PATH: A career path is about identifying alternative paths of an employee progress and that may require higher skills and consequent promotional opportunities

EQUAL EMPLOYMENT OPPORTUNITY: It is the right of all persons of community to work & progress on the basis of merit, ability, skill, competencies without regard to race, caste, religion, nationality, origin, disability etc.

FRINGE BENEFITS: This term refers to all the employment benefits other than the wages and salaries. For example, medical insurances, annual leaves, bonus, profit sharing, pension etc.

HARASSMENT: Any repeated behaviour by one or more employee towards another employee or group of employees which the affected employees consider annoying, insulting, bullying or intimidating and has a detrimental effect on an employee's performance.

SEXUAL HARASSMENT: This is a form of harassment involving use of implicit or explicit sexual overtones including inappropriate promise of rewards in exchange of sexual favours. It also refers to unwelcome sexual advances or any other conduct physical or verbal of sexual nature.

JOB DESCRIPTION: It is a written description of a particular job title detailing its duties and responsibilities. It includes Job title, roles and responsibility, scope and duties to be performed.

JOB SPECIFICATION: A list of job's "human requirements," that is requisite education, skills, personality and so on.

JOB ENLARGEMENT: This refers to increasing the overall job profile in terms of duties and responsibilities. This could mean adding or combining more responsibilities to the existing job at the same level.

JOB ENRICHMENT: Job enrichment is about adding more dimensions to an existing job with an aim to make it more motivating and meaningful. This may be adding extra tasks, giving more decision-making authority and giving constructive feedback.

JOB ROTATION: This is a management approach where employees are moved to different verticals of business to give them more exposure, to break monotony of work and to test their skills and competencies to place them at the most suited place.

RESIGNATION: When an employee terminates his own employment voluntarily, it is called a resignation.

TERMINATION: This term refers to end of an employee's work in an organization.

SKILL: Any observable competency to a perform a particular learned act is called skill.

ATTRITION: This term is used in HR to refer to reducing the workforce of a company. It may be due to resignations or terminations.

BEST PRACTICES: This is a set of practices which have proven to be instrumental and effective in achieving organizational goals and objectives. Such practices could also be learned from other organizations and be implemented in another organization with an aim of improve overall results.

BLUE COLLAR WORKERS: This term is used to express the workforce which is paid per hour for physical and manual labour.

GREEN COLLAR JOB: This job refers to jobs in the environmental sectors such as energy conservation, sustainability etc.

WHITE COLLAR WORKERS: This refers to the mid-level to higher levels of jobs, for example those who work in environment of cubicles and desks on their computers and are not involved in manual labour.

OUTSOURCING: This is the process of hiring an organization to perform a particular service.

TALENT MANAGEMENT: This is used in HR when it is with reference to ensuring to recruit, retain, develop, manage the best people in an organization. Management & HR are both involved in developing, implementing talent management.

GOLD COLLAR JOBS: This refers to those resources who are highly qualified like a scientist or a specialist, extremely creative engineer who are rare and hence high in demand

BREACH OF CONTRACT: This phrase is used to express a situation whereby in a contract one party has violated one or more terms on the contracts stated on his part making him breaching the contract.

BUDDY SYSTEM: It is effective method used during orientation whereby a new employee's gets the opportunity to work closely with a senior employee. The senior employee guides the newly hired employee about various aspects of the job and also introduces him to the other employees at work like a buddy.

CAREER PLATEAU: This term is used in HR for an employee who has reached the highest level of an organizational growth possible and cannot be promoted any further. This may be due to the way the corporate hierarchy is designed or any other factor that may have nothing to do with his skill set.

CORE COMPETENCIES: These are an organizations strength from a competitive company which creates its competitive advantage in the market place. It may be a defining skill, product, service, capability that gives a competitive advantage to a business.

CORPORATE CULTURE: This refers to a company's values, belief's, environment and ethics. It is shared valued, social order & defines nature of the company. It shapes attitudes and behaviour of the team of the company. A company's culture is what makes it unique and is very difficult to be copied by another company.

DOWNSIZING: This term refers to reducing the number of staff in the organization and the objective is to reduce the overall workforce sometimes this may be for restructuring.

EMPLOYEE RETENTION: This refers to creating a great work culture with the support of leadership and employee friendly policies and procedures which boost an employee's moral and engagement which makes him stay with the company

KPI: KEY PERFORMANCE INDICATOR: This is a tool for performance measurement of critical indicators of progress towards an intended result. This aims at providing focus to efforts towards a desired target and to be effective, its measures a company's or an individual performance against the set of targets or objectives. KPI is used to track the performance of a department, project, organization or an individual.

KEY RESPONSIBILITY AREAS (KRA): This term outlines the scope of the job profile, its description of the job and capatures the work role and its key responsibilities. KRA'S are the broader topics/subjects on which an employee is required to concentrate on. KRA aims to connect the employees with the organizational objectives. KRA's are larger goals.

ONBOARDING: All the set of activities required to be done after joining new in an organization is called on boarding. Activities like paper work required to be done, knowing policies and procedures, getting to the employees etc.

360 DEGREE FEEDBACK: This is approach to employee's performance assessment whereby a feedback is taken from every individual who is familiar with an employee, even the self-assessment of the employee is taken into consideration. Software can also be used.

TEAM BUIDLING: This refers to an activity or training etc. which are aimed at employees understanding the benefits and value of working together.

DISCRIMINATION: This is a practice of treating people differently from others in an unfair way. This also refers to treating people in an organization unfairly or with prejudice etc.

EMPLOYEE ENGAGEMENT: Employee engagement is how an employee feels connected with an organization, how he feels for an organization and what energy and willingness to do work they bring at work.

EMPLOYEE SATISFACTION: This term refers to how happy, valued or fulfilled employees feel at their work. This is an inclusive term that reflects their satisfaction as whole towards their manager, kind of work, work environment, colleagues etc.

CHANGE MANAGEMENT: It is the process of communicating information about changes in an organization such as change of leadership, mission or policy procedures, or overall change in the way a company is managed. Change management is an opportunity to improve employee's engagement and earn more trust.

EMPLOYEE TURNOVER: It is the rate at which employees of a company leave.

CORE VALUES: These are a set of values, that are at the core of the business/organization based in which an, organization functions. It is kind of guiding principles of an organization.

COMPANY CULTURE: Company culture refers to values, work environment, ethics, mode of communication, recognition of work, employee empowerment. In a way it reflects the personality of an organization.

COMPANY VISION: Where a company envisions itself in the future after having achieved its mission

COMPANY MISSION: Organizations purpose and reason of being in the business

NEPOTISM: This term refers to hiring of friends and relatives even though certain more qualified and competent individuals are available. This kind if favouritism is called nepotism

BACKGROUND CHECK: Investigating or verifying the facts and information about a candidate with regards to the details provided in the resume.

SUCCESSION PLANNING: This is a method by which top executives are evaluated by senior management to assess their strengths and weakness. The concept and purpose is to prepare second in command to be ready as a back-up option for senior officials of the company

FIRED FROM JOB: Is to remove someone from the job.

MISCONDUCT: An unacceptable behaviour by an employee.

CTC (Cost to Company): Is the term for the total amount that an organization spend either directly or indirectly on an employee during a year.

GROSS SALARY: Gross salary is the total monthly or yearly salary before deducting any taxes and other deductions.gross salary is the total of basic salary and allowances provided by the organization.Gross salary consists of:

- Basic Salary
- House rent allowance
- Special Allowance
- Conveyance Allowance
- Medical allowance. Etc.

Gross Salary = Basic Salary + HRA + Other Allowances.

IN HAND SALARY: In hand salary or net salary or take-home salary is the total amount which an employee gets at the end of each month, in other words the actual amount an employee gets after various deductions.

REMUNERATION: Remuneration is the money along with the non cash benefits an emplyee is paid by the orgnanization . It may onclude salary/wages, bonuses, incentives, meals , travel allownace or any other perks that may be provided by the organization.

DIFFERENCE BETWEEN RECRUITMENT & SELECTION

SELECTION	RECRUITMENT
It is an activity of establishing contact between employers and applicants.	It is a process of picking up more competent and suitable employees.
It encourages large number of candidates for a job.	It attempts at rejecting unsuitable candidates
The candidates do not have to cross over many hurdles.	Many hurdles have to be crossed
Positive approach.	Negative approach
It proceeds recruitment	It is done after selection

DIFFERENCE BETWEEN TRANING & DEVELOPMENT

TRAINING	DEVELOPMENT
This is designed for non-managers as well as mangers.	It involves only managerial personnel.
It is a short-term process.	Long term in nature.
Managerial personnel learn technical knowledge and skills.	Managerial personnel learn conceptual and theoretical knowledge.
The objectives of training are specific job-related purpose.	The objectives have broader overview and consider general knowledge.
Training is concerned with the immediate improvement of the employee, i.e. the ways to make the employee more effective in his current role.	Development is a process to make the employee efficient enough to handle critical situations in the future, i.e. how well he can equip himself for the future demands.
Training means learning new things and refreshing old ones.	Development means implementing the learned session and finding new ones.

BUSINESS MANAGEMENT

KEY MANAGEMENT CONCEPTS & TERMS THAT ARE ESSENTIAL FOR MANAGERS TO BE EFFECTIVE

DEFINITION OF MANAGEMENT:

MARY PARKER FOLLET: Management is the art of getting things done thorough people

HAROLD JOONTZ: Management is the art of getting things done through & with people in formally organized groups

LAWRENCE APPLLEY: Management is the accomplishment of results through the efforts of other people

HENRI FAYOL: To manage is to forecast and to plan, to organize, to command, to co-ordinate and to control

PETER DRUCKER: Management is a multi-purpose organ that manages a business, manages managers and manages workers and work

WHAT IS BEING EFFECTIVE AND BEING EFFICIENT?

EFFECTIVE: Is about "Doing Right Things" This would mean doing the right tasks and is a goal-oriented approach.

EFFICIENT: Is about "Doing Things Right". This would mean doing things optimally, may be doing

them faster or may be completing the task at a lower cost.

MBO- MANAGEMENT BY OBJECTIVE

The term was first outlined by management guru Peter Drucker in his 1954 book, *The Practice of Management*. The key focus of this tool is to improve the performance of an organization by way of clearly defining the objectives that are agreed by the management as well as the employees. According to this theory having a say in the setting of the goals and planning activities encourages participation & increases commitment & acceptance of the objectives. This strategy was formulated by Peter Drucker in 1950's and includes the following five steps that organizations should follow:

1. Determine or review or revise organizational objectives for the entire organization
2. The second step is to ensure that these objectives are translated to employees. Ensuring that the objectives set are measurable
3. Step three is all about encouraging participation of the employees in setting individual objectives. This results in increased motivation of the employees and they feel empowered to achieve larger organizational goals
4. Step four is about monitoring the performance and progress of the employees against the established measurable (SMART Goals-specific-measurable-acceptable-realistic-time bound)
5. The step five is about recognizing & rewarding the employee progress. This includes giving honest feedback about what is achieved and what has not been achieved

MANAGEMENT FUNCTIONS

PLANNING & DECISION MAKING: Planning & Determining Course of action. This function refers to decision making with regard to the goal setting and determining future course of action and making choices amongst the set of alternatives. This step aims at goal setting and the paths chosen to achieve them. A manager must be able to foresee and visualize and look ahead purposefully and with clarity

ORGANIZING: Co-ordinating Resources & Activities. This function is about the process of establishing formalized structure or roles, positions & responsibilities within a company. This also aims at establishing relationship between different positions. The purpose of an organization is to create an environment for optimizing human performance. This function also establishes rules, polices and assigning tasks and allocation of resources. Staffing being a part of organizing is about filling and keeping the positions filled in the organizational structure. Promotions, discharge, dismissal, remunerations, transfers etc. are functions included in staffing. Organizing is about: who will do what job/tasks, who will report to whom, how and where decisions will be made and about resources allocations

LEADING: Motivating, Managing & Directing people. Leading is the skill of about influencing people towards a directed/specific purpose. It is one of the most challenging role in an organization. Leadership aims are a collaborating and positive environment whereby teams work towards a common organizational goal with high motivation & team work. Leadership aims at teams to co-ordinate and becoming effective as well as efficient towards the organizational goal.

CONTROLLING: Monitoring & Evaluating activities. This function is about comparing results with targets, establishing variance with established standards and finding reasons for variances. This also aims to control the utilization of resources against the budget. The aim of controlling is to correct the rouse of action and stay on course with the established standards and budgets. It is about measuring the results of the actions taken to achieve organizational goals

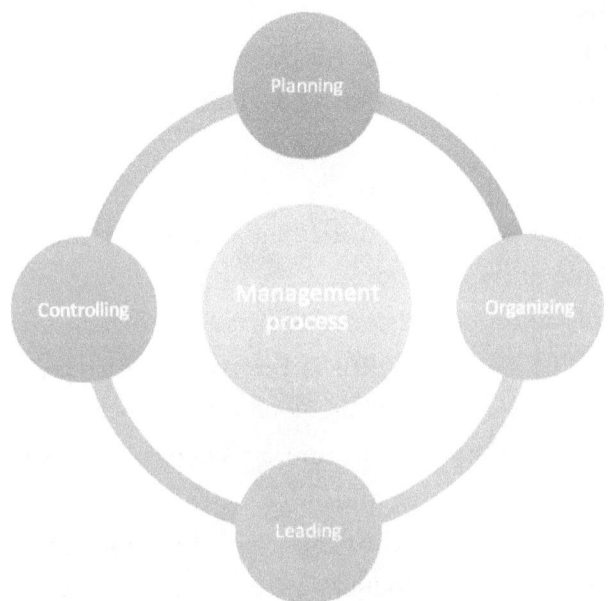

QUALITY: W.Edwards Deming defined quality as follows: Good quality means a predictable degree of uniformity and dependability with a quality standard suited to the customer. The underlying philosophy of all definitions is the same – consistency of conformance and performance, and keeping the customer in mind.

Juran defined quality as "fitness for use":

Quality is about getting it right first time everytime

Quality is always planned and never accidental.

QUALITY DIMENSIONS:

- Performance
- Reliability
- Durability
- Serviceability
- Aesthetics
- Features
- Perceived Value
- Reliability

DIMENSIONS OF QUALITY

CONFORMANCE: Conformance is the precision with which the product or service meets the specified standards. How well the product conforms to the customer's expectations

E.g.-Mileage,

DURABILITY: Durability measures the length of a product's life. That means useful life of the product

E.g. - Useful life in miles, resistance to rust & corrosion

SERVICEABLITY: Serviceability is the speed with which the product can be put into service when it breaks down, as well as the competence and the behavior of the service person. Refers to after sales service

E.g. - Handling of complaints and/or requests for information

AESTHETICS: Aesthetics is the subjective dimension indicating the kind of response a user has to a product. It represents the individual's personal preference. Appearance, feel, smell, taste

E.g. - Interior design, soft touch,

PERCEIVED QUALITY: Perceived Quality is the quality attributed to a good or service based on indirect measures! How a customer perceives the quality of the product based on his perception and the knowledge he has gathered about the product indirect evaluation of quality (e.g. reputation)

E.g. - Top-rated car

PERFORMANCE: Main characteristics of the product/service

E.g. - Everything works, fit & finish ride, handling, grade of materials used

ADVANTAGES OF QUALITY

- Freedom from harmful effect
- Economies of cost
- Benefits to producer and consumer
- Accountability for resource conservation
- Maximise use of human talent
- Brand perception

- Competitive advantage
- Value for money
- Cost control
- Internal acceptance

QUALITY MANAGEMENT

Aims to achieve and maintain the desired quality within an organization. It aims to achieve consistency in product and services of an organization. It is a combination of overseeing all the acts and process that are aimed towards achieving the desired quality standards aimed at. It also includes having a quality policy and is a continuous process of improvement also named as TQM (Total Quality Management).

FOUR STEPS IN QUALITY MANAGEMENT

QUALITY PLANNING: The process of establishing the quality standards and how they will be achieved in an organization

QUALITY IMPROVEMENT: A purposeful change in the process to improve the overall confidence or reliability of the resultant product/ service

QUALITY ASSURANCE: (QA) Is a way of preventing mistakes or defects in manufactured products and avoiding problems when delivering solutions or services to customers

QUALITY CONTROL: (QC) Is a system of maintaining standards in manufactured products! QC focuses on identifying a defect. It is about detecting problems or quality issues and is reactive in nature.

QC & QA are very closely linked to each other, both are part of Quality Management QA process is designed to prevent a defect and QC process is designed to identify a defect

SERVICE QUALITY & DIMENSIONS

Gronroos (1984) identified two service quality dimensions the technical aspect that is "what" service is provided and functional aspect and "how" the service is provided. The customers perceive what he/she receives as the outcome of the process in which the resources are used that is the technical quality. But he also and more often importantly, perceives how the process itself functions that is the functions quality.The SERVQUAL instrument developed by Parasuraman et al (1991) is being used in many studies of service quality. This is because it has a generic application and is a practical approach to any area. SERVQUAL instrument is designed to identify and measure the gaps between customers' expectations and perceptions of the service received. Service quality from the consumer's perspective depends on the direction and degree of difference between the expected service and the perceived service. Thus by comparing customer's expected service with customer's perceived service, hotels, for example can determine whether its service standard is appropriate. The gap between expectations and perceptions of performance determines the level of service quality from a customer's perspective.

DIMENSIONS OF SERVICE QUALITY:

TANGIBLES: This is about physical appearance which includes employees,facilities, equipment, design etc .For example in a hotel: interior design, menu card, staff appearance, lobby look & feel, room designs etc

RELIABILITY: It is the ability of the service firm to perform the service promised dependably and accurately. It is the ability to perform the promised service accurately.

For example: Making accurate bills, performing standardised services or as promised services

ASSURANCE: It refers to the knowledge and courtesy of the employees of companies and their ability to inspire trust and confidence in the customer mind.

Example: Showing courtesy, competence & credibility

EMPATHY: It is the caring individualized attention the service firm providers to each customer, it is the ability of the service provider to feel & think like customer

Listening to customer needs, showing care & Understanding, personalized attention

RESPONSIVENESS: It is the willingness to help customers & serve them promptly

For example: serving customers promptly, Willingness to serve, helpfulness

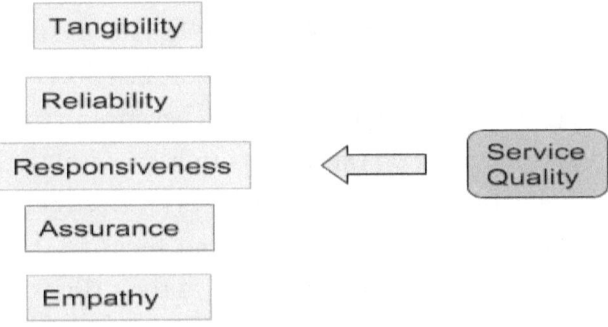

PARETO PRINCIPLE: Man behind the concept -Vilfredo Federico Damaso Pareto was born in Italy in 1848. He would go on to become an important philosopher and economist.

It's a theory that says that the connection between inputs and outputs is not a balanced one and that 80% of the effects come from 20% of the causes or 80% of the results are based on 20% of the efforts. The essence of this principle is to differentiate between Vital Few from Trivial Many. The tool helps in focusing, more on the aspects that are vital to the efficiency or performance. It also helps work force to prioritize there work better, whereby they commit more time energy and focus to the aspects that matter the most rather than spending most of their time on aspects that have little or almost no effect on the output

Some of the examples of Pareto's Principle are:

- 20% of the employees produce 80% of the results
- 20% of the criminal's o 80% of the crimes
- 80% pollution is caused by 20% of the factories
- 20% of the customers give 80% of business
- 20% of stocks yield 80% of the stock market results
- 80% of our output is from out 20% time of work

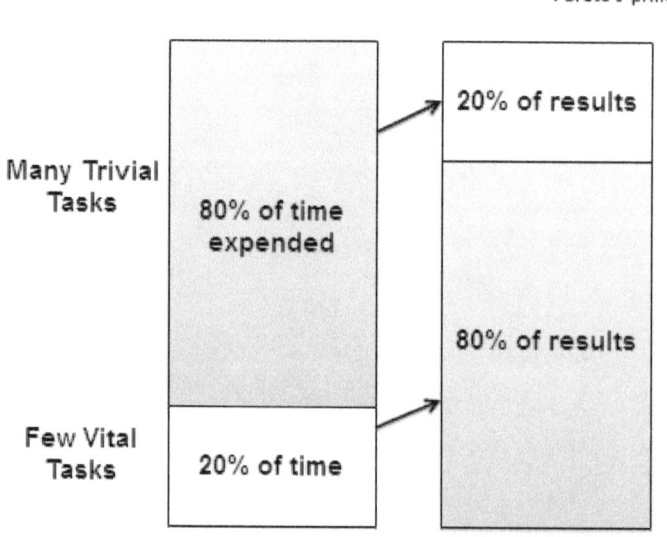

Pareto's principle

SWOT ANALYSIS: SWOT is a strategic planning technique that helps a person or business to assess four crucial aspects i.e strengths, weaknesses, opportunities & threats. It is used to evaluate a company's competitive position & strategic planning. It also plays a vital role in assessing viability of projects or investments.

STRENGTH: Refers to the aspects which an organization is good at or may be expert at. It could be a unique patented technology; it could be extraordinary customer service or unique delivery process.

WEAKNESSES: This is the aspect of business which an organization is weak at, compared to its competition or it could even be certain factors that stop a company to perform at its best. For example- high amount of loans, cash crunch, high employee turnover etc.

OPPORTUNITIES: These are favourable external factors that an organization can take advantage of. For example, a tapping new untapped market overseas where the government is providing support for new entrants

THREATS: All those factors that have the potential to harm an organization. It could be growing cost, labour scarcity, increasing completion etc.

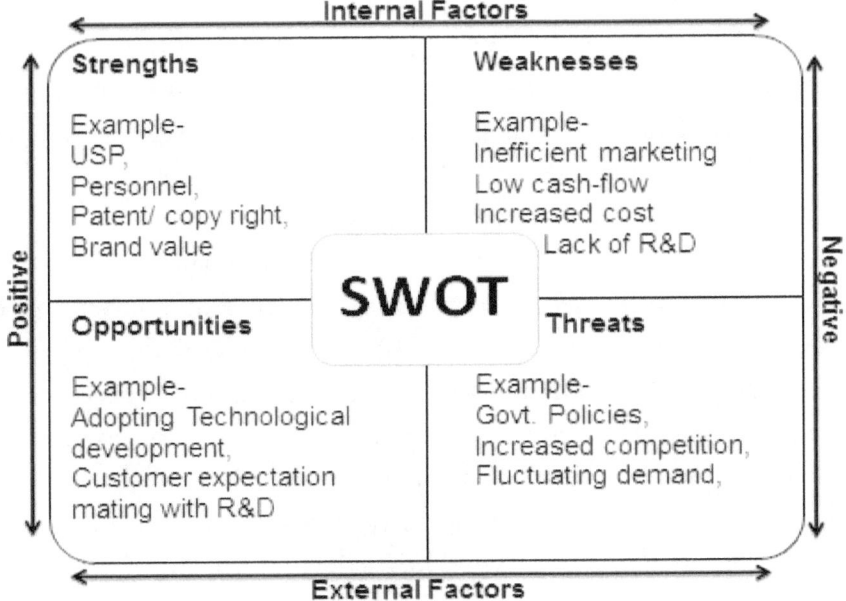

MASLOWS HIERARCHY OF NEEDS

Abraham Maslow proposed his Hierarchy of Needs Theory in 1943. This theory classically depicts human motivation. These five needs are

PHYSIOLOGICAL NEEDS: These are the basic necessities of life like needs of air, water, food, clothing and shelter.

SAFETY NEEDS: these include physical, environmental and emotional safety and protection. For instance- Job security, health security, etc.

SOCIAL NEEDS: Social needs include the need for love, affection, care, belongingness, and friendship.

ESTEEM NEEDS: Esteem needs are of two types: internal esteem needs (self- respect, confidence, competence, achievement and freedom) and external esteem needs (recognition, power, status, attention and admiration).

SELF ACTUALIZATION NEEDS: This include the urge to become what you are capable of becoming/what you have the potential to become. It includes the need for growth and self-contentment. According to Maslow, individuals are motivated by unsatisfied needs. As each of these needs is significantly satisfied, it drives and forces the next need to emerge. Maslow grouped the five needs into two categories - **Higher-order needs** and **Lower-order needs**. The physiological and the safety needs constituted the lower-order needs. These lower-order needs are mainly satisfied externally. The social, esteem, and self-actualization needs constituted the higher-order needs. These higher-order needs are generally satisfied internally, i.e., within an individual. Thus, we can conclude that during boom period, the employees lower-order needs are significantly met.

PARADOX OF CHOICES

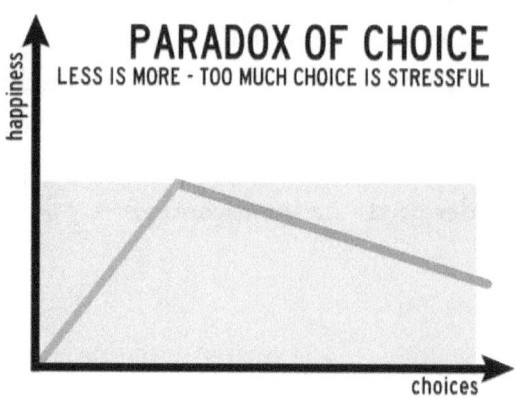

The Paradox of Choice principle was explained by the American psychologist Barry Schwartz in his book The Paradox of Choice – Why more is less (2004). Schwartz explains and convicnes how, rather than increasing our capacity to make a decision, an abundance of choice can often lead to feelings of anxiety, loneliness and depression. Even though we belive that we'd be happier if given a larger range of choices in everyday life, we actually make better decisions and end up happier and more satisfied when fewer options are presented to us. Reducing choices reduces consumer anxiety as too many options is overwhelming for our brains and, having to choose just one option from a large selection of "desirable" options often leads us to feel unsatisfied and keep pondering on those other possibilities we missed out on. The more choices we have, the higher our expectations become and the lower our sense of final accomplishment and satisfaction. It can even lead to "overanalysis and no action", where we are so overwhelmed by the choice on offer that we fail to make any decision.

S.M.A.R.T GOALS

Goals are part of every aspect of business/life and provide a sense of direction, motivation, clarity and focus. By setting goals for yourself, one gets motivated to aim at precise target.

A SMART goal is used to help guide goal setting. SMART stands for **Specific, Measurable, Achievable, Realistic,** and **Timely.** Therefore, a SMART goal incorporates all of these criteria to help focus your efforts and improves as well as increase the chances of achieving your goal.

- **SPECIFIC:** Well- defined
- **MEASURABLE:** Measure how much progess one has made, and the progess should be measurable against the established goal
- **ACHIEVABLE:** Challenging yet attainable/achievable
- **REALISTIC:** Within the availability of resources, knowledge and time
- **TIME BOUND:** Enough time to achieve the goal, & define a time line to achieve the goal

PRODUCT LIFE CYCLE

Product life cycle is the historical study of (sales of) the product. It includes when it was introduced; when it was getting fast acceptance; when it was at its peak of its position; when it started dropping from the peak; and when it vanished from the marketplace. Product passes through certain stages during its life span.

Product Life Cycle

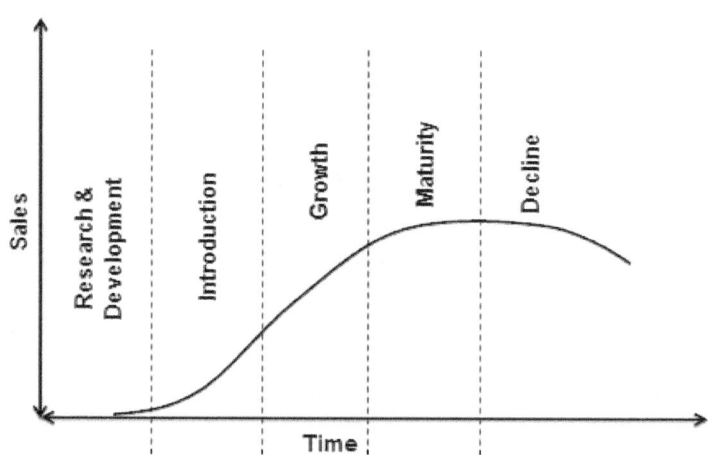

- A product life cycle is the amount of time a product goes from being introduced into the market until it's taken away or discontinued from the market.
- There are four stages in a product's life cycle—introduction, growth, maturity, and decline.
- The concept of product life cycle helps improve overall business decision-making, from pricing and promotion to expansion or cost-cutting
- Innovative and more competitive successful products push older ones out of the market.

CBA (COST BENEFIT ANALYSIS): Jules Dupuit, a French engineer and economist, introduced this great concept in 1840's. It became popular as a simple way of weighing up project costs and benefits, to help decide whether to go ahead with a project.

As its name suggests, Cost-Benefit Analysis involves adding up the benefits of a course of action, and then comparing these with the costs associated with it. A cost-benefit analysis is a process, businesses use, to analyse decisions. The business or analyst sums the benefits of a situation or action and then subtracts the costs associated with taking that action. Some consultants or analysts also build models to assign a dollar value on intangible items, such as the benefits and costs associated with living in a certain town.

- A cost-benefit analysis (CBA) is the process used to measure the benefits of a decision or taking action minus the costs associated with taking that action.
- A CBA involves measurable financial metrics such as revenue earned or costs saved as a result of the decision to pursue a project.
- A CBA can also include intangible benefits and costs or effects from a decision such as employee morale and customer satisfaction

PARALYSIS OF ANALYSIS: It is not enough to be busy, so are the ants. The question is what are we busy doing.

Henry David Theory

Paralysis of analysis is about over thinking or over analysing of a situation that it may lead to delayed or often no decision taking at all. It about being in situation whereby one is torn between-to do or not to do situation for a very long time and spends most of the time analysing the situation and gets sucked into no action.

In spite of the best of the analysis we cannot be 100% sure of any decision and there is always some risk involved in all endeavours. Paralysis of analysis is a vicious cycle which ends up in taking no action. It happens due to overthinking and taking enough action.

WHAT CAUSES PARALYSIS OF ANALYSIS:

- Inability to take decision
- Fear of consequences of a decision
- Fear of failing or making a mistake
- Habit of procrastination, laziness,
- Feeling overwhelmed by the situation and over information & options
- Over analyzing, overcomplicates an otherwise simple decision
- Over analyzing situation for long time to look for a perfect solution

HOW TO ESCAPE TRAP OF PARALYSIS OF ANALYSIS: Understand that it is not practical to keep collecting all information in the world before the decision is taken

We must set a date by the decision must be made

We must select not all the information but only the most relevant information which will help us take the decision

Align the decision making with the teams and the experts

INNOVATION CURVE: Innovation curves based on the willingness to adapt new technology and helps categorize customers in categories. The concept emphasizes that the market place has consumers who differ in their enthusiasm to adopt new introduced products/technology.

Innovation curve

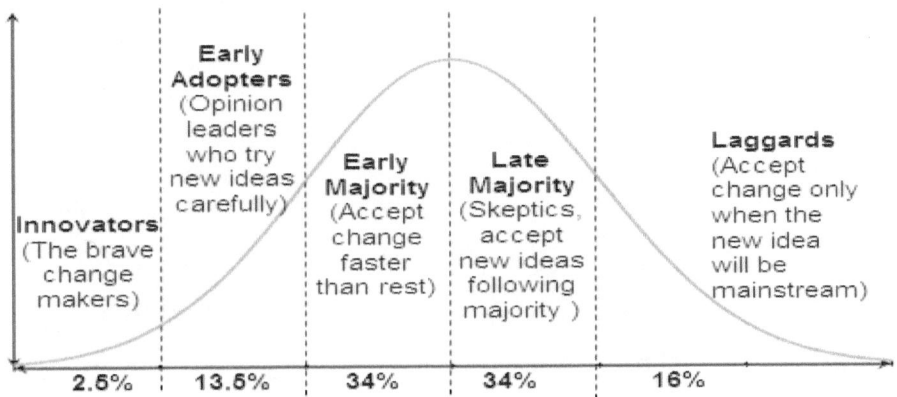

INNOVATORS: Customers of this category are small in size i.e. 2.5% of the population but are the first ones to adopt a new technology.

EARLY ADOPTERS: This category comprises 13.5% and this category is comparatively young in age & high on influence and leadership.

EARLY MAJORITY: Third category comprises of 34% which takes longer time than innovators & early adopters but is much higher in % than the first two categories.

LATE MAJORITY: This category takes longer to adopt a new technology as they are often sceptical of the technology and indulge in information collection and research before they are completely convinced to adopt. This segment is 34% of the population.

LAGGARDS: This category is reluctant to change and adopt any new technology. They are happy doing things the old ways with old technology as the feel comfortable using that. By the time they adopt the new technology, the technology is almost on the verge of becoming obsolete.

BREAK EVEN POINT EXPLAIN: In simple words, the **break-even point** can be defined as a point where total costs (expenses) and total sales (revenue) are equal. Break-even point can be described as a point where there is no net profit or loss. The firm just "breaks even." Any company which wants to make abnormal profit, desires to have a break-even point. Graphically, it is the point where the total cost and the total revenue curves meet.

Break-Even Point

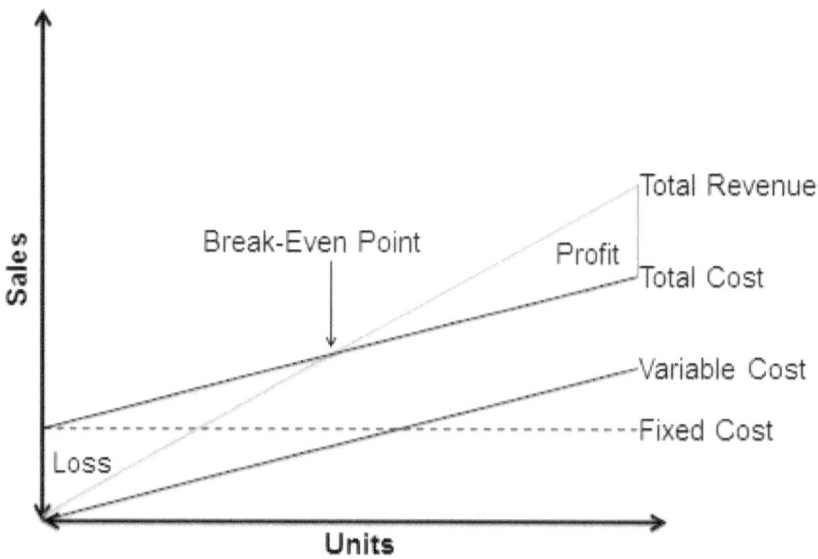

BCG MATRIX

Boston Consulting Group: The purpose of this tool is to identify which products a company should invest in more and which products a company should divest in

It an extremely effective tool that provides graphical representation of the product portfolio of an organization, based om their market share and industry growth rate as below.

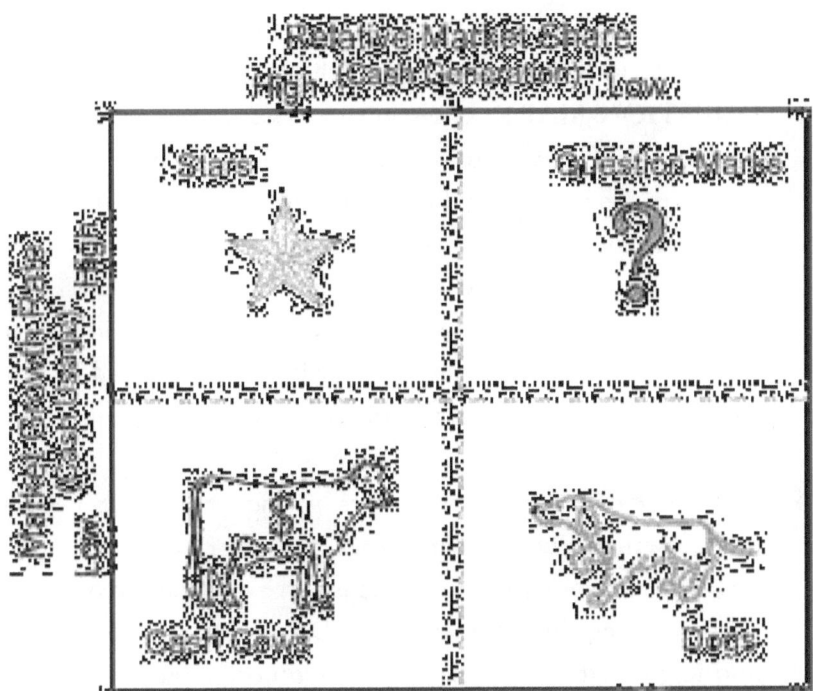

This grid helps the leaders to allocate resources to the product line based on their position in the market place. The four cells of this matrix have been called as stars, cash cows, question marks and dogs. Each of these cells represents a particular type of business

Resources are allocated to the business units according to their situation on the grid.

1. **STARS**: Represent business units having large market share in a fast-growing industry. They may generate cash but because of fast growing market, stars require huge investments to maintain their lead. If the stars become successful they become cash cows when the industry matures.

2. **CASH COWS**: Cash Cows represent business units that have large market share in a mature, slow growing industry. Cash cows require little investment and generate cash that can be utilized for investment in other business units. These businesses

or product are the key source of cash flow for the organization. Organizations stay focused on such products.

3. **QUESTION MARK:** Question marks represent business units having low relative market share and located in a high growth industry. They require large amount of cash to maintain or gain market share. Question marks are generally new product or services which have a good future prospective. Most new businesses start as question marks & the company tries to enter a high growth market. Questions marks have potential to become stars but if ignored and not managed well they may turn into dogs.

4. **DOGS:** Dogs represent businesses having weak market shares in low-growth markets. They neither generate cash nor they require huge amount of cash. Unless dogs serve a specific reason on the portfolio they should be divested. Dogs have weak market share and low profits. Number of dogs in an organizational portfolio should be avoided.

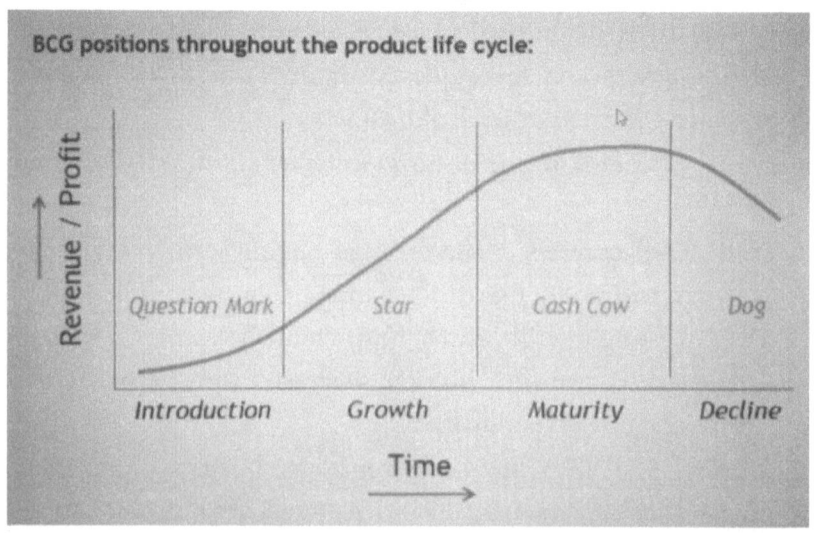

PDCA CYCLE: PLAN-DO-CHECK-ADJUST

Also called Deming Cycle/Wheel by Dr William Deming

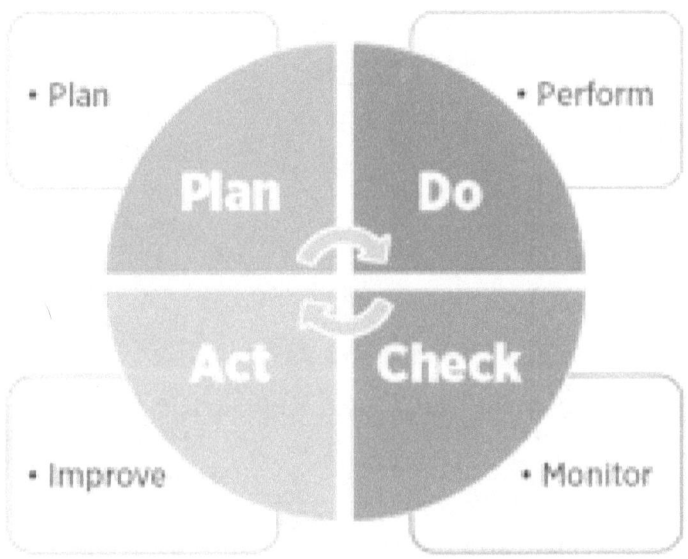

This is a four-step model for carrying out change, solving problems, continuous improvement of processes and products.

PLAN: Identify and understand the problem. Explore the information and generate and screen ideas and draft a strong implementation plan

DO: Implement and test the safety and effectiveness of the solution as pilot test. The pilot could be in one department of a company before implementing in the entire organization or may be in a geographical restriction before using it across the country. After running the pilot test gather data to show whether the change has worked or not.

CHECK: At this level check the result and compare it against the expectations whether the idea was a success. If the plan worked advance to step 4. If the plan has failed than return to step 1.

ACT: At this level you apply and implement the solution. Even if the plan works still continue to look for more solution to make the process better

KAIZEN

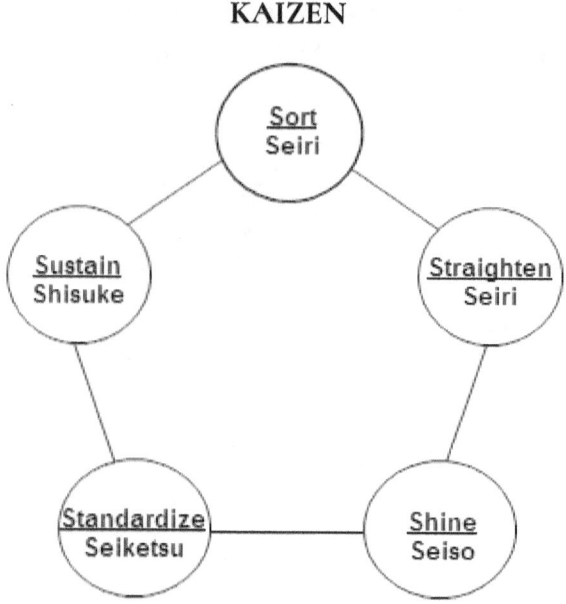

- Seiri; Sort, Clearing, Classify
- Seiton; Straighten, Simplify, Set in Order
- Seiso; Sweep, Shine, Scrub, Clean and Check
- Seiketsu; Standardize, Stabilize, Conformity
- Shitsuke; Sustain, Self Discipline, Standardization

Kaizen is a Japanese business philosophy that focuses on gradually improving productivity by involving all employees and by making the work environment more efficient.

Kaizen translates to "change for the better" or "continuous improvement." The small changes used in kaizen can involve quality control, just-in-time delivery, standardized work, the use of efficient equipment, and the elimination of waste.

Changes can come from any employee anytime and don't have to happen slowly, although kaizen recognizes that small changes now can have big future impacts.

MCKINSEY'S 7 S MODEL

McKinsey's & S Fra+mework

Structure is the organization of business units & flow of info.

Strategy is the way of seeking competitive advantages

Systems are the processes & procedures that company follows

Shared Values are companies guiding norms and standards

Skills are the abilities & competences of firm's manpower.

Staff this includes the company's personnel policy & budget.

Style Represents the top managements way of leadership

The McKinsey 7S Model is an organizational tool that assesses the wellbeing of seven internal factors of an organization as a means of determining whether a company has the structural support to be successful.

The Model comprises a mix of hard elements, which are clear-cut and influenced by management, and soft elements, which are fuzzier and influenced by corporate culture.

The 7S Model specifies seven factors that are classified as "hard" and "soft" elements. Hard elements are easily identified and influenced by management, while soft elements are fuzzier, more intangible and influenced by corporate culture.

THE HARD ELEMENTS ARE:

- **STRATEGY:** This is the overall approach of achieving of goals and objectives. This is about clearly articulating an organizational vision and mission statement. This includes short term as well as long term goals in order to achieve competitive sustainable advantage.

- **STRUCTURE:** This refers to the organizational chart, and defines who is responsible for what
- **SYSTEMS:** Are the process and procedures of a company. How activities are done

THE SOFT ELEMENTS ARE:

- **SHARED VALUES:** These are at the core of the Mckinsey's 7S Model. these are the core values of the organization, based on which the culture of the company is formed.
- **SKILLS:** The skills of the organization and their competencies
- **STYLES:** This refers to the leadership style of the organization
- **STAFF:** This refers to the overall staff and their capabilities

MARKETING MIX: This term refers to the set of actions, or tactics, that a company uses to promote its brand or product in the market. The 4Ps make up a typical marketing mix - Price, Product, Promotion and Place. Marketing mix todays world includes several other Ps like Packaging, Positioning, People and even Politics as vital mix elements.

Product	Price	Place	Promotion
Quality	Discounts	Retail	Advertisement
After sales services	Credit	Wholesale	Special offers
Warranty	terms	Direct sales	Direct marketing
Brand value	Bundling	E-commerce	
Packaging			

PRICE: refers to the value that is put for a product. It depends on costs of production, segment targeted, ability of the market to pay, supply - demand and a host of other direct and indirect factors. There can be several types of pricing strategies, each tied in with an overall business plan. Pricing can also be used a demarcation, to differentiate and enhance the image of a product.

PRODUCT: refers to the item actually being sold. The product must deliver a minimum level of performance; otherwise even the best work on the other elements of the marketing mix won't do any good.

PLACE: refers to the place/point of sale. All marketers aim at catching the eye of the consumer and making it easy for them to buy it this the main aim of a good distribution or 'place' strategy. Retailers pay a premium for the right location. The key to successful retail business is 'location, location, location'.

PROMOTION: this refers to all the activities initiated & focused to make the product or service known to the user and trade. This includes advertising, word of mouth, press reports, incentives, commissions and awards. It may also include consumer discount schemes, direct marketing, contests and prizes.

TQM (Total Quality Management): When we buy up any service/ product or even buy fruits from the roadside vendor, quality is an important parameter to consider and so to provide quality, total quality management comes into the picture. According to ISO (International Organization for Standardization) describe TQM as "a management approach of a system centred on quality, based on the aid of all its associate and focus at deep-rooted success through customer satisfaction and profit to all associate of the organization and society."

STEPS IN TQM (total quality management):

1. Project Selection
2. Set up data collection system
3. Connect and analysis data
4. Diagnose root cause
5. Select and Implement solution
6. Confirm validity of solution
7. Standardize new way of business
8. Set up maintenance system
9. Review Improvement price

CHARACTERISTICS OF TQM

- Committed management.
- Quality is an attitude
- Do it right first time
- Top management is involved
- Adopting and communicating about total quality management.
- Closer customer relations.
- Closer provider relations.
- Benchmarking.
- Increased training.
- Open organization
- Employee empowerment.
- Flexible production.
- Process improvements.
- Process measuring

SEVICE GAP ANALYSIS: The Gap Model of Service Quality (aka the Customer Service Gap Model or the 5 Gap Model) is a framework which can help us to understand customer satisfaction.

The model shows the five major satisfaction gaps that organizations must address when seeking to meet customer expectations. The model was first proposed by A. Parasuraman, Valarie Zeithaml, and Leonard L. Berry in 1985.

In the Gap Model of Service Quality, customer satisfaction is largely a function of perception. If the customer perceives that the service meets their expectations then they will be satisfied. If not, they'll be dissatisfied.

The Gap Model of Service Quality is a framework which can help us to understand common customer satisfaction issues.

FIVE COMMON GAPS WHICH OCCUR:

- The Knowledge Gap
- The Policy Gap
- The Delivery Gap
- The Communication Gap
- The Customer Gap

JIT- JUST IN TIME: The just-in-time inventory system is a management strategy that aims at minimizing inventory and increases efficiency.

Just-in-time (JIT) manufacturing is also known as the Toyota Production System (TPS) Toyota adopted the system in the 1970s.

The success of the JIT production process depends on steady production, high-quality workmanship, no machine breakdowns, and reliable vendor.

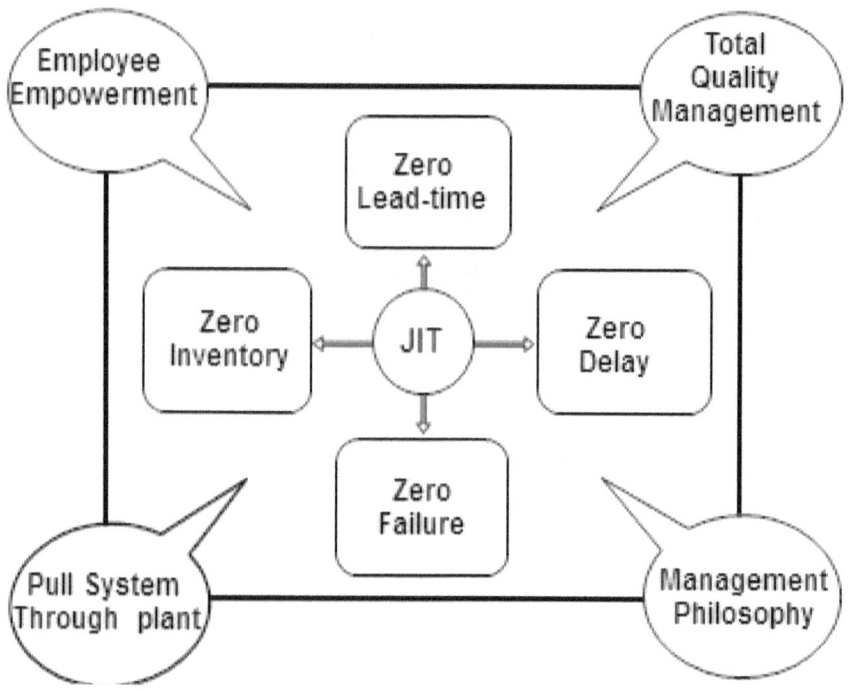

PORTERS FIVE FORCES ANALYSIS

Porter's Five Forces Tools

Threat of New Substitutes	Threat of New Entrants
Bargaining Power of the Buyers	Industry Rivalry / Bargaining Power of the Suppliers

Porter's Five Forces analysis includes a critical analysis of five separate forces that shape the overall extent of competition. Developed by Michael Porter (1979).

THREAT TO NEW ENTRANTS: Profitable industries that yield higher returns will definitely attract new firms. New entrants will decrease the profitability for other firms in the industry.

THREAT OF SUBSTITUTES: A substitute product will use a different technology/innovation to solve the same economic need in the market.

BARGAINING POWER OF CUSTOMERS: The ability of customers to put the firm under pressure also affects the customer's sensitivity to price changes.

BARGAINING POWER OF SUPPLIERS: Suppliers of raw materials, components, labor, and expertise to the firm can be a source of power over the firm when there are few substitutes.

COMPETITIVE RIVALRY: Having an understanding of industry rivals is vital to successfully market a product. Positioning plays an important role. An organization must be aware of its competitors' marketing strategies and pricing.

BUSINESS MANAGEMENT CONCEPTS:

UNIQUE SALES PROPOSITION: Is that point or special feature about your product that stands out amongst the competition. It gives a great advantage if you have a product or service which has a feature which your completion does not have, but even though the competition has that feature but has not been talking about it in the market place it is open for you to be taken and build your marketing campaign around it. Having a USP gives a distinct advantage to the company in the market place.

USP does not necessarily mean that you are doing it best than anyone else it means that you were first one to claim that USP as long as it matters to the customers. Anyone claiming the same USP after your will feature as a second and not a pioneer. It is all about focusing on a single feature or a factor that would make that company special.

To discover ones USP one must as some questions –

1. What do customers want?
2. What can your company do that no other company does?

The idea of the USP was introduced by Rosser Reeves of Ted Bates & Company in the US in 1940. Reeves believed that the purpose of advertising is to sell. Towards this end, he developed television commercials that featured the unique selling proposition of the product. This was typified in an advert he designed for Anacin, an analgesic for headaches. The ad lasted for seven years, grated and annoyed most viewers, and was successful in tripling the product's sales.

You may also want to consider what competitors do and talk about so you can avoid this in your USP. Although it is less fashionable than a customer value proposition, the unique selling proposition.

IDENTIFYING COMPETITION SET: A Competitive Set (or Comp Set) is a group of hotels that are seen as direct competitors to your own hotel. Hotels will often compare their performance against Competition set hotels, in order to find ways to make their own offering more competitive. Competitive sets are used for benchmarking purposes, market penetration analyses and to help develop positioning strategies. Many hotels use rate shopping tools to compare their current pricing with the ones of their competitors in order to make proper pricing decisions. The purpose of a competitive set in a hotel study is to provide a context for analysing the historical performance of a hotel and a basis for making projections. A competitive set should not be selected based on one element but rather on a thorough analysis of the total supply in the market. The main factors to consider and research are location, brand, product type, quality, and ADR relative to the subject property or the proposed subject hotel. By weighing these factors, an appropriate competitive set can be identified, which will provide a good base for conducting supply and demand projections and give a more accurate picture of the existing competitive market.

BENCHMARKING: Benchmarking is a process of measuring the performance of a company's products, services, or processes against those of another business which are considered to be the best in the industry, aka "best in class". This strategy helps in comparing one's business with the best in class business and make essential changes to become more competitive in the marketplace.

LEVERAGING: Leverage results from using borrowed capital as a funding source when investing to expand the firm's asset base and generate returns on risk capital. Leverage is an investment strategy of using borrowed money—specifically, the use of various financial instruments or borrowed capital—to increase the potential return of an investment. Leverage can also refer to the amount of debt a firm uses to finance assets.

BACK WARD INTEGRATION: Backward integration is a form of vertical integration in which a company expands its role by doing a process which was earlier done by another company or was outsourced. For example, a chain of coffee café stores, acquires a coffee plantation lands would be backward integration which means to start doing something themselves which was a process before the production of their product or service

FORWARD INTEGRATION: Forward integration is a business strategy that involves a form of vertical integration whereby business activities are expanded to include control of the direct distribution or supply of a company's products. This type of vertical integration is conducted by a company advancing along the supply chain.

FOMO (FEAR OF MISSING OUT): Too many choices often lead to fatigue to choose. Too many choices may lead to paralysis of decision making. This concept challenges the notion that more choices give more happiness or more choices give more freedom. Too many choices often lead to raised levels of anxiety, depression and wastage of time analysing and comparing them.

ECONOMIES OF SCALE: Economist Adam Smith identified the division of labour and specialization as the two key means to achieving a larger return on production. Through these two techniques, employees would not only be able to concentrate on a specific task but with time, improve the skills necessary to perform their jobs. The tasks could then be performed better and faster. Hence, through such efficiency, time and money could be saved while production levels increased.

When more units of services and products are made at a large scale and along It refers to the concept that as the company grows and produces more quantity it has increased chances to bring down the cost per unit.

DIS-ECONOMIES OF SCALE: Diseconomies of scale happen when a company or business grows so large that the costs per unit increase. It takes place when economies of scale no longer function for a firm. With this principle, rather than experiencing continued decreasing costs and increasing output, a firm sees an increase in costs when output is increased. Diseconomies of scale occur when the expansion of output comes with increasing average unit costs. Diseconomies of scale can involve factors internal to an operation or external conditions beyond a firm's control. Diseconomies of scale may result from technical issues in a production process, organizational management issues, or resource constraints on productive inputs.

OPPORTUNITY COST: Opportunity cost is the forgone benefit that would have been derived by an option not chosen.

To properly evaluate opportunity costs, the costs and benefits of every option available must be considered and weighed against the others. Considering the value of opportunity costs can guide individuals and organizations to more profitable decision-making

Calculation of Opportunity Cost: Opportunity Cost=FO-CO
- FO=Return on best foregone option
- CO=Return on chosen option

Opportunity cost is one of the key concepts of economics, but is not an accounting concept so does not show in financial records. It is basically a financial analysis concept. It means that every decision has a cost and not even that every decision that has not been taken has a cost too. It is about making a choice and whenever we make a decision or a choice, we have to let go another opportunity or options. It is also mentioned as a "trade off"! The concept refers to the next best or highest value alternative use of the resources (time, money or efforts). Opportunity cost may not always be money, it could also be time, energy and efforts. For example, if we plan to spend time and money watching a movie and the next best option was to read a book on motivation, and we ended up watching the movie then the opportunity cost of the movie is the cost of the movie ticket + the loss of not having gained the knowledge for having not read the book.

- The concept is extremely crucial because life and time is limited. It is all about scarcity. If we choose a certain profession, we have to let go some other profession.
- Concept may be understood as what is the next best option that we are giving up to gain something else. It is about forgone opportunities
- For example, if we have Rs. 100000/we may have option to invest in business, keep in bank as fixed deposit, invest in stock market but if we choose one we have to forgo all the other opportunities.
- It could also be decisions like paying college fee earning higher education and expecting to earn many folds in the coming years in corporate jobs
- It could be spending money on a holiday trip or paying the car mortgage

EXPLICIT OPPORTUNITY COST: A cost involving monetary payment is known as an **explicit cost**. These costs have a definite, readily identifiable value. Employee wages, utilities, and equipment are all examples of explicit costs. Even bartered goods and services are considered explicit costs, because they have a specific monetary worth.

IMPLICIT OPPORTUNITY COST: An **implicit cost** is the opportunity cost that occurs from allocation of resources for a specific purpose, which cannot easily be assigned a monetary value. Business expenses that cannot be assigned to any specific good or service are also implicit costs. For instance, the time required to train a new employee is an implicit cost. Maintenance activities such as taking a robot offline for routine service are also implicit costs. Many opportunity costs are implicit costs—the cost of giving up the next best alternative.

BOGO- BUY ONE GET ONE or **"two for the price of one"** is a common form of sales promotion. Economist "Alex Tabarrok" has argued that the success of this promotion lies in the fact that the price actually considers the fact that two items are being sold. The price of "one" is somewhat nominal and is typically raised when used as part of a buy one get one free deal. Whilst the cost per item is proportionately cheaper than if bought on its own, it is not actually half price shoppers generally overvalue the benefits of "free" even when compared to higher-quality items at a discounted price. BOGO is a great discount technique to use to appeal to consumers. Buy One, Get One is a great tool that can help you get rid of your less desirable inventory quicker and maintain profitability at the same time. Sales can be one of the most effective types of promotions. If executed properly, you can see higher sales, bigger orders, and better conversion rates. A well-executed Buy One, Get One deal is a plus for your business and for your shoppers, which is why it is understandable that retailers have jumped on the BOGO hype.

FEASIBILITY STUDY: A feasibility study is an analysis that takes all of a project's relevant factors into account—including economic, technical, legal, and scheduling considerations—to ascertain the likelihood of completing the project successfully. Project managers use feasibility studies to discern the pros and cons of undertaking a project before they invest a lot of time and money into it. Feasibility studies can provide a company's management with crucial information that could prevent the company from entering blindly into risky businesses.

Sales and Marketing

SALES & MARKETING

Sales & Marketing are two key functions of an organization- both have a crucial impact on lead generation & sales of the product and services. Sales refers to all the activities that leads to the selling of the products and services. On the other hand, marketing activities lead to getting people interested in the products. Sales is crucial to create revenue and growth of the organization but to have sales, it is essential that organizations have a strong marketing plan.

Sales is a transaction between a buyer and a seller, whereby the buyer receives the goods and services against exchange of money or may be an asset.

Sales teams are responsible for managing relationship with clients and explain and provide them solution that eventually leads to sales

Sales process is about closing a sale and it consists of interpersonal interactions. Sales is about one to one interaction, through meetings and through a lot of networking

Marketing is all those activities that ignite customer interest towards the products and services that a company has to offer. Marketers employ lot of research and information about the customers and their interest so that they can come out with strategies and marketing campaigns that attract people towards their products and services

DIFFERENCE BETWEEN SALES AND MARKETING

SALES	MARKETING
Sales refers to all the activities that leads to the selling of the products and services.	Marketing activities lead to getting people interested in the products.
Narrow concept.	Wider concept.
Is a PUSH approach	Is a PULL approach
It is a part of marketing process.	It involves a set of activities.
It revolves around needs and interest of the seller.	It revolves around needs and interest of the buyer.

DIFFERENCE BETWEEN ADVERTISING AND PERSONAL SELLING

ADVERTISING	PERSONAL SELLING
• This is impersonal	• This is personal
• There is uniformity of messages which means message is same for all.	• The message has no uniformity which means keeps changing.
• It lacks flexibility.	• Completely flexible.
• TV, radio, newspapers are media.	• Through salesman.
• Role is to create & maintain interest in product.	• It immediately affects decision to Purchase
• Reach can be carried to numerous people at same time.	• Reach is to a single person or a group of persons at a time.

WHAT IS A BRAND?

A **brand** is a product, service, name, logo, word, sentence that any company uses to distinguish itself in the market. It could be a combination of one or two or more of the above elements to create a distinguished brand.

TRADEMARK: Brands those are legally approved are Trademarks

BRAND POSITIONING: Brand positioning has been defined by Kotler as "the act of designing the company's offering and image to occupy a distinctive place in the mind of the target market". Brand positioning takes place in the minds of the customers. And its all about perception. Positioning aims to achieve how different is one brand from another and wants the customers to perceive their brand in a certain way.

BRAND MANAGEMENT: Brand management is a function of marketing that aims to achieve an increased perceived value of a product line or brand over a period of time. Successful brand management enables the price of products or services to go up and adds customer loyalty by creating positive brand associations and images or a strong awareness of the brand.

BRAND EQUITY: Brand Equity is about the value of the brand in the customer's mind which is determined by consumer perception and their experiences with the brand. If customer feels highly of the brand and hold a positive image of it in their minds than it reflects that the brand equity is high

POSITIONING: Positioning refers to the place that a brand occupies in the mind of its consumers. Also, it is about how different and distinguished a brand is, as compared to the similar or competitive products or services.

DIFFERENCE BETWEEN STRATEGY AND TACTIC?

As said in the "Art of War" by Sun Tzu about 2500 years ago

"Strategy without tactic is the slowest route to victory & Tactic without strategy is noise before the defeat"

Strategy defines the long-term approach, how we are going to achieve our goals. Strategy talks about the path you would need to achieve an organizational goal

For organizational success Michael Porter has suggested key three strategies

1.   Cost leadership (Without frills)
2.   Differentiation (Uniqueness in Product & Services)

3. Focus (Staying focused in the product and service category and achieving specialization in that)

Strategy and tactic are not against each other but are part of the same team as is often said in the organizations Think Strategically and act tactically. Strategy and tactic must work in line with each other.

Tactic is much more specific than that and is more concrete and smaller steps around shorter time frames & compliment the strategy. A good tactic has a clear purpose to achieve and must aid the strategy. Tactic are those numerous smaller initiatives or specific actions that you will be taking to achieve your goals.

KEY MARKETING TERMS & CONCEPTS

RE-POSITONING: Re-positioning involves changing the market's perceptions of an offering so that it can compete more effectively in its market. It is about making major changes in the positioning of the brand/product. It refers to the process and activities to change the existing space that the brand occupies in the mind of its customers.

BRAND EQUITY: Brand equity refers to a value premium that a company generates from a product with a recognizable name when compared to a generic equivalent. Companies can create brand equity for their products by making them memorable, easily recognizable, and superior in quality and reliability.

MARKETING PLAN: It is a detailed document that explains a company's overall marketing strategy. It explains how a company will implement the complete strategy and allocation of resources to marketing activities.

GREY MARKET: It is unofficial market or a parallel market. It refers to the trade of a commodity through distribution channels that are not authorized by the original manufacturer.

DIGITAL MARKETING: Digital marketing is a component of marketing that is done through internet technologies. Digital marketing refers to marketing delivered through **digital** channels such as search engines, websites, social media, email, and mobile apps. It has become increasingly essential for an organization's growth and transformation as more and more customer spend increasing time online and consume more data digitally

ADVERTISING: Advertising is a paid marketing tactic that involves paying for space to promote a product, service, or cause by the sender of the message. The purpose such message is to influence the purchasing behaviour of customers and persuade them favourably to buy a firm's products and services. Such a paid form of message communication is called advertisement.

MEDIA PLANNING: It is a decision process of identifying and selecting various media in the achievement of marketing goals. It is the process by which marketer plan out where, when how often to run advertisement to achieve increased engagement and return on investment. Some of the areas addressed by media plan are:

- Achieving advertising objectives.
- The selection of appropriate media.
- Frequency of running advertisement campaigns
- Ensuring an appropriate timing of advertising.
- In allocating advertising budget.

Media planning is helpful in setting goals, determining prospective, future planning, conducting a research.

CUSTOMER SUPPORT: Customer support is a range of customer services that a firm offers to its customers to ensure that their customer get the most of its product functionality and to resolve problems if any. Some of the customer support areas are assistance in planning, installation, training, troubleshooting, maintenance, upgrading, and disposal of a product

CONSUMER BEHAVIOUR: Consumer behavior is the study of how individual or consumer groups behave, function, choose select, buy or dispose or repurchase product and services to satisfy their requirements. This study also focuses in consumer emotional, behavior responses, economy, spending pattern etc.

B2B MARKETING: B2B stands for (business-to-business) marketing of product and services. Any company that sells products or services to other businesses or organizations (vs. consumers) is called to be using B2B marketing strategies.

B2C MARKETING: Business-to-consumer marketing or B2C marketing, refers to the tactics and strategies in which a company promotes its products and services to individual people

SALES PROMOTION: Sales promotion is the process of persuading and influencing, a potential customer to buy the product. Sales promotion is often used as a short-term tactic to boost sales.

SALES STRATEGY: Sales strategy is a plan that defines how to go about selling product and service and how to increase sales and profits. The sales strategy can be for an individual sales man or for an organization

MARKET SHARE: Market share refers to the % of a market that is captured by a brand or an organization. Market share is calculated as-

Company sales over a period of time/total sales of the industry over the same period x 100.

Market share is said to be a key indicator of market competitiveness, it reflects, how well a firm is doing against its competitors?

DISTINCTIVE ADVANTAGE BENEFIT (DAB): A distinctive advantage is when a firm's products or services differ from its competitors' offerings and is a competitive advantage for an organization. Some of the examples are superior technology, patented products or processes, exceptional customer service and strong brand identity are all drivers of differential advantage.

LOW HANGING FRUIT: This phrase is used to accomplish a task that is easy to complete or may solve a problem which is easier or may be achieve a target that is extremely easy like catching a low hanging fruit from a tree

MARKETING MIX: The marketing mix is a foundation model for businesses.

The marketing mix has been defined as the *"set of marketing tools that the firm uses to pursue its marketing objectives in the target market"*. Thus the marketing mix refers to four broad levels of marketing decision, namely: product, price, place, and promotion.

In services marketing, an extended marketing mix is used, typically comprising **7 Ps**, made up of the original 4 Ps extended by process, people, and physical evidence.

7P'S OF MARKETING

The extended marketing mix (7P's) is the combination of seven elements of marketing that aim to work together to achieve the objectives of a marketing strategy. These 7 elements are: product; price; place; promotion; people; process and physical.

The marketing mix is the combination of elements used by a business to enable it to meet the needs and expectations of customers.

It is called a marketing mix because each element of the marketing mix is related to the others. The challenge for marketing is to ensure that the elements of the mix work together to achieve the marketing objectives. Traditionally the marketing mix has been taken to comprise four elements: (product, price, promotion and place)

However, in recent years it has become more common to add three new elements to the traditional marketing mix, making a combined 7p's. This is the so-called extended marketing mix. The 7p's extended marketing mix therefore comprises the following elements:

PRODUCT: The good or service that the customer buys

PRICE: How much the customer pays for the product

PLACE: How the product is distributed to the customer

PROMOTION: How the customer is found & persuaded to buy

PEOPLE: The people who make contact with customers in delivering the product

PROCESS: The systems and processes that deliver a product to a customer

PHYSICAL: The elements of the physical environment the customer experiences

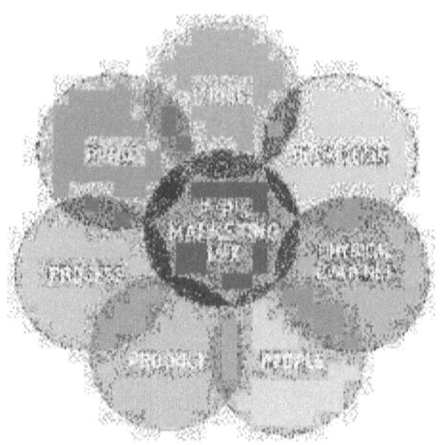

CONCEPTS OF MARKETING

NICHE MARKETING: Niche marketing is an advertising strategy that focuses on a unique target market. Instead of marketing to everyone who could benefit from a product or service, this strategy focuses exclusively on one group—a niche market—or demographic of potential customers who would most benefit from the offerings.

SNOB VALUE: Is all about show off, snob customers see higher price as an indicator of exclusivity or a privilege and this lures them to fancy such products or services as this makes them feel special and not included in popular regular brands or products. Snob is a person who seeks to be, or is, a member of the upper classes and somewhat has a feeling of superiority and brand take advantage of this strategy to create excusive, limited edition or exceptionally high-priced premium luxury products and services

MARKETING SEGMENTATION: The key aim of market segmentation is to get to know more about your customers and the more the marketer know its customers the more effectively they can positively influence them towards their products and services. Marketing segmentation splits the market into various groups that have similar characteristics based on age, gender, income, behavior, personality traits etc.

According to Philip Kotler: "Market segmentation is sub-dividing, a market into distinct and homogeneous subgroups of customers, where any group can conceivably be selected as a target market to be met with distinct marketing mix."

ADVANTAGES OF MARKET SEGEMENTATION:

- Identify most effective marketing tactics
- Create more targeted marketing communication/messages
- Differentiate the brand from competition
- Develop Niche market opportunities
- Attract quality leads from the markets
- Optimize utilization of marketing resources
- Staying focused

LEVELS OF MARKET SEGMENT

MASS MARKETING: Mass marketing is the strategy to communicate the same marketing message to the entire potential population. This method does not target the customers as per the needs of then customers

SEGMENT MARKETING: This marketing strategy is when the company divides its target market into different segments based on their needs and requirements. This is about segmenting the market in terms of similar needs and wants and purchasing powers and buying attitudes.

NICHE MARKETING: Niche marketing is focused on that particular segment of customer who have unique needs and preferences and who are ready to pay a premium. Organizations than tries to deliver a better solution for such customers. Niche does not mean a smaller market in size but a segment with niche requirements.

PSYCHCOGRAPHIC SEGMENTATION: This type of market segmentation targets lifestyle, opinions and interests, aiming primarily about psychological aspects of the customer's response.

LOCAL MARKETING: This Marketing strategy is tailored to the needs and wants of local customer groups in trading areas, neighborhoods, etc. this trend is called grass roots marketing. e.g.- Spiderman 3 was released in 5 different languages in India.

INDIVIDUAL MARKETING: Ultimate segmentation- segments of 1 or customized marketing or one to one marketing. Customization- empower the customers or public to design the product or service offering of their choice.

e.g.- paint companies have started doing this Asian paint, nerolac, Berger paints.

BEHAVIOURAL SEGMENTATION: This category of segmentation is about dividing people in the basis of behavior they exhibit. This also means that the same segment customers react same to the same communicated message.

SALES AND MARKETING TERMINOLOGY

ADVERTISINMENT: Advertisements are paid form of communications with the product or services users. The objective of advertisement is to influence or inform the receivers to purchase the product or service advertised over the competition.

PUBLICITY: Publicity is a component of marketing. In marketing terms publicity is all about visibility in public or creating awareness about a product or service or an organization via media.

COLD CALLING: Cold calling is a sales technique to solicit customers who have not yet expressed their interest in the product or services that the sales person has to offer. It's a very popular technique for telemarketing or even one to one contact like door to door selling. It may also refer to a sales person going to a potential company expecting them to be interested in the products or services.

BRAND LOYALITY: It occurs when customers choose to repeatedly purchase a product by same company instead of substitute product produced by a competitor.

BRAND: Brand is the name given to a product or service that identifies itself differently in the market. It could be a term, symbol, name or any other feature which differentiates it from the other similar products or services.

VALUE PROPOSITION: An additional benefit or offer made by a company to make it more lucrative to the prospective buyer is value proposition.

AIDA: Awareness-Interest-Desire-Action.

There are four steps in thee purchase funnel, the four steps mark the journey of a customer from awareness to action that is buying.

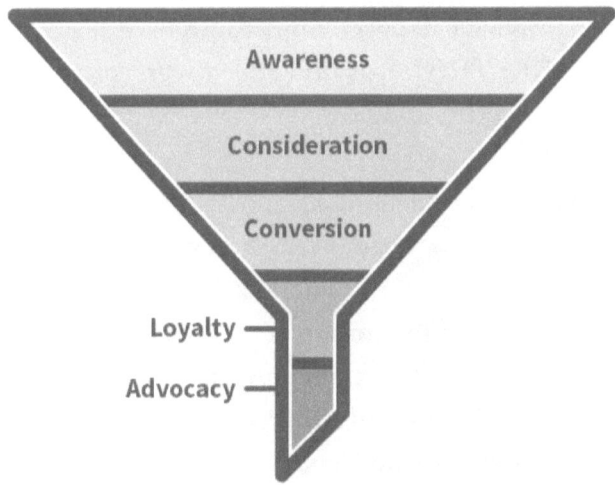

TOFU: Top of the funnel, is under problem identification stage.

MOFU: Middle of the funnel, option consideration stage may or may not buy.

BOFU: Bottom of the funnel, abut to take decision.

CROSS SELLING: When a sales person has more than one product or services to sell, he sells more than one product or service to the customers, this refers that he was able to cross sell another product as well.

UPSELLING: When a sales person is able to sell a higher version or the more premium product in the range of product or services than what initially a customer was wanting to, this effort of salesmanship is upselling.

DECISION MAKER: The final person who will make the call to buy the product or service is called as the decision maker as he will only make the final decision to buy or not to buy the product or service a sales person is pitching to sell.

BANT: Budget Authority Need Timeline. This helps sales man to understand if the prospective buyer is ready to make a purchase.

SMARKETING: This word means to align the sales and marketing efforts or to have efforts and activities synergized of both sales & marketing.

LOW HANGING FRUIT: It is a phrase refer to easy-to-accomplish task or easy-to-solve problems in particular situation.

REFERRAL MARKETING: It is also called word-of-mouth marketing. It is method of promoting products or service to new customer through referrals.

E-COMMERCE: It refers to buying and selling of goods and services or transmitting of funds or data, over an electronic network, primarily internet.

FMCG: FMCG or fast-moving consumer goods or CPD (consumer packed goods), refers to product that are sold quickly off the shelf.

ICP: (IDEAL CUSTOMER PROFILE): Is that ideal profile of the customers which matches the prospective customer for your product and services. It helps to target the market.

TARGET AUDIENCE: That group of people who match your ideal customer who would be keen to buy your product or services.

ROI: Return on Investment. In marketing this refers to measuring efficiency or profitability because of running marketing campaign.

CREATIVE BRIEF: This may also be called advertising or marketing brief, this forms the foundation or guideline of advertisements and marketing campaigns.

KPI (Key Performance Indicators) – These are specific numerical marketing metrics that organization track in order to measure their progress towards a defined goal within your marketing channel on their job role. These responses are called KRA and are described in the employee's job document.

BOUNCE RATE: Bounce rate is an Internet marketing term used in web traffic analysis. It represents the percentage of visitors who enter the site and then leave rather than continuing to view other pages within the same site.

BRAND AWARENESS: Brand awareness refers to the extent to which customers are able to recall or recognize a brand. Brand awareness is a key consideration in consumer behavior, advertising management, brand management and strategy development.

DEAL CLOSING: When a prospective customer agrees to buy the service or the product and finally does the transaction is called deal closing

DIRECT COMPETITION: Companies that offer and sell similar kind of services and products as compared to what your company sells than they become your direct competition. This also means that companies offer similar product and services and targeting similar customer profiles are in direct competition to each other.

USP: Unique sales proposition. Is that aspect of your product or business that makes your business or service stand out between the competition. Being unique is a strong value proposition in itself. It is that statement that a form chooses to communicate why & how their product or service is different from the competition.

Digital Marketing

DIGITAL MARKETING

DEFINITION: Digital Marketing is the discipline which involves the marketing conducted digitally for a brand, company, product or a service. In the present times everything is going online and therefore rises the need for advertising, marketing and promoting online.

Digital marketing encompasses all marketing efforts that use an electronic device or the internet. Businesses leverage digital channels such as search engines, social media, email, and other websites to connect with current and prospective customers.

While traditional marketing might exist in print ads, phone communication, or physical marketing, digital marketing can occur electronically and online. This means that there are a number of endless possibilities for brands including email, video, social media, or website-based marketing opportunities.

ROLE OF DIGITAL MARKETEERS

Digital marketing professional or digital marketers are responsible for creating awareness regarding the brand, website or a product on online platforms like social media, search engines, websites and emails. Digital marketing career is growing these days due to increase in connectivity on internet among people.

TYPES OF DIGITAL MARKETING:

1. **SEO-SEARCH ENGINE OPTIMIZATION:** Optimizing a website so that it appears on the initial pages or on higher ranks

of a search result. SEO helps in increasing the organic traffic for a website.

2. **CONTENT MARKETING:** The process of creation, marketing and promotion for content to increase awareness about the brand. The creation of content to increase traffic for website and bring more customers is known as content marketing.

3. **SOCIAL MEDIA MARKETING:** The practice of brand promotion on various social media platforms to create awareness about the brand, increase new traffic and for generation of new customers.

4. **PAY PER CLICK:** The method for driving traffic to a website with the help of paying for every time the ad is clicked to the publisher. Pay per click is used by major website for top slots in the search engine result pages to increase the traffic on website.

5. **Email MARKETING:** Marketing practices conducted by a company with the help of emails to promote their content.

KEY TERMS IN DIGITAL MARKETING

COST PER ACQUISITION: The measure of cost related to acquiring a customer who clicks on a website link.

COST PER IMPRESSION: The measure of total number of times an ad appears on a website. It doesn't matter if the customer actually interacts with the ad or sees it. The appearing frequency of an ad and its measurement is the Cost per impression.

CALL TO ACTION: A attention seeking button which is used for attracting a customer to click on it which will make them purchase, sign up or interact with the website. It is an important part of every social media campaign.

CALL THROUGH RATE: The measurement of the users who click on a link in the terms of percentage. CTR is a significant measure to find out how many users have clicked a link.

TYPES OF DIGITAL MARKETING

SEO: Search Engine Optimization This is the process of optimizing your website to "rank" higher in search engine results pages, thereby increasing the amount of organic (or free) traffic your website receives. The channels that benefit from SEO include websites, blogs, and infographics.

CONTENT MARKETING: This term denotes the creation and promotion of content assets for the purpose of generating brand awareness, traffic growth, lead generation, and customers.

SOCIAL MEDIA MARKETING: This practice promotes your brand and your content on social media channels to increase brand awareness, drive traffic, and generate leads for your business.

PPC: Pay Per Click, PPC is a method of driving traffic to your website by paying a publisher every time your ad is clicked. One of the most common types of PPC is Google Ads, which allows you to pay for top slots on Google's search engine results pages at a price "per click" of the links you place.

AFFILIATE MARKETING: This is a type of performance-based advertising where you receive commission for promoting someone else's products or services online.

NATIVE ADVERTISING: This type of advertisement matches the form and function of the platform so much that it seems that feels it belongs there. Hence the word native, the product promoted blends well with the content and reduces consumer ad recognition within the content.

MARKETING AUTOMATION: refers to the software that serves to automate your basic marketing operations. Many marketing departments can automate repetitive tasks they would otherwise do manually

EMAIL MARKETING: Companies use email marketing as a way of communicating with their audiences. Email is often used to promote content, discounts and events, as well as to direct people toward the business's website.

ONLINE PR: Online PR is the practice of securing earned online coverage with digital publications, blogs, and other content-based websites. It's much like traditional PR, but in the online space

Inbound Marketing: Inbound marketing refers to a marketing methodology wherein you attract, engage, and delight customers at every stage of the buyer's journey.

SPONSORED CONTENT: With sponsored content, you as a brand pay another company or entity, advertiser, influencer or publisher to create and promote content that discusses your brand or service in some way.

CONTEXTUAL MARKETING: Contextual marketing is all about delivering the right content at the right moment based on a potential client's preferences using behavioural targeting and enabling brand awareness, recall and engagement. It fuels targeted ads based on user information such as recent searches and web histories.

BLOG MARKETING: This is a process of advertising of a business, website, brand, service etc. through the medium of writing blogs.

DIGITAL MARKETING TERMS

CPA: COST PER ACQUISITION: This is a metric used to determine how much it costs to acquire one customer.

CPA: Cost Per Action- This is a metric or a pricing strategy whereby an online advertising agency allows an advertiser to pay for a specified action from a target customer.

QUALITY SCORE: Quality Score is Google AdWords' rating of the relevance and quality of keywords used in advertisements, landing pages. This refers to how relevant are your key words used in landing pages, ads to the person who views them.

CPI: Cost Per Impression CPI measures how many times your ad appears on a site whether or not the users actually sees or interacts with it. This is similar to the marketing term "reach" but reach measures how many people see your content and impressions measure how many times yr ad or content was displayed.

ENGAGEMENT RATE: This is a metric which helps analyzing the effectiveness and efficiency of a brand campaign. Engagement rate refers to the consumer engagement with the brand which is reflected by likes, comments and social sharing. This reflects how much users are interacting with the brand.

REMARKETING: Is a method of reconnecting with the prospective customers who previously interacted with your website or mobile app. This strategy helps reach out to such customers and position advertisement in front of them with the reason to build your brand awareness and impacting them to make a purchase.

RELEVANCY SCORE: This is based on the kind of feedback an advertisement campaign receives, positive or negative. The more the positive interactions about an advertisement the more the relevancy score. The relevancy score reflects how well the advertisement resonates with the audience or your customers.

CTA: Call to Action: A call to action is usually a button used to get customers attention and make them click. This phrase is used to tell the user what action to take and how to take that action when they are at a website or an advertisement campaign.

IDEAL CUSTOMER PROFILE: This refers to the ideal customer profile of, a perfect customer for the product & services that your company offers/produces. In a way Ideal Customer Profile helps understand the requirements and expectations of your ideal customers and helps an organization understand customers better. Also helps in higher customer retention.

CTR: Click-Through Rate is a metric that measures the number of clicks an advertiser receives on their advertisement per number of impressions. In short it's a measures the percentage of people who viewed the ad and then further clicked the advertisement as well

CPA: Cost per Acquisition – This is a marketing metric that measures the cost incurred to acquire one paying customers for a campaign or channel. Its in a way measurement of a marketing campaign or channel success.

Total campaign cost/conversions x 100

CPC: Cost per Click Cost per Click is a pricing model which simply means you pay for each click that you get on your advertisement. Companies are charged by publishers for every click people make on a displayed/test ad which leads people to your website

CPM: Cost per Thousand Cost per Thousand is a marketing term as well as a pricing model where advertising impressions are purchased and companies are charged according to the number of times their ad appears per 1,000 impressions. This metric counts the number of ad views or viewer engagements, that an advertisement receives. This model is recommended for increasing the brand awareness.

CONVERSION: When a visitor takes the desired action while visiting your site, it is called conversion. This can be filling up a from, registrations, purchase, membership signup, download or registration for newsletter.

IMPRESSIONS: This term defines the number of times a company's advertisement appears on a user's screen. Impressions are not action based and its only defines the users potential viewing of the advertisements.

KEYWORD: A keyword is word or phrase that searchers may use to search for relevant topics on search engines. This is also called search queries. For a flower shop, a relevant key words used by the searchers would be "*Buy Red Roses*" or "*online purchase flowers*"

ORGANIC TRAFFIC: This refers to all the visitors to your site as an organic (unpaid) traffic search results. Organic traffic is not generated by paid advertisements, it is in fact just the opposite of the paid traffic i.e. unpaid traffic

PAID TRAFFIC: Paid search is when a company bids on keywords and makes advertisements around those keywords to be displayed on search engines. These results appear separately, either on the top, bottom or right side of a search results page. Paid traffic also encompasses any form of paid advertisement that directly points to your website.

SEO: Search Engine Optimisation, it is a process of improving your site's visibility for relevant searches. The better visibility results in better attention and helps in attracting prospective and existing customers to your business.

SEM: Search Engine Marketing, companies use this to get higher placement on search engines by bidding on the search terms. It also helps increase the visibility of a website by both organic as well as paid ways.

SERP: Search Engine Results Page, is the list of results that are provided by a search engine after a search query is made.

DOMAIN AUTHORITY: This is a scale from 1-100 that search engines use to determine how authoritative a company's website is, 1 being the lowest rank and 100 being the highest. The higher your domain authority the more Search Engines trust you.

KEYWORD STUFFING: This is the practice of using too many keywords in content in hopes of making it more visible on search engines. You will be penalized by search engines if you resort to it. Never keyword stuff, just provide great and valuable content.

META DESCRIPTION: The META description is the few lines of text that appear on the search engine results page about your website for the viewers to read, the challenge is that has to be conveyed in a very few words.

SUBSCRIBER: A subscriber is a person who allows a company to send him/her messages through email or other personal communication means. These subscribers are high value to publishers and businesses alike. Subscribers keep coming back!

HYPERLOCAL: Hyperlocal means an area close to home—the people within walking or driving distance to a particular destination or those united in one identifiable community. Hyperlocal marketing is the process where the potential customers in the nearby vicinity or geographical locations are targeted the focus is on people who conduct a search near "me"

GLOCAL: Reflecting or characterized by both local and global considerations. Glocal management is about "think globally" and "act locally"

VIRAL MARKETING: This is a way of marketing where the audience is encouraged by companies to pass on their content to others for more exposure. Any message that spreads across at a very high speed like a virus, quickly from one person to another hence the name viral marketing. Viral content sometimes has a viral strategy behind it but often contents get viral because of luck. Such content is often funny or unique. A successful viral content can work miracles for the brand or a company.

SOCIAL MEDIA MARKETING: Use of social media platforms to connect with your audience to build a brand or to increase the traffic on your website or to increase sales of your product of services. This would also mean publishing content of various platforms, running advertisement campaigns, engaging with the customers and reviewing results. Some of the key platforms are YouTube, Facebook, Instagram, Twitter, LinkedIn, Pinterest & Snapchat

LANDING PAGE: This is the page on a company's website that is optimized to act as the entry page to a site. This is where the visitor lands after having clicked the link in an advertisement or link or search result.

CONTENT MARKETING: Content writing can be defined as the form of online writing which is has a consistent content, and has a very focused approach towards creating valuable and relevant content to attract and retain a particular audience.

REVENUE MANAGEMENT

REVENUE MANAGEMENT: Revenue management is an approach used for forecasting, strategizing and applying tactics to sell the product to the right customer at the right time for the right price to boost sales and revenue. Revenue Management aims at optimizing financial results Revenue management in the hospitality industry refers to application of various strategies and tactics to sell hotel's products to the guests at prices which help in maximizing revenue.

IMPORTANCE OF REVENUE MANAGEMENT

Every hotelier, regardless of size, is facing rising operating costs and increased competition. Having a revenue management strategy allows you to maintain profitability and achieve revenue growth even though you can't physically increase the number of rooms you have to sell.

- Connecting with guests, helping them enjoy extraordinary experiences and create lasting memories is at the core of why all of us work in hospitality. Having a revenue management strategy reflects a hotel's unique market, guests, and property will give a strong, lasting foundation for a thriving business.
- The primary purpose behind revenue management and its rise in usage since the 1980's is the maximization of revenue and profits.
- Many attributes in the hospitality industry, including perishable products, high fixed costs, low variable costs and fixed capacity, help drive increases in margins and profits as the result of revenue

management. These include hotels and other lodging providers, rental car companies, vacation package and tour providers, restaurants and cruise lines.

- Revenue management primarily benefits companies by allowing them to leverage price discrimination through market segmentation. Different customer segments have different needs and wants.

- Effective hotel revenue management strategies can also help hoteliers:

  - Protect against overstaffing during slow periods
  - Ensure adequate numbers of staff are working during the busiest times
  - Helps in increasing profitability of the organization.
  - Gives boost to sales and helps in operating in a highly competitive market.
  - Better resource management
  - Revenue management works on the principle of market segmentation which leads to a high market share for the company.

The term revenue management refers to a business practice designed to optimize the revenue potential of an asset through all market conditions. Revenue management is the strategic use of performance data, local market data, competitor rates, and other applied analytics to help predict consumer demand in order to optimize pricing and distribution in a way that maximizes revenue and profits.

Hotel revenue management involves forecasting demand by understanding the unique characteristics and buying behaviours of prospective traveller segments, then matching that demand by optimizing prices and inventory to secure their bookings. In other words, attracting the right travellers by selling rooms at the right time, for the right price and thus increasing top-line revenue.

BENEFITS OF REVENUE MANAGEMENT SOFTWARE:

- Improved business forecasting
- Helps achieve maximum revenue generation per booking
- Creates a dynamic/flexible room pricing
- It allows to advertise across various distribution channels and maintain rate parity & drive bookings
- It encourages direct bookings
- Saves valuable time of administration
- Increases profits
- Create real time pricing 24/7/365
- More control over pricing strategy
- Helps in achieving competitive pricing

ELEMENTS AND PRINCIPLES OF REVENUE MANAGEMENT

- Market Segmentation
- Historical Demand and Booking Patterns
- Demand Forecast and Displacement Analysis
- Pricing and Inventory Management
- Overbooking
- Information Systems

REVENUE MANAGEMENT KEY CONCEPTS:

MARKET SEGMENTATION: Each customer has different wants; it becomes important for a company to segment the market according to their different demands. Market segmentation helps in targeting the right customer by selling him/her the product according to their tastes and interests.

DEMAND FORECAST: It helps in estimating the future with the help of past records. Demand forecasting helps In predicting the demand and therefore strategize accordingly.

PRICING & INVENTORY MANAGEMENT: Approach used for changing price according to the demand for a product. Inventory management strategy is essential for a hotel to sell the existing inventory at a price which will yield the maximum revenue possible for the inventory item.

OVERBOOKING: Overbooking helps in increasing the chances of maximizing the capacity of the hotel, if one guest refuses to visit the hotel, overbooking will ensure that the room is sold to another potential guest.

HOSPITALITY DISTRIBUTION CHANNEL: Distribution channel is hospitality about getting your product to the end consumer. This term describes different methods/channels/platforms through which hotel rooms/services have been booked. A channel could be a hotel booking engine or a direct booking through a call made to the hotel or may be an email query directly made to the hotel. Hotel use multi-channel to book their inventory

DISTRIBUTION STRATEGY: This strategy is about deciding that through which channel hotel plans to sell its hotel rooms, this decision is achieved upon analysis of cost of acquisition of the individual channel. By choosing the cost-effective distribution channel for driving business, hotels can maximise their profitability. Hotels have many choices of distribution channels the key of them are:

DIRECT SELLING: Booking through hotels website & hotels sales team

GDS: GLOBAL DISTRIBUTION CHANNEL: This is a worldwide platform that serves to connect the travel brokers & suppliers like hotel and other accommodation providers. The key benefit of participating on this platform is that this attracts demand from across the world. This platform shows real time rates.

CRS: CENTRALIZED RESERVATION SYSTEM: This centralized reservation system could be for a chain of hotels that manages reservation for all the properties at different locations. This helps better management of inventory, rates, yield through a single unified platform for the group of hotels

OTA's: Online Travel Agent. Online travel agents are those online companies that sell different hotels at their platform/website. Hotel participates with OTA's as it increases the chances of the hotel to reach the potential customers, as OTA's often market themselves aggressively.

METASEARCH ENGINES: A metasearch engine is a tool that aggregates data from other search engines and produces results to the user. In the travel industry, the metasearch engines aggregate rates and availability of hotels from different sources mainly from OTAs and sometimes directly from hotels. This makes things quite easy for users. All they have to do is find the type of hotel they want, enter their journey dates and compare the different options.

Metasearch engines do not do the actual booking; they just list the price and availability. When you select a particular hotel, you will be redirected to the OTA in which the fare was displayed to make the actual booking.

TERMS USED IN REVENUE MANAGEMENT

ROOM BLOCK: A group of guestrooms which are ranging between 10 or more in quantity are sold on special rates to guests.

OTA: Online travel agency is an online source or a website which deals in various travel products. OTA's sell travel products like hotels, cruise packages, flights, car rentals etc.

BEST AVAILABLE RATE: BAR is the rate which is said to the lowest rate available for the guests to book for a day.

BEST RATE GURANTEED: BRG is the rate guaranteed to a guest by the hotel as a promise that the rate found of their rooms on hotel's website is the best rate in the market.

CANCELLATION CLAUSE: Cancellation clause means the contract which is between the guest and the hotel, it lists down the terms and conditions of the hotel booking being conducted.

CHANNEL MANAGEMENT: Channel management involves the management of various distribution channels to sell room inventory to different agents globally.

CENTRALISED RESERVATION SYSTEM: CRS is a software used by hotels to manage reservations and other related tasks like inventory management, rate allocation.

CLOSE TO ARRIVAL: A revenue management tactic used as a restriction for closing arrival on particular days.

CLOSE TO DEPARTURE: A particular set of days where guests may not have the option to depart and it is applied to a room plan.

EBITDA: Earnings before interest, taxes, depreciation and amortization. It measures the profitability of a business.

EBITDA = Revenue – Expenses.

GROUP RATE: Hotels that frequently accept bookings for groups, group rates are offered special rates depending on the volume/size of the groups.

OCCUPANCY RATE: Shows how occupied your property is over a given period of time.

ADR: Average Daily Rate- The average daily is the average rate of all the rooms sold over a given period of time. It is calculated by dividing Total Room revenue of one night by the total number of rooms sold of all types.

BOOKING ENGINE: The software that is used to make the reservations online

FORECASTING: Process used to predict future business trends by using the present and future data

LOS: Length of stay, this term is used to show the duration of stay of a reservation booking

MICE: This term refers to Meetings, Incentives, Conferences & exhibitions. This is the term used to separately show the generated business from this business stream and also to this segment has very special requirements to cater to

PMS: Property Management System- This refers to the software that the is installed in the hotel to manage a property including reservations. The core of this system is Reservations, billing & housekeeping

RMS: Revenue Management System, this refers to the tool that a hotel uses to optimize revenue. This software application helps the hotel to control supply and price the room inventory accordingly achieving revenue maximization.

PACKAGE: It's a fixed price that may be offered to the make it easier for the traveller to include services like transportation, meals, accommodation etc.

RATE PARITY: This is a strategy that different distribution channels show similar rates with same terms and conditions for a particular type of room. This strategy encourages customer towards more loyalty and book through the hotel website as where they may find more flexibility in policy and offers

RFP: Request for proposal, this is a hotels formal proposal

WEB ANALYTICS: This is about monitoring the visits of the customers on your website. This helps understand the effectiveness of the website

YIELD MANAGEMENT: Hotel yield management is about understanding, anticipating & reacting to the customer behaviour and demand patterns with an aim to price inventory accordingly to achieve revenue maximization

REVENUE MANAGEMENT FORMULAS

Rev Par (REVENUE PER AVAILABLE ROOM): Revenue per available room (RevPAR) is a metric used in the hospitality industry to measure hotel performance. The measurement is calculated by:

RevPAR = Rooms Revenue/Rooms Available

REV POR (REVENUE PER OCCUPIED ROOM): Revenue per occupied room (RevPOR) is a performance measure for companies in the hotel and lodging industries.

RevPOR = **Total Revenue/Occupied Rooms**

AVERAGE DAILY RATE= Average daily rate is used for measuring the hotel's average room rate of an occupied room on a daily basis.

ADR= Total rooms sold/Room Revenue earned

ALOS: (AVERAGE LENGTH OF STAY): ALOS is used for calculating the minimum number of days a guest lives in the hotel. One can calculate the average length of stay by dividing the total occupied rooms nights by the number of bookings.

ALOS= Total occupied room nights/Total bookings

AVERAGE ROOM RATE= The metric used to calculate the average rate levied for a room.

ARR = Total room revenue/Total rooms occupied

COST PER OCCUPIED ROOM= CPOR is calculate to find out the average cost per occupied room

CPOR= Total rooms department cost/Total rooms sold

REV POR (REVENUE PER OCCUPIED ROOM): Revenue per occupied room (RevPOR) is a performance measure for companies in the hotel and lodging industries.

RevPOR = **Total Revenue/Occupied Rooms**

BAR: (BEST AVAILABLE RATE): BAR stands for Best Available Rate which is the lowest rate of the day that is available for guests to book. The BAR rates are available to the general public, does not require pre-payment and does not impose cancellation or change penalties and/or fees, other than those imposed as a result of a hotel property's normal cancellation policy

BRG: (BEST RATE GUARANTEE): The hotel makes a promise that the room prices found on their website are the best rates compared to other any other sites.

Hotels implement the BRG policy, to drive consumers to book directly via their own website, instead of the third party OTA. OTA's are of course giving the same promise as they want to encourage consumers to book their hotel stay with them.

ROOM BLOCKS: A room block is a group of guest rooms that a hotel puts on hold at a specific "negotiated" rate for a group of people. A room block typically needs to have 10 or more rooms to qualify for the potential for special rates or concessions.

GROSS REVENUE: A hotel's gross revenue is the money generated by all its operations before deductions are taken for expenses. Revenue can come from the sale of the hotels products or services, from the sale of surplus equipment or property, or from the sale of shares of stock in the hotel company.

ADS (ALTERNATE DISTRIBUTION SYSTEM): Alternative Distribution System, in short form ADS is a term used to describe the distribution via 3rd party websites.

- This includes online travel agencies (OTA), travel portals, travel search engines/directories, online hotel consolidators, airline websites with online reservation options.

OTA: Acronym for Online Travel Agency. An OTA is a travel website that specializes in the sale of travel products to consumers. Some agencies sell a variety of travel products including flights, hotels, car rentals, cruises, activities, and packages e.g: Booking.com, Expedia.com, Hotels. com., Agoda.com.

CTA: (CLOSE TO ARRIVAL): It is a yield tool used to close days from reservations arriving on a particular day.

- When requesting a stay on the hotel's website, with such a day as check-in date, it will show as not available. However you can book rooms arriving before and stay through such date.

CTD: (CLOSE TO DEPARTURE): It is a specific set of days' guests cannot make their reservation for with this date as check-out.

EBITDA: EBITDA stands for: **Earnings Before Interest, Taxes, Depreciation and Amortization.**

- This KPI is used to determine how profitable a company or business is with regard to its operations (the profit on the products it produces and sells).
- EBITDA is calculated by taking the company's earnings before interest, tax, amortization and depreciation and subtracting them from the company's total amount of revenue.
- EBITDA Formula: Revenue – Expenses

EBITDAR: EBITDAR stands for: **Earnings Before Interest, Taxes, Depreciation, Amortisation, and Rent**

- It is the same calculation as EBITDA, with the exception that rents and/or restructuring costs are excluded from the expenses.

FAIR MARKET SHARE: Fair Market Share is an indication that a hotel's overall performance stacks up against its immediate competitors. A hotel within a competitive set can work out if it's getting its Fair Market Share through a simple calculation: **Fair Market Share** = Total number of rooms at the hotel /Total number of rooms in the comp set

CANCELLATION CLAUSE: The term cancellation clause refers to the terms mentioned in the hotel booking contract, in which the hotel states under which terms & conditions a cancellation can occur.

The kind of cancellation clause differs depending on if only one/multiple rooms are booked – or the customer is booking whole blocks of rooms (for Events/Conferences etc.).

CHANNEL MANAGEMENT: Channel management is the process of managing online distribution channels in order to sell hotel inventory to various agents across the globe. It is the only way to effectively reach a global audience without risking overbookings.

CRS (CENTRALIZED RESERVATION SYSTEM: CRS or Central Reservation System is a type of reservation software that is used to update and maintain information of a hotel pertaining to inventory and rates so that hotels are able to manage guest reservations and the process around such reservations in real time.

- These reservations are managed across distribution channels such as the 3rd party booking websites, direct internet booking engines, the global distribution system (GDS), wholesalers and more.
- A CRS centralises the data from the property management systems (PMS), distribution channels, call centres and phone reservation systems used across one or many properties.

GDS: (GLOBAL DISTRIBUTION SYSTEM): A global distribution system (GDS) is a computerised network system owned or operated by a company that enables transactions between travel industry service providers, mainly airlines, hotels, car rental companies, and travel agencies

YIELD: Yield are basically the earnings that have been generated and realized on an investment over a period of time. It is expressed in percentage. It includes-interest earned/dividends received from holding security.

- Yield is a return for an investment over a period of time.
- It is measured in percentage.
- Yield includes price increases as well as any dividends paid that is calculated as the net realized return divided by the principal amount.
- Higher yields mean lower risk and higher income, but a high yield may not always be a positive.

FOOD SCIENCE AND NUTRITION

HEALTH	FITNESS
Health is the state of an entire body and the system.	Fitness is also described as the state of the body, but it focuses more specifically on the nervous system, the muscular system, and the skeletal system.
Health is the main category.	Fitness is a sub-category of health.
Health is measured in cholesterol numbers, blood sugar levels, blood pressure levels, etc.	Fitness is measured in terms, to be able to do certain activities, sports etc
Health is a much broader term and varies from individual to individual.	Fitness is a state/condition of being physically active.
Health is not as easily measured or defined as fitness.	Fitness is a measurable state which is partially determined by genetics.

FOOD: Food is basically any substance which nourishes the body and provides energy to the body as well helps in growth and maintenance and regulating various processes within the body.

NUTRIENTS: The chemical substances present in food are known as nutrients. The six major groups of nutrients, are proteins, carbohydrates, fats, vitamins, minerals, and water.

NUTRITION: The discipline which includes studying of the various components which are essential for nourishing the body and for preventing health related risks to ensure the body is fit.

MALNURITION: Malnutrition is a condition which is a result of deficiency, excess or an imbalance of intake of nutrients in a person's diet.

UNDERNUTRITION: Undernutrition occurs due to a deficiency of calories or nutrients within the diet.

OVER NUTRITION: Over nutrition refers to the condition in which a person's intake of calories is excessive and it may lead to the person becoming overweight or obese.

DIET: A diet may refer to a plan or a bunch of food items which will be consumed by a person according to his/her bodily requirements.

CLASSIFICATION OF NUTRIENTS: The essential components of food that are required for the proper bodily functions are known as nutrients. Nutrients are majorly placed in six categories -proteins, carbohydrates, fats, vitamins, minerals, and water.

BALANCED DIET: A term given to the proper intake of nutrient rich foods in suitable amounts which help to keep the body healthy. Balanced diet is a mixture of various types of foods in adequate amounts to prevent under or over nutrition.

MEAL PLANNING: Meal Planning is the process of planning what to eat, how much to eat and when to eat. The meals are planned, what all nutrients are required accordingly the food to be consumed is thought of. The meal planning ensures that one eats only what is needed and not more than the required quantities. The meals planned should not only ensure that nutrients are adequately met but also be flexible enough to take advantage of easy availability and lower prices if seasonal foods and meet the needs and choices of family members. Meal planning involves planning a balanced meal which is colorful, attractive, appetizing, and palatable and within the economic means of the individuals concerned. A balanced diet is one which provides all the nutrients in the amount and proportion required according to one's age, gender and activity.

GOOD NUTRITION: This is about providing all essential nutrients in correct balance which are further utilized to promote the highest level of physical and mental health. Such a state of nutrition can be attained through balanced diets.

BALANCED DIET: Can be defined as one which contains different types of foods (from all food group) in such quantities and proportions that needs for all the nutrients are adequately met and a small extra allowance is made as a margin of safety.

SAFETY MARGIN: Is taken into account due to individual variations, losses during cooking and processing and also minor illnesses.

A balanced diet along with inclusion of various food groups focuses on the RDA for various nutrients.

RDA (Recommended Dietary Allowances) is defined as the estimates of intakes nutrients which individuals in a population group need to consume to ensure that the physiological needs of all subjects in that population are met.

RDA varies with age, sex, physiological state etc.

Meal planning involves decision making regarding what to eat and how much to eat each day at each meal.

BALANCED DIET: When the diet is able to meet all the needs of an individual and also it provides an extra allowance for minor stresses and strains, the individual is said to be in a state of optimum nutrition.

OPTIMUM NUTRITION: Is also known as adequate nutrition or good nutrition

JUNK FOOD: Junk food includes the food items which are considered to have very less or almost no nutritional value as well as have ingredients which are unhealthy if consumed on a regular basis. The term "Junk Food" was coined in 1972 by Michael Jacobson, director of the Centre for Science in the Public Interest. Example of junk food: Wafers, Soft Drinks, Burgers, Pizza, Fries, Ice Cream etc.

ADVANTAGES & DISADVANTAGES OF JUNK FOOD

ADVANTAGES	DISADVANTAGES
Easy & quick to prepare	Contain high amount of calories and fat.
Are attractive and appeal to the palate.	Unhealthy and Unhygienic

Less expensive	Less nutritional value
Provides salt, sugar & fat that are required for the energy of our body.	If consumed on a regular basis, it triggers off many diseases.

HEALTHY FOOD VS. JUNK FOOD

HEALTHY FOOD	JUNK FOOD
Rich in nutrients viz. protein, carbohydrates, dietary fibers, fats, vitamins, minerals, etc.	Low or no nutrients, but rich in saturated fats, salt, sugars, artificial flavour etc.
Prevents consumers from cancer, diabetes, heart diseases, and obesity	Causes the consumers to have cancer, diabetes, heart diseases and obesity
Not convenient to access and prepare	Very convenient to access and mostly prepared and ready to eat
Mostly natural	Mostly artificial

HEALTH EFFECTS OF JUNK FOOD

- Most Junk foods contain colours that are carcinogenic.
- It can induce early heart attacks, osteoporosis, & Hypertension.
- Obesity leading to less energetic body.
- Less concentration of mind in children, especially.

JUNK FOOD AND ITS EFFECT ON HEALTH: Junk food is used to describe food and drinks low in nutrients (e.g. vitamins, minerals and fibre) and high in kilojoules, saturated fat, added sugar and/or added salt. They are also known as discretionary choices.

HEALTH ISSUES: It has been brought forth that fast foods are characterized by high-fat content, high calories, high cholesterol, and quick, high sodium concentration and made from ingredients that are cheap such as fat meat and refined grains. All these pose a greater risk to human health. Too much eating of fast food with such health problems as obesity, high blood pressure, cardiovascular disorders, and liver problems.

HEART ATTACK: Fast foods are prepared using Trans-fat which is an artery-clogging fat. Increased high blood pressure:

Fast food contains a good deal of sodium concentration, this aggravates the risk of high blood pressure.

OBESITY: Continual eating of such kinds of food means that we accumulate a lot of calories in our body that are not useful leading to individuals being obese.

LIVER PROBLEM: Since the liver is responsible for purification/filtering of harmful substances as well as producing substances that help breakdown fats, when fast foods are consumed every now and then, the liver will be overloaded and damaged. This, in turn, leads to very serious health problems that can be fatal.

ADDICTION: It has been documented that fast food is addictive. What this means is that individuals who are used to eating such foods cannot go for long without having a bit of such food.

FAMILY BOND: The issue of fast food has been brought forth as another factor that jeopardizes family bonds. This is because no or very minimal time is used in preparing food together, leave alone eating together. Young people are spending more of their time in having a meal with their fellow friends other than their family members.

LOWER NUTRITIONAL CONTENT: Fast food has been linked and it is a fact that most of them apart from pizza lack dietary fibre as well as essential micro-nutrients such as vitamins and minerals. It is worth mentioning that food that lacks fiber brings with it several stomach complications such as constipation.

EXPENSIVE: Although previously it was stated that fast food is inexpensive, that was only true when considering an individual buying such kind of food cooking at home. It is important to note that a family visiting or buying fast food once in a while is not that expensive, but when this is done more often, then the amount of money spent can be quite much more as compared to if the family could just buy the food in supermarket, take the time to prepare it and enjoy a dinner or lunch together as a family

FOOD: Food can be defined as any substance which nourishes the body and is fit to eat. It may be solid or liquid. Food provides the body with materials for providing energy, growth and maintenance, and regulating various processes in the body. These materials of which food is made up of are termed as nutrients.

NUTRIENTS: Nutrients are the chemical substances present in food, which the body needs to carry out its functions. There are six major groups of nutrients, namely, proteins, carbohydrates, fats, vitamins, minerals, and water.

NUTRITION: Nutrition is the science of nourishing the body. It includes much more than just consuming a balanced diet. Nutrition is a study of various nutrients, their characteristics, functions, requirement and sources. The effect of deficiency, excessive intake, digestion, absorption and utilization in the body as well as the interrelationships that occur among some nutrients is an important part of nutrition.

HEALTH: Health is the ability of a biological system to acquire, convert, allocate, distribute, and utilize energy with maximum efficiency.

RELATION OF FOOD AND HEALTH

MALNURITION: Malnutrition is an impairment of health resulting from a deficiency, excess, or imbalance of nutrients in the diet. It includes both under nutrition or deficiency and over nutrition or excessive consumption.

UNDERNUTRITION: It refers to a deficiency of calories and/or one or more nutrients in the diet. An undernourished person is underweight.

OVER NUTRITION: It refers to an excess of calories and/or one or more nutrients in the diet. An excessive intake of calories results in overweight which can lead to obesity. An excessive intake of fat soluble vitamins can cause hypervitaminosis or vitamin toxicity.

DIET: A diet means the kinds and amounts of food and beverage consumed every day. A diet may be normal diet or it may be a modified diet which is used in the treatment of specific disease or condition.

NUTRITIONAL STATUS: The nutritional status of an individual is defined as the condition of health as influenced by the utilization of nutrients in the body. The nutritional status of an individual or a community can be assessed by surveying the kind and amount of food being consumed, signs of ill health or deficiency symptoms if present, height, weight, and other measurements as well as level of nutrients in the blood and excreted in the urine.

CLASSIFICATION OF NUTRIENTS: Nutrients are the essential constituents of food that are required by the body in suitable amounts. There are approximately fifty nutrients which are placed in six categories, namely, proteins, carbohydrates, fats, vitamins, minerals, and water.

TYPES OF NUTRIENTS

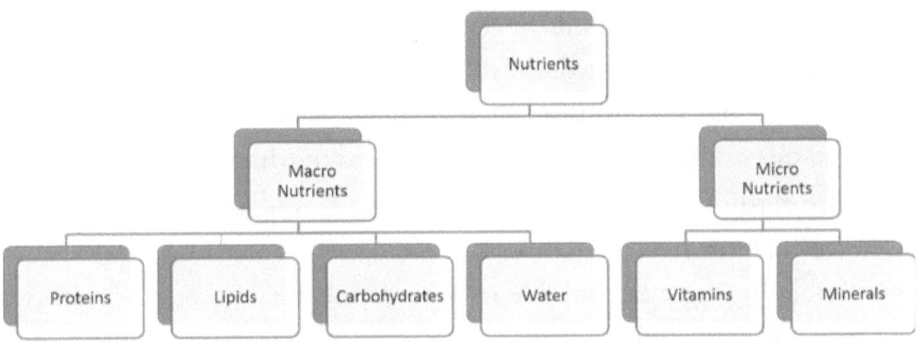

KEY FUNCTIONS OF FOOD

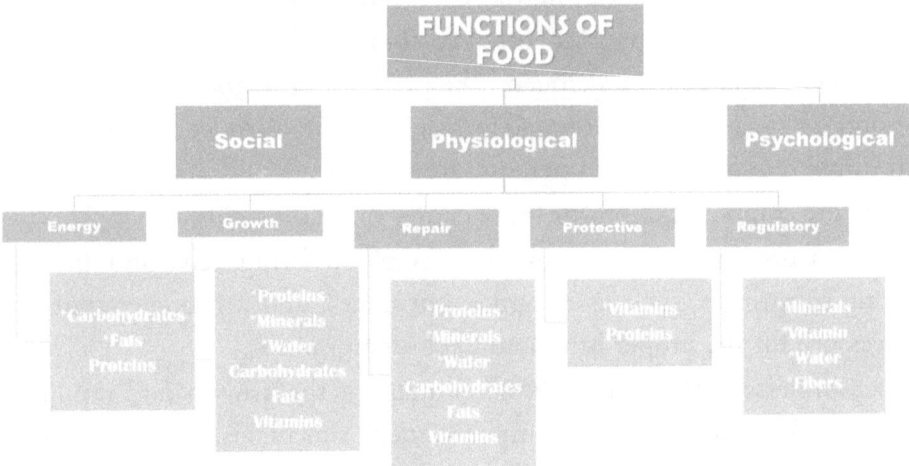

Food is composed of three main constituents, namely, carbohydrates, proteins, fats and their derivatives.

In addition, these constituents, inorganic mineral elements and diverse organic compounds such as vitamins, pigments, enzymes and acids are also present.

The variation in structure, texture, color, flavor and nutritive value is because of the varying proportions and arrangement of these constituents. Knowledge of these constituents, their properties and reactions with other constituents is necessary for a person who processes, severs and stores food.

The basic use of fats and oils in cookery is to add richness and flavor to food and as a cooking medium to fry or cook food. They improve the texture of various preparations such as cakes, pastries and biscuits.

Fats and oils are found in plants, animals and marine foods.

They are organic compounds composed of C, H and O

Collectively known as LIPIDS

Immiscible in water but soluble in organic solvent. (Ether, Chloroform, Benzene and Acetone)

Unlike carbohydrates – contains small proportion of O and larger proportion of H and C

Provide more energy per gram than carbohydrates

Proteins are large, complex, organic compounds made up of carbon, hydrogen, oxygen, and nitrogen. The presence of nitrogen distinguishes proteins from carbohydrates and fats. Apart from nitrogen, elements such as sulphur, phosphorus, copper, and iron are also found in some proteins. They are composed of one or more chains of amino acids.

Proteins are fundamental components of all living cells and include many substances, such as enzymes, hormones, and antibodies that are necessary for the proper functioning of an organism.

They are essential in the diet of animals for the growth and repair of tissue and can be obtained from foods such as meat, fish, eggs, milk, and legumes.

Vitamins are Organic molecules with a wide variety of functions

Cofactors for enzymatic reactions

Essential, supplied in the diet

Two distinct types: Fat soluble (A, D, E, K)

Water soluble (B – complex, C)

MINERALS: Minerals are natural compounds formed through geological processes. Minerals are needed by the body in small amounts to help it function properly and stay strong. Iron, calcium, potassium, and sodium are some of essential minerals. Humans need small amounts of about 14 minerals to maintain normal body function and good health.

CARBOHYDRATES: These are also called as carbs. , they are types of macronutrients found in certain food and drinks like sugar, starches, fibre are carbohydrates. Body needs them to stay healthy. Some examples are

- Dairy. Milk, yogurt, and ice cream.
- Fruit. Whole fruit and fruit juice.
- Grains. Bread, rice, crackers, and cereal.
- Legumes. Beans and other plant-based proteins.
- Starchy Vegetables. Potatoes and corn.
- Sugary Sweets. Limit these! Soda, candy, cookies, and other desserts.

Responsible Hospitality

RESPONSIBLE HOSPITALITY

Every profession must act responsibly, hence it is essential that Hospitality professionals must be aware of certain aspects & concepts which will help them deliver better and be responsible professionals.

RESPONSIBLE HOSPITALITY

The act of practicing hospitality in a smart yet responsible manner to safeguard the interests of the present as well as future generations.

CORPORATE SOCIAL RESPONSIBILITY: Is about ethical behaviour, of organizations towards the society which reflects its commitment towards sustainability and development of the society

It being responsible towards: Society, Government, Shareholders, Environment, Employees & Customers

KEY TERMS

BUSINESS ETHICS: This is the study of how a business should be conducted in controversial or challenging situations. These are those set of business principles that define what is wrong & right conduct & what is the appropriate behaviour at workplace

SUSTAINABLITY: This is a responsible business approach whereby an enterprise conducts its business aiming at creating long term value and operates responsibly towards ecological, social and economic environment

GOODWILL: It an intangible asset that an organization has in the market place or may have gained with purchase of one company

LABOUR RIGHTS: This is also called as worker rights which are enforced legally as well as by human rights, pertaining to labour relations between workers and employers

HUMAN RIGHTS: Every person has certain basic human and freedom rights from birth till death

SOCIALLY RESPONSIBLE COMPANY: An organization which behaves responsibly i.e conducts its business in an ethical and responsible manner pertaining to employees, society, environment & government Its conducts its business under an ethical framework which contributes towards the overall society.

CORPORATE IMAGE: This refers to the image of an organization, it is about how a firm/business conducts itself in business which reflects its overall image or how its image is in the market place

RESPONSIBILITY OF ENGINEERING DEPARTMENT

- Conduct Preventive Maintenance
- Renovating Guest rooms and public areas from time to time as approved by the management
- Maintain escalators and elevators in top condition & duly certified as per legal compliances
- Fire alarm systems & Test Fire prevention periodically
- Ensure that all equipments of the hotel. work safely & efficiently
- Repair any water leaks
- Repair all light & electrical failures & emergency Lights
- Ensure energy optimization and conduct regular energy audits
- Check smooth and efficient functioning of HVAC (Heating, ventilating and air conditioning)
- ETP (Effluent treatment plant) & STP (Sewage treatment plant)
- UPS (Un-interrupted power supply) & DG set (diesel generator)
- Attending & resolving guest complaints to their satisfaction
- Attending to different departments maintenance calls across the hotel
- Waste disposal & its recycling
- Safe environment and encouraging go green practices
- Maintain all equipments of health club & spa & swimming pool & water bodies across hotel
- Maintain building exterior in good condition
- Maintain laundry machines, washers, extractors, dryers and calender machines
- Maintain telephone & EPABX system
- Keep a watch on the energy consumption & its readings
- Co-ordinate any 3rd party maintenance
- Maintains ceilings, roofs, windows, any electronic equipments, in room as well as across the hotel
- Hot & cold water supplies & water storage tanks
- Sanitary fixtures and fittings

- Maintain pigeon wires
- Maintain Building structure, interior finish, wall papers & FF&E (Furniture, Fixtures and Equipments)
- Establishing budgets for the Engineering/maintenance department
- Ensuring the team is well trained and follows the established standards of maintenance that is safe and efficient
- Maintain well stocked as per par stocks maintenance store, for parts which are required for time to time maintenance
- To establish well negotiated and effective third party contracts to ensure smooth flow of operations

TYPES OF MAINTENANCE

PREVENTIVE MAINTENANCE: This is done when we do maintenance before the failure has occurred, the aim & objective of this maintenance is to minimise failure & prevent failure

CORRECTIVE MAINTENANCE: This is done when the failure has already occurred and the objective is to restore the functionality of the equipment.

TYPES OF PREVENTIVE MAINTENANCE:

Time Based Maintenance (TBM): This refers to maintenance that is done after a fixed time/interval regardless of the condition of the equipment

Failure Finding Maintenance (FFM): This refers to finding detecting hidden failures and to be protective in nature. The aim of this is to detect failure

Risk Based Maintenance (RBM): Risk = Likelihood x consequence

This refers to a maintenance process that effectively reduces the total risk of failure across your plan/equipment in the most economical way

Condition Based Maintenance (CBM): Often failure is not always age related, some failures failurs shor some sort of a warning before they occur. This is to find a faikure in its early stage and prevent that

Predictive Maintenance (PDM): This is a more about a next level approach to the condition-based maintenance, whereby advanced process gauging pramaters are used to determine if the equipment is moving /performing away from the standard performance parameters

TYPES OF CORRECTIVE MAINTENANCE:

1. **Deferred Corrective Maintenance:** This maintenance requires detailed planning and scheduling though it is crucial for example changing the repair and maintenance of the chiller plant units of the entire hotel etc

2. **Emergency Maintenance (EM):** This type of maintenance is urgent and cannot be delayed and must be attended to and resolved immediately as it disrupts the smooth flow of operation/ plant. It is the most expensive cost amongst the maintenance categories. However as a thumb rule not more than 2% of the maintenance should fall in this category

3. **Breakdown Maintenance:** This is simply corrective maintenance

RESPONSIBLE ALCOHOL SERVICE

Always Serve Alcohol Responsible

If you are not serving responsibly-DO NOT SERVE AT ALL

If you are pregnant or breastfeeding, it's safest for your baby if you don't drink.

Responsible Alcohol service means serving alcohol to customers in a responsible manner and conducting oneself and the alcohol business in a responsible manner that is in tune with all legal compliances. The management, managers, bartenders should serve, sell and supply alcohol in a very responsible manner or they may be held accountable for their behaviour

Responsible Alcohol services ensures never serving to minors or under-age,

Never serve more alcohol to an already intoxicated person &

Staying responsible to taking care if anyone is noticed drunk

Responsible alcohol service avoids any unruly or rowdy behaviour of drunk guests and is also a reflection of your business ethics, which shows that you truly care about the safety and wellbeing of all customers

1. Keep an eye on any customers who is intoxicated, as this can lead to an uncontrollable behaviour and could be a nuisance to other customers. Do not serve more alcohol to such customers

2. Serve one drink at a time when you observe that the customer is consuming alcohol very fast

3. Always serve alcohol to patrons who are above minimum age prescribed as per the law applicable

4. Must check the ID's of the customers for serving alcohol unless you are absolutely sure of the age of the customer

5. Always serve alcohol during the time and within premises as prescribed by the governing law & its guidelines

6. One may also have a restaurant or bar guidelines towards establishing the maximum alcoholic drinks to be served per customer

7. Always keep a track of the number of drinks a customer has consumed

8. Try and recommend food with the drinks as this slows down the impact of alcohol

9. Inform your manager in advance that you are going to refuse alcohol service to a particular guest so that you have his support when you refuse alcohol service

10. The bar tending team should be trained not to aim at increasing the bill of beverages as the sole aim of performance and rather responsible alcohol service should be appreciated, that is to point out when its enough for a particular guest

11. In spite of all the best responsible practices someone will get intoxicated, so always offer to call a cab for such customers to ensure their wellbeing & it is advised to have their car stay parked overnight in your parking lot

12. Display minimum age prescribed as per the law

13. Display that you have a call a Cab facility by simply asking the bartender a cab will be called

14. Always serve drinks that are measured before being served, to avoid any over pouring of the drinks

15. Also display and encourage the practice of -have a designed driver in your group. This refers to encouraging those coming in groups to ensure that one person is a designated driver who will not be drinking

16. Install surveillance cameras to record incase any unruly /rowdy event takes place

SIGNS OF AN INTOXICATED PERSON

- Difficulty in maintaining their balance
- Sudden aggressive change in the behaviour
- Shows sudden slurred speech
- One may notice that the intoxicated person may show difficulty in his body co-ordination
- Blooshot shot & glazed eyes

How to Slow down alcohol consumption of an intoxicated person:

Every time the server serves drink to the person, he or she should assess the intoxication level of the customer

Recommend some non-alcoholic drink/ food to bring down the alcohol levels of the customer

Tone down the level of music/entertainment to allow the customer to be able to converse, as conversations will slow down alcohol intake

HOW TO HANDLE AN INTOXICATED GUEST

- Stay calm & deal with the situation in a very calm and friendly way.
- Try and invite guest to be taken away from the other guests, where one can talk without making a nuisance for the other guests
- Never argue with the intoxicated guest.
- Always try never to embarrass the guest, especially in front of other people.
- Listen and empathize with your guest.

DIFFERENTLY ABLED GUESTS-GENERAL GUIDELINES

1. Have dedicated rooms for differently abled guests
2. Have well-equipped bathrooms for special needs, elevators with wheel chair in the elevators
3. Braille sign on every call button and an audio announcement for each floor.
4. Restaurant tables at the hotel-designed in a way that seats guests in own wheel chair
5. Fire alarms to have both audio & visible signals
6. Exclusive marked parking space with a sign post, nearest to the entrance to be made available
7. Ramp at the entrance wide enough for the movement of the wheel chair
8. Easy provision to enter from the door to the lobby
9. Public area not to have any protruding objects that may be dangerous to visually challenged
10. Provision of one toilet in the lobby similar to those in differently abled guest rooms
11. Door of the guest room should be wide enough for the wheel chair to enter
12. No split-level floor in differently abled rooms
13. Provision for grab bars alongside the toilet as prescribed
14. Faucet operation with closed fist – by applying pressure of the hand
15. Toilet seat to be 17" to 19" above the floor
16. Toiletries & towels easily accessible at an arms-length

OPERATIONAL GUIDELINES FOR DIFFERENTLY ABLED GUESTS

- Information of this guest should be made to all departments so that special attention & care is extended from all departments
- Offer an in-room check in & check out
- Front office to explain in detail about the facilities of the room and inquire if any special requirements are to be provided for
- Also it must be explained how simply the guest can connect to reach out for any assistance of service
- All departments should serve with a pro-active approach for all requests
- All departments to ensure that a same guest respect attitude as for all others guests
- During the case of fire/earthquake etc housekeeping & security specially incharge for the floor should be well trained to rescue and evacuate specially-abled guest as a top priority

SAFE USE OF SWIMMING POOL IN HOTELS

It is essential to comply by the rules while in the swimming pool area for everyone's safety and wellbeing as non-compliance to pool rules can be life threatening

- Take a shower before entering the swimming pool
- Read the sign board and guidelines of the pool before entering the pool
- Always wear swimming suit when in the pool
- Be careful when you get in and get out of the pool
- It is always better to go swimming with someone, never swim alone
- Never allow children swim without supervision
- The pool guard should be trained in CPR (cardiopulmonary Resuscitation)
- Ensure that the life guard is around while swimming
- Use non slip material in the pool deck area
- Do not drink alcohol or consume food while you are in the pool
- Never swim after taking alcohol beverages or after medications
- Never use any glassware near the pool
- Have the right safety equipment around the swimming pool at all times
- Chewing gum is not permitted in the swimming pool
- Do not leave your valuables unattended while you are swimming
- Avoid swimming pool usage if you have a medical restriction like an open wound or a cut or a contagious medical condition
- It is not permitted to smoke while you are in the pool side area
- It is not advisable to run around the swimming pool and make loud noises in that area
- Diving & jumping is not allowed in the swimming pool
- It is not permitted to wear jewellery while you are in the pool – like chain, bracelet, rings etc

- Assess your swimming abilities and swim as per your capabilities & do not show off
- While using water slides always use feet first
- Keep the pool clean and hygienic all times
- Regularly maintain and conduct deep cleaning of the pool

RISK MANAGEMENT:

HAZARD: Any potential source of harm, so hazard is something that may cause harm or adverse health effect on something or someone. Often hazard and risk are used together

RISK: Risk is the probability or chances that a person will be harmed or experience an adverse health effect if he/she is exposed to a hazard. Hazard + Possibility= Risk

Risk is the probability or likelihood of developing a disease, suffering adverse effect or getting injured on the other hand Hazard is the agent itself that is responsible for this adverse effect.

IMPORTANCE OF RISK MANAGEMENT: It's a continuous process of identifying possible risks, disasters or problems before they happen. This approach helps organizations to plan and set up procedures that avoid those risks and their impact and also be prepared to cope up better with its impact.

Four aspects of risk management are:
- IDENTIFY RISKS
- ANALYSE RISKS
- PLAN RISK RESPONSE
- MONITOR/CONTROL RISKS

DO'S AND DONT'S OF KITCHEN
WHEN STORING FOODS:
- Place all meat and fish in bottom shelf of the refrigerator: to prevent them dripping onto other foods
- Place all meat and fish in sealed, covered containers
- Place all cooked foods/meats above raw foods/meats
- Place all dairy products on the highest shelf
- Keep eggs away (above) from fresh meats and fish and powerful smelling foods
- Discard any cracked eggs

WHEN PREPARING FOODS:

- Do not allow pets within the kitchen
- Do not blow nose within the kitchen
- Do not smoke when preparing foods
- Do not lick fingers/taste food with fingers
- Do not mix different foods on the work bench or chopping board: raw meats with cooked, meats with fish etc.
- Thoroughly rinse all fruit and vegetables before peeling or cutting
- Thoroughly cook meats in order that juices run clear with no signs of blood
- Thoroughly wash work bench, chopping boards, knives etc. between tasks in hot soapy water
- Thoroughly scrub hands between tasks in hot soapy water

WHEN WASHING/CLEANING UP:

- Use hot soapy water: as hot as your hands can stand, even better is using gloves so on ready to increase the water temperature
- Allow dishes to drip dry: tea towels are public enemy #1 and spread bacteria
- Wash work surfaces with hot soapy water: boiling water (100C) will sanitize and water at 80C will disinfect much more efficiently, quicker and cheaper than chemicals. Wipe dry with paper towels or quickly with a dish towel (placing in washer afterwards)
- Keep cleaning sponges during a mild bleach solution (changed daily)

FOR PERSONAL HYGIENE:

- Always wash your hands after getting to the toilet
- Always wash your hands after smoking
- Always wash your hands after handling garbage
- Always wash your hands after handling chemicals
- Always wash your hands after touching any part
- Always wash your hands after blowing nose

- Take daily showers
- Thoroughly dry after a shower/bath, particularly within the following areas: between the toes, behind knees, groin, and navel, armpits.
- Use only mild or unscented deodorants/anti-per spirants

PERSONAL HYGIENE:

Food handlers shall avoid certain hand habits such as scratching nose, running finger through hair, rubbing eyes, ears and mouth, scratching beard, scratching parts of bodies etc.

Behavioural & Personal Cleanliness

1. All food handlers shall wear suitable clean protective clothing, head covering, face mask, gloves and footwear.
2. Food handlers shall always wash their hands with soap and clean potable water, disinfect their hands and then dry with hand drier or clean cloth towel or disposable paper.
3. Food handlers shall always wash their hands at the beginning of food handling activities immediately after handling raw food or any contaminated material, tools, equipment or work surface, where this could result in contamination of other food items or after using the toilet.
4. No Food handlers shall be engaged in smoking, spitting, chewing, sneezing or coughing over any food and eating in food preparation and food service areas.
5. The food handlers should trim their nails and hair periodically.
6. Food Handlers shall avoid certain hand habits such as scratching nose, running finger through hair, rubbing eyes, ears and mouth, scratching beard, scratching parts of bodies etc. When unavoidable, hands should be effectively washed before resuming work after such actions.
7. Street shoes inside the food preparation area should not be worn while handling & preparing food.
8. Food handlers should not handle soiled currency notes/cards to avoid cross contamination

FOOD SAFETY

It means assurance that food is acceptable for human consumption according to its intended use.

FOOD SAFETY MANAGEMENT SYSTEM: Means the adoption of Good Manufacturing Practices, Good Hygienic Practices, Hazard Analysis and Critical Control Point and such other practices as may be specified by regulation, for the food business.

FOOD SAFETY HAZARD: Biological, Chemical or Physical agent in food, or condition of food, with the potential to cause an adverse health effect.

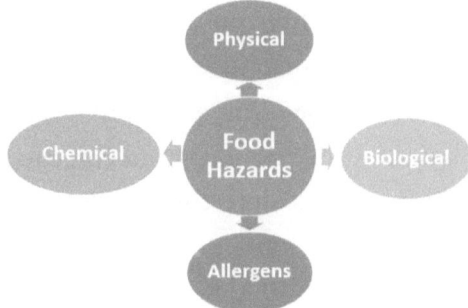

PHYSCIAL HAZARDS: Any foreign object found in the food or a naturally occurring object (bone in fillet), that poses; a hazard is called a 'Physical Contamination'.

Common Physical Hazards include: Glass, chipped pieces of cutlery and crockery, metal shavings from cans and foils, Stapler pins, Blades, plastic films used for wrapping or chipped pieces of disposables, Non edible garnishes, lint and threads, Band- aids, Hair, Finger nails, Bones, Jewellery pieces.

CHEMICAL HAZARDS: Naturally occurring and Process Induced Chemical substances that can cause a food borne illness is called a 'Chemical Contaminant or Hazard'.

BIOLOGICAL HAZARDS: Biological hazards are organisms, or substances produced by organisms, that pose a threat to human health. They are a major concern in food processing because they cause most food borne illness outbreaks.

ALLERGENS: An allergen is any normally harmless substance that causes an immediate allergic reaction in a susceptible person. Food allergens are almost always proteins although other food constituents, such as certain additives, are known to have allergenic (allergy-causing) properties.

Food allergy is a potentially serious immune response to eating or otherwise coming into contact with certain foods or food additives.

A food allergy occurs when the immune system:

- Identifies a particular food protein as dangerous and creates antibodies against it
- The next time the individual eats that food, immune system tries to protect the body against the danger by releasing massive amount of chemicals including Histamine
- Histamine is a powerful chemical that can cause a reaction in the respiratory system, gastrointestinal tract, skin or cardiovascular system.
- In the most extreme cases, food allergies can be fatal. Although any food can provoke an immune response in allergic individuals, a few foods are responsible for the majority of food allergies.

FOOD SAFETY:

The practice of keeping food safe and healthy to be consumed. From preparation till service, each step of food handling is hygienic and carefully conducted.

It is necessary for hospitality professionals to be trained in food safety education and its enforcement to ensure safety in organizations.

3e's of Safety Training

1. Safety education
2. Safety engineering
3. Safety Enforcement

SAFETY EDUCATION: To educate the employees about the theoretical part of safety and it should begin on the orientation of any employees.

SAFETY ENGINEERING: To impart knowledge regarding how to include safety related features in various equipment, furniture and other important tools which should be handled with care.

SAFETY ENFORCEMENT: To implement what has been studied in Safety education.

To ensure safety and discipline at work.

To promote proper supervision of all tasks being done at workplace.

To enhance the quick reaction to emergencies

FOOD DANGER ZONE
(FOOD DANGER ZONE)

There are various conditions for growth of bacteria such as moisture, food, acidity, oxygen, time and other one is temperature which can cause **"DANGER ZONE"**

Bacteria or pathogens grow best or they enjoy warm temperature between 5- 57 degree Celsius or 40- 135-degree F and at this temperature it promotes the growth of harmful bacteria and this range of temperature is known as **"FOOD DANGER ZONE"**. That's why it is advised that cold food items should be stored or served at temperature which is as low as 4 degree Celsius & hot food items above 60 degrees Celsius. Always cook the food item till the internal temperature reaches 75 degrees Celsius.

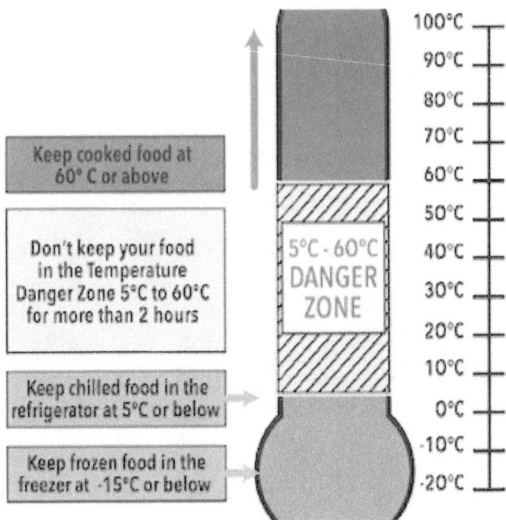

FOOD SAFETY: The safety of food produced, served & consumed is of utmost importance to everyone, more so to those who habitually eat outside their homes and are unaware of the intrinsic quality of food that is served to them, even though their taste buds approve it

Food safety is defined as keeping food safe to eat at every stage of (purchasing, receiving, storage, preparing, cooking, holding, cooling, reheating, and serving) handling as it passes through the flow of food from farm to table.

FOOD SPOILAGE: Food spoilage means the original nutritional value, texture, flavour of the food are damaged, the food become harmful to people and unsuitable to eat. Major reason for food spoilage are -

Foreign matter: Human hair, stapler, metal particles, fabric, plastic, alkali etc. are big threats to food safety and can cause food spoilage. Anything that is not considered as food or food substance is considered as foreign matter.

Storage of food in the refrigerator

Separate Fridge is required for storing Veg & Non- Veg food

If separate refrigerator is available:

Sequence in Veg Refrigerator---Ready to eat and salad at the top shelve, cooked vegetables at next top shelves and raw vegetables at the lower shelves.

Sequence in Non-Veg Refrigerator----- Ready to eat and non-veg salad at the top shelve, cooked Non-Veg at next top shelves and raw Non-veg at the lower shelves.

If separate refrigerator is not available:

Ready to eat and salad at the top shelve, cooked vegetables at next top shelves, Cooked Non-Veg in the next top shelves and raw food at the lower shelves

Preparation of fruits/vegetables

Use fruits and vegetables that are protected from cross-contamination and properly conserved.

whole fruits and vegetables should be washed in potable water before being cut, mixed with other ingredients.

whole fruits & vegetables should be washed (intend is to sanitize) with 50 ppm chlorinated water before cutting, peeling or serving.

non-absorbent food grade material, equipment, containers shall be used for preparing fruits & vegetable.

prepared fruits/vegetables should be kept in clean and properly covered food grade containers at a required temperature.

PRE –PROCESS:

Washing of raw vegetable with water

- Washing will help reduce bacteria, including *e.coli,* from the surface of fruit and vegetables.

- Most of the bacteria will be in the soil attached to the produce. Washing to remove any soil is, therefore, particularly important.

- When you wash vegetables, wash them under a running tap and rub them under water, for example in a bowl of fresh water. Start with the least soiled items first and give each of them a final rinse.

- Washing loose produce is particularly important as it tends to have more soil attached to it than pre-packaged fruit and vegetables.

- Peeling or cooking fruit and vegetables can also remove bacteria.

Washing of raw vegetable with chlorinated water –

Thawing -

There are three method approved for thawing of food:-

1. Temperature control (cool room/refrigerator)
2. Microwave oven
3. Cold running water (conditional)

HAZARD ANALYSIS CRITICAL CONTROL POINT

HACCP (Hazard Analysis Critical Control Point) is an internationally accepted technique for preventing microbiological, chemical and physical contamination along the food supply chain.

The HACCP technique does this by identifying the risks, establishing critical control points, setting critical limits, and ensuring control measures are validated, verified and monitored before implementation.

Conduct a hazard analysis:

A food safety hazard is any biological, chemical, or physical property that may cause a food to be unsafe for human consumption.

Determining the food safety hazards and identifying the preventive measures to plan and control these hazards.

Identify critical control points:

A critical control point (CCP) is a point, step, or procedure in a food manufacturing process at which control can be applied and, as a result, a food safety hazard can be prevented, eliminated, or reduced to an acceptable level.

Establish critical limits:

For each critical control point, a critical limit is the maximum or minimum value to which a physical, biological, or chemical hazard must be controlled at a critical control point to prevent, eliminate, or reduce to an acceptable level.

Establish critical control point monitoring requirements:

Monitoring activities are necessary to ensure that the process is under control at each critical control point.

Establish corrective actions:

Corrective actions are intended to ensure that no product is injurious to health or otherwise adulterated as a result of the deviation enters commerce.

Establish verification procedures:

Validation ensures that the plants are successful in ensuring the production of a safe product.

Establish Documentation:

The HACCP regulation requires that all plants maintain the documents, including its hazard analysis and written HACCP plan, records documenting the monitoring of critical control points, critical limits, verification activities, and the handling of processing deviations.

Implementation involves monitoring, verifying, and validating of the daily work that is compliant with regulatory requirements in all stages all the time.

WHAT IS A DISASTER?

A sudden accident or a natural catastrophe that causes great damage or loss of life.

It a sudden, calamitous event that disrupts the normal functioning of the society, community and causes human, economic and environmental loss that the community and society is not prepared to handle with the resources that they may have at their disposal at that given time.

TYPES OF DISASTER:

1. **NATURAL DISASTER**: Natural Disaster-Floods-Earthquake-Hurricanes-Tsunami-Volcanic eruptions

2. **ENVIRONMENTAL DISASTER:** Such emergencies include an technological or industrial accident, forest fires

3. **PANDEMIC EMERGENCIES:** Pandemic Emergency-Sudden emergence of a contagious disease which affects health & disrupts business, economy & day today activities in society

4. **COMPLEX EMERGENCIES:** Complex Emergencies are major crisis situation which may be a combined result of political instability, violence, social inequities, poverty etc combined together

WHAT IS DISASTER MANAGEMENT?

Disaster management can be defined as the organization and management of resources and responsibilities for dealing with all humanitarian's aspects of emergencies, in particular preparedness, response and recovery in order to lessen the impact of disaster.

STEPS IN DISASTER MANAGEMENT:

1. **DISASTER PREPAREDNESS:** This refers to all the measures that have been taken to prepare for and reduce the impact of disasters. This means to predict where possible, prevent and mitigate disaster impact and respond and cope effectively with the consequences of the disaster. Disaster preparedness is a continuous process which involves a huge range of risk reduction

activities, resources and also including training and logistics, healthcare and livelihood aspects as well

2. **RESPONSE:** This is the second phase of the disaster response cycle.This step focuses in immediate threats to people, property and business. The key focus of the disaster response phase is safety of people, prevent the next disaster and provide for basic needs of the people. In short. this step is about restoring, redeveloping, and revitalizing communities impacted.

3. **RECOVERY:** Disaster recovery is the process of resuming normal operations followed by the disaster impact. This phase is focused in restoration.

4. **PREVENTION & MITIGATION:** This step refers to taking measures and actions ahead of time, to be ready for any emergency. The objective is to reduce vulnerability to disaster impacts and decrease risks and damages caused by a disaster.

KEY CONCEPTS IN ENVIRONMENT MANAGEMENT

ENVIRONMENT MANAGEMENT

Environment management is about understanding the structure and functioning of planet earth and how humans fit into that. It is a multifaceted subject which includes studying environmental changes, reasons for environmental degradations. It aims about creating a win win situation benefitting the environment, economy and humans.

This is a combination of activities and initiatives with the goal to maintain and improve the overall state of environmental resource which are impacted by human activities.

This is also defined as management of the interactions and impact of human activities on the natural environment.

ENVIRONEMENTAL CONCERNS:

GLOBAL WARMING: Gradual heating of earth's surface, oceans & atmosphere by human activity, primarily by burning fossil fuels which releases methane and carbon-di-oxide and other greenhouse gases in the atmosphere. Continuous use of fossil fuel brings a discharge of greenhouse gases which impacts the environment. There is a requirement to move to renewable sources of energy.

ACID RAIN: This term is used when any form of precipitation includes acidic components such as nitric acid or sulphuric acid that falls on the ground from the atmosphere in wet or dry form. Acid rains are a result of having specific poisons in the climate. For example, corrosive downpour may be because of fossil fuel usages, volcanic eruptions etc.

AIR POLLUTION: Air pollution is caused by solid and liquid particles suspended in air which are detrimental to human and planet as a whole. Most of the air pollution is caused by use of energy and production. Burning of fossil fuels releases chemicals and gases into air which not only pollutes air but also contribute to climate change. Air pollution in the form of Carbon di oxide and methane, increases earth's temperature which forms smog

SOIL & LAND POLLUTION: Soil pollution is defined when there is presence of toxic chemicals in soil in such a high concentration that it poses a threat to human health and ecosystem. It would also be termed as soil pollution when the level of toxic chemicals exceeds natural levels. This simply means degradation of earth's surface because of human activities like mining, deforestation, construction and industrial activities. Impact of the land pollution is huge on adding to air pollution which creative problems in human health,

WASTE DISPOSAL: Everything that no longer has a use or purpose and needs to be disposed of. The term waste is mostly used for solid waste, sewage, hazardous waste and electronic waste.

OZONE LAYER DEPLETION: Ozone layer is an undetectable layer of protection around our earth that keeps us safe from the unsafe beams of sun. The depletion of this layer

WATER POLLUTION: Water pollution happens when toxic substances enter water bodies like oceans, rivers, lakes and remain suspended in water or may get deposited in the bed of the water body. One of reason for polluting water bodies is city sewage and industrial waste discharge. This degrades the overall quality of water. Clean water is slowly becoming a scarcity as more and more population battles for the need of clean water. Waste from industrial and agricultural activities is polluting water resources of their profits continuously

CLIMATE CHANGE: Some of the impact of the climate change are – melting of the polar ice, change in seasons, new diseases and overall change in the climate across the world

DEFFORESTATION: Deforestation is a large-scale removal of tress. It is clearing or thinning or destruction of tress to make way for agriculture, roads and urban development. Loss of all of trees and forests is not intentional, it may also be because of wildfires in forests. Deforestation is a huge problem and it is continuing to grow. More and more wooden areas are being lost, t

CARBON FOOTPRINT: According to WHO-a carbon footprint is a measure of the impact your activities have on the amount of carbon dioxide (CO_2) produced through the burning of fossil fuels and is expressed as a weight of CO_2 emissions produced in tonnes.

AGRICULTURAL POLLUTION: Use of pesticide in agriculture to deal with local pests contain chemicals which when sprayed in the crops does not disappear but seeps into ground and sometimes harm plants and crops

LITTERING: Littering means disposing of garbage, waste improperly and irresponsibly. For example, simply throwing it anywhere rather than trashing it in a dustbin or a recycling bin.

NATURAL RESOURCE DEPLETION: Non-renewable resources are limited and will get exhausted. Use of fossil fuels can lead to increased global warming which can increase sea levels and melting of polar ice.

MAJOR TYPES OF POLLUTION ARE;

WATER POLLUTION: When harmful substances like chemical or micro-organisms contaminate a water body- stream-river-ocean thereby degrading the water quality and making it toxic for humans and its environment

River dumping

Sewage & waste water- Sinks-showers & toilets

Agricultural pollution- fertilizers, pesticides

Effluent from factories & refineries

Oil pollution- big spills from cars, trucks, factories, sea tanker

Radio-active susbstances- Uranium mining, nuclear power plants,testing of weapons, radio active research and medicines

LAND POLLUTION: Land pollution is a major problem around the world and is caused by a variety of factors. Some of main causes of soil pollution include deforestation and consequent erosion, agriculture, industry, mining, landfills and illegal dumping of waste as well as urbanization and construction

AIR POLLUTION: This refers to the release of pollutants into the air that is detrimental/toxic to the human health and for planet as a whole

- Emission from Power stations
- Vehicle Pollution
- Industrial Pollution
- Burning of Fossil Fuels
- Burning of Solid Wastes
- Forest Fires
- Volcanic eruptions

NOISE POLLUTION: This refers to regular exposure to elevated levels of sound that have an adverse effect in humans and living beings.

- Industries
- Places of entertainment
- Road traffic
- Community Noise
- Animals
- Machinery

WATER CONSERVATION

Water is an essential element for everybody and also for the hospitality industry. Hotels use water in almost every department for e.g. Housekeeping (Laundry), Horticulture, F&B services, Kitchen stewarding etc. It is the duty of hotels to save water and to use it judiciously.

Water conservation practices

1. Create a water conservation team which will audit the usage of water on a regular basis and will find ways to save it.
2. Ensure maximum participation from all departments to increase conservation of water.
3. Set up a rainwater harvesting system.
4. Create new standard operating procedures keeping in mind minimum usage of water.
5. Give guests an option if they do not want a daily linen change in the guestrooms.

ENVIRONMENTAL CONCERNS

The environmental concerns are energy pollution, water pollution, waste generation and noise pollution. It is necessary to solve the problem of concerns related to environment by shifting towards a greener world. Hotels should focus on increasing green initiatives which will boost their market image as well as help the environment to replenish.

SUSTAINABLE PURCHASING POLICY

- A sustainable purchasing policy outlines an organizatios environmentally and socially conscious purchasing practice. It shows the organization's commitment to support of green. Purchasing from local vendors and choosing products made from recycled materials.

- The benefit of green and sustainable purchasing policy can reach beyond our organization and local community too. Green purchasing policies have the power to make a large scale of environment change. In addition, contrary to popular conception reen product are often less expensive than more traditional options.

NOISE, AIR QUALITY AND LANDSCAPE INTEGRATION

Just like any other type of pollution, noise has an impact on the quality of life and on health. Hotels are, above all, meant to be places where one can relax and rest. This often proves difficult because of the noise level. It affects hotel guests and the staff, as well as the hotel's surroundings. Exposure to noise pollution above 60 has an impact on mood, the quality of sleep, and stress levels. It can also give rise to auditory fatigue. Prolonged exposure to high noise levels, above 90 represents a hazard to hearing.

LANDSCAPE INTEGRATION AND PROTECTION OF NATURAL RESOURCES

Areas with high natural diversity or with an important historical heritage are favorite tourist destinations.to respond to the increasing demand, construction linked to the tourism industry has expanded rapidly. This situation creates certain abuses linked with gradual modifications of the environment and landscape that may become irreversible. The growth of tourism and its aesthetic requirements have direct impacts on soil, landscape and on the surrounding ecosystems. In some places developments on the coastline can lead to severe conflicts. Intensive construction practices are harmful to the environment, especially when the building materials used are not in harmony with traditional architecture.

WASTE MANAGEMENT

Waste management concept refers to various initiatives to manage and dispose waste.

This may be discarding, processing, recycling, controlling or reusing.

Define Waste: Waste are those material which are discarded after primary use, are worthless, defective, unwanted & unusable.

BIODEGRADABLE WASTE: This is the waste that comes from our kitchens like food waste, remains etc. Bio degradable waste decomposes itself over a period of time depending on its material. They are non-toxic, non-pollutants, eco-friendly to the environment.

NON- BIODEGRADABLE WASTE: These are the waste that comprises of broken glasses, plastics, cans etc also known as dry waste. Dry waste can be recycled and can be re used. Non-biodegradable waste does not decompose themselves and are pollutants. They remain in the environment for a very long time harming the overall environment & planet earth

The Three R's of Waste Management are:

REDUCE: This refers to cut down on the amount of waste being generated

REUSE: This refers to finding new ways to use things that otherwise has been discarded or thrown away

RECYCLE: This means to create something new and useful from something that is old, useless and discarded.

WASTE DISPOSAL & DUSTBIN COLOR CODE:

GREEN DUSTBIN: BIO DEGRADABLE

BLUE DUSTBIN: NON-BIO DEGRADABLE

SAFETY & SECURITY

SAFETY	SECURITY
The term safety is used with reference to such things as disaster, emergencies, fire, prevention and protection, and conditions that provide for freedom from injury and prevent damage to property.	The term security is used with reference to freedom from fear, anxiety, and doubts concerning humans as well as protection against terrorism and thefts of guest, employee, or hotel property.

SAFETY AND SECURITY PRACTICES IN HOTELS: A floor should have at least two exits

- Every guestroom should have an emergency evacuation plan
- Fire extinguishers should be installed on all floors of the hotel.
- Fire plan should exist for every hotel.
- Baggage scanning machines and metal detectors should be used on the entrance of the hotel
- CCTVs should be installed in the hotel premises.

FIRE SAFETY

It is a set of practices with an objective to reduce the destruction caused by fire. This includes practices that are preventive in nature & practices that are used to limit the development and its effect after the fire has started

Fire safety is everyone's responsibility.

FIRE

The process of combustion with light, flame and heat is called fire

ESSENTIAL COMPONENTS OF FIRE: Fuel + Oxygen + Heat = Fire

Fire is a chemical reaction initiated by presence of heat energy in which a substance combines with oxygen (from air). The process involves giving out heat energy (exothermic reaction), light and sometimes sound.

A) FUEL

B) OXYGEN

C) HEAT

D) CHAIN REACTION PROCESS

CLASSIFICATION OF FIRES & TYPES OF FIRE EXTINGUISHERS:

Broadly following extinguishers are generally used.

1. ABC stored pressure
2. CO_2 gas
3. DCP dry powder
4. Clean Agent (K Type)
5. Water CO_2

To be able to effectively extinguish fire it is important that the most appropriate fire extinguisher is installed and used. To do that we must first understand the classes of fire as below:

TYPES OF FIRES:

CLASS A: Fire involving solid combustible materials of organic nature such as rubber, paper, wood, plastic etc where cooling effect of water is essential to extinguish the fire.

Suitable extinguishers – Water, Foam, ABC dry powder and clean agents.

CLASS B: Fires involving – flammable liquids or liquefiable solids or whereby a blanketing effect is essential.

Suitable extinguishers – Foam, Dry powder, clean agent and carbon dioxide.

CLASS C: Fire involving flammable gases under pressure like LPG, where it is necessary to inhibit the burning gas which is at a fast rate with an inert gas, powder or vaporizing liquid for extinguishment.

Suitable extinguishers – Dry powder, clean agent and carbon dioxide.

CLASS D: Fire involving combustible metals such as zinc, magnesium, aluminum, sodium, potassium etc. where the burning metal reacts with water, CO_2, halogenated hydrocarbons.

Suitable extinguishers – Special dry powder extinguishers.

** Kindly refer to the updated/revised guidelines as per the governing body

HOTEL FIRE SAFETY SYSTEM INCLUDES:

- Fire sprinkler
- Smoke and fire detector
- Automatic alarm system
- Emergency lights
- Exits and exit signs
- Fire department standpipes
- Fire resistivity of construction
- Pressurized stairways
- Smoke control systems
- Portable fire extinguishers
- Staff emergency response teams
- Gas supply shut-off devices
- Connection between air handling unit sand alarm systems.
- Water sprinklers
- Smoke detectors/alarms
- Manual alarms
- Fire escape routes
- Escape drills
- Fire lights

GENERAL CAUSES OF FIRE

Most fires start because of carelessness of staff and guests. Newspapers, periodicals or clothes left lying too close to a fireplace, misuse of electricity by overloading, using faculty equipment, covering of lamps and heaters with damp clothes, etc. could be some common causes of a fire in the hotel.

SMOKING: No smoking should be allowed in restricted areas. All cigarette ends must be extinguished completely. Adequate ashtrays should be provided.

ELECTRICAL: Regular checking and maintenance of electrical appliances, building wiring. Train staff not to use faulty equipment. Do not permit overloading of electrical outlets.

HEATING EQUIPMENT: Use fire guards where possible. Position fire away from furnishings or inflammable material. Apply fire retardant finishes to all furnishings.

STORAGE OF CHEMICALS: All chemicals, including cleaning agents, must be stored in specific stores. Inflammable liquids should be stored in dark colored bottles away from naked light or direct light.

SAFETY

SAFETY SYSTEMS COVER THE FOLLOWING AREAS:

GUEST: Protection from abduction and health hazards from outsiders, hotel staff, pests, food poisoning etc.

STAFF: Providing staff lockers, insurance, health schemes, provident funds etc. protective clothing, shoes, firefighting drills, supply of clean drinking water use of aqua guards, sanitized washrooms etc.

GUEST LUGGAGE: Secure luggage, store rooms and proper equipment such as luggage trolley and bellhop trolley should be provided.

HOTELS EQUIPMENTS: Lifts, boilers, kitchen equipment, furniture and fittings and building etc. must be protected and for these the safety should cover up fire safety equipment, water floods security system, earthquake safety system, and security system etc.

PROTECTION OF GOODS, RAW MATERIAL & PROVISIONS: For this the safety system should cover proper storage and pest control systems, apart from the application of total material management system.

PROTECTION OF FUNDS & CASH: This is the duty of the hotel safe the salary in the form of provident fund and employee insurance. Safety of the budget in the form of food cost, labour cost and over-head cost.

SAFETY OF FOOD: This is a prime concern of the hotel to provide safe and hygiene food to the guest that's why every hotel has HACCP department.

IMPORTANCE OF SAFETY STANDARDS:

- To maintain guest safety
- To avoid the loss of business
- To avoid law suits
- To maintain the guests trust
- To maintain quality standards
- To eliminate hazards before they cause any serious problem

CLASSIFICATION OF SAFETY STANDARDS:

- Building safety
- Fire safety
- Service safety
- Food safety
- Employee safety
- Property safety

SECURITY ENHANCEMENT

- Digital CCTV
- Vehicle checkpoint
- Established checkpoints at entrances
- Barricades were installed
- Metal detector screening all
- Luggage screening
- Limited times for deliveries
- Laminated glass
- In room safe
- Electronic key system
- Luggage inspections, using X-ray machines
- Onsite security personnel (including local police or military, preferably)
- Round-the-clock security officer(s)
- Explosives-detecting dogs
- Surveillance detection program

SAFETY AND SECURITY WITH RESPECT TO HOTELS IN GENERAL

- Every floor should have at least two exits & display fire exit route
- The emergency staircase should connect at least 3-4 outlets in a hotel
- Directional sign boards (visible) should be placed at each entry and exit point.
- Every guestroom should have a visible emergency exit map or plan behind the door and this should never be concealed with any kind of decoration.
- Fire extinguishers should be placed at all convenient points.
- Water sprinklers and smoke detectors or a well planned fire plan should be a part of every hotel design.
- Metal detectors or baggage scanners can be placed at the main entrance to prevent entry of unauthorized material.
- Each and every room door should have a 'peephole' for the occupant
- Every exit area should open into an open area.
- Concierge and reception should be located at strategic points- a location from where the receptionist is able to view the movement from the main entrance. For this reason, reception is located between the main entrance and the guest elevators
- The hotel's parking lot should preferably be adjacent to the main building rather than in the basement. If this is unavoidable, the hotel parking lot should require the guest to cross the lobby and the reception area in order to reach the car park. CCTV surveillance is recommended for the car park area especially if in the basement.
- Valet service should be suggested to single guests to avoid the occurance of skippers and walk outs.

- At the main entrance of the hotel a rear view mirror may be placed in order to keep a check on the vehicles moving in and out of the hotel premises.
- Boom barriers should be installed to prevent unauthorised entry and exit of vehicles.
- Hotels must scan and search the underneath of cars and the car bonnets and car booth (luggage box at the rear)
- A house maid should make sure not to place the maids trolley at the entrance of the room to avoid any unauthorized or unsuspected entry of anyone while busy in cleaning

SECURITY MANAGEMENT BASIC TERMINOLOGY

Acceptable documentation: Original, or certified copies of records providing evidence of a fact or an event that have been deemed authoritative, acceptable, and reciprocal by law, or practice by a government or industrial body or company.

Alarm system: Combination of sensors, controls, and annunciators (devices that announce an alarm via sound, light, or other means) arranged to detect and report an intrusion or other emergency.

ARMED: A private security officer who is equipped with or has access to a weapon (fireman), such as pistol or rifle.

BACKGROUND SCREENING: An inquiry into the history and behaviours of an individual under consideration for employment, credit, access to sensitive assets (such as national defence).

CLOSED-CIRCUIT TELEVISION (CCTV): It is TV system in which signals are not publicly distributed but are monitored, primarily for the surveillance and security purposes.

CRISIS MANAGEMENT TEAM (CMT): A group of individuals functionally responsible for the directing the development and execution of the plan, and providing direction during the recovery process, both pre-and-post disruptive incident.

CRITICAL CONTROL POINT (CCP): A point, step, or process at which controls can be applied and threat or hazard can be prevented, eliminated, or reduced to acceptable levels.

DURESS ALARM: A device that enables a person placed under duress to call for help without arousing suspicion.

HAZARD: Possible source of danger, or conditions (physical or operational) that have a capacity to produce a particular type of adverse effect.

INFORMATION SECURITY RISK MANAGEMENT PROGRAM: The overall strategy used to assess threats, their impacts to critical information and resources, recommended countermeasures to mitigate those impacts, and continual management of the security process.

INTRUSION DETECTION SYSTEM: A system that uses a sensor to detect an impending or actual security breach and to initiate an alarm.

MANUAL EVACUATION: The physical removal of people and property by hand to another, more secure location.

MITIGATION STRATEGIES: Implementation of measures to eliminate the occurrence or impact of a crisis.

PHYSICAL SURVEILLANCE: A form of monitoring where the subject is kept under physical observation

QUALITY ASSURANCE AND SECURITY MANAGEMENT SYSTEM (QASMS): Systematic and coordinated activities and practices through which an organisation manages its operations and security risks.

SECURITY SURVEY: A thorough physical examination of a facility and its systems and procedures, conducted to assess the current level of security.

RESPONSE AND RECOVERY PLAN: Documented collection of the procedures and information that is developed, compelled, and maintained in readiness for the use in an accident.

FIRE ESCAPE: A fire escape is a staircase on the outside of the building, which can be used to escape from the building if there is a fire.

EVACUATION: Oganised, phased, and supervised dispersal of people from dangerous or potentially dangerous areas.

EMERGENCY RESPONSE TEAM: The response team at the scene to resolve the critical incident.

ENERGY CONSERVATION

- Responsible hospitality is incomplete without Energy conservation, it involves making sure to optimize energy usage and to reduce costs related to energy.

ENERGY CONSERVATION PRACTICES:

- Start an energy conservation team in various departments of the hotel, to ensure maximum participation of employees.
- An energy conservation program should be introduced which should involve weekly tasks and responsibilities so that everyone gets to lead an initiative once in a while.
- Ensure minimum consumption of energy by regulating the lighting and temperature levels.
- Do not run laundry equipment which are partially full.
- Try to avoid use of bright lighting.

ENERGY CONSERVTION IN HOTELS:

Let us now learn some general methods for energy conservation which can be followed by the hotel throughout the property. Switching off lights and air-conditioning in the rooms not in use: The first step of energy conservation activities is elimination of waste. Being aware of importance of making thorough efforts to small matters will result in great energy conservation.

Energy conservation during guest room cleaning: Consider switching off in room air conditioning units while cleaning guest rooms. As even when the indoor air-conditioning units (fan coils and others) are turned off, room corridor air-conditioning units are still operational. Hence, turning off the fan coils during room cleaning would not cause poor work environment.

Open curtains whenever possible to utilize sunlight during the cleaning work, so that electricity is used only in a dark place, such as a bathroom. All small initiatives being practiced should be documented in a manual and implemented by the cleaning supervisor.

Lighting control in banquets: Significant amounts of lighting are used in banquet halls. Banquet halls lights can be categorized into two -general lighting to keep enough illuminance in the rooms, and directive illumination such as chandeliers. The latter consumes greater electricity than the former. Use only general lighting during preparation and cleaning periods and turn off the directive lighting

ABOUT THE AUTHOR- NEERAJ CHANDHOK

Neeraj Chandhok is an author, academician, corporate trainer, hospitality consultant and an entrepreneur. CEO & founder of Building Block Customer Services (Hospitality Training & Consulting Company). He has rich experience of more than 25 years in Hospitality Luxury brands and has proven expertise in Customer Experience Management, General Management, Leadership, Food & Beverage Management, Cost Control, Budgeting, Complaint Management, Strategy, Feasibility Studies, Profit centre head and Consulting Hospitality Projects. An alumnus of IHM Pusa, New Delhi himself , Neeraj has been a visiting faculty for M.sc In Hotel Administration at IHM Pusa for over 15 years & also teaches at various Hotel Management Institutes across the country. He is also visiting faculty at Indian Culinary Institute and teaches Strategy, Entrepreneurship & Business Fundamentals. As a corporate trainer he has been conducting Training/Workshops for leading hotel brands & various MNC's across Asia on Customer Centricity, Customer Experience Management & Leadership.

He is driven by the vision to help organizations and individuals excel & succeed!!

- 3 Year Hotel Management (IHM Pusa, New Delhi)
- Masters in English Literature
- F&B Management from American Hotel & Motel Association,
- Specialization in Strategy Thinking from eCornell
- Specialization in Social Media & its impact from eCornell
- Founder of www.the10dayhm.com (Online Quizzes on Hotel Management)
- Author of: 1. Customer Plus 2. Leadership Plus 3. The 10 day Hotel Management

All Books available @ www.neerajchandhok.com

He also served as Master Trainer/Assessor for FSSAI trainings on Food safety. He is also a member of Board of faculty for Hotel Management at Manav Rachna International Institute of Research & Studies. (2020).

Also served with CII for PMKVY Pradhan Mantri Kaushal Vikas Yojna for F&B & Front Office. In addition to being a keen sportsman who loves to play tennis, badminton and volleyball, he is a passionate musician artist & trained in Indian Classical music and, often performs live.

Connect with Neeraj for Virtual/Onsite Trainings/Workshops

Connect with Neeraj for Professional Developments @ www.neerajchandhok.in

www.ingramcontent.com/pod-product-compliance
Lightning Source LLC
Chambersburg PA
CBHW021348210526

45463CB00001B/16